I0803212

IMAGES
of America

Mullica Hill and Old Harrison Township

ON THE COVER: AMERICAN STORE, C. 1925. The American Store Company was a Pennsylvania-based grocery store chain founded in 1917. Located at 54 South Main Street, the grates below the windows still bear the company's initials, ASCO. The American Store was considered modern, in contrast to the traditional country stores that were still operating in Mullica Hill and most of the adjacent villages. (Courtesy of Wilbert Reed.)

IMAGES
of America

Mullica Hill and Old Harrison Township

James F. Turk and Karen E. Heritage with
the Harrison Township Historical Society

ARCADIA
PUBLISHING

Copyright © 2018 by James F. Turk and Karen E. Heritage with the Harrison Township Historical Society
ISBN 978-1-4671-2971-8

Published by Arcadia Publishing
Charleston, South Carolina

Printed in the United States of America

Library of Congress Control Number: 2018934776

For all general information, please contact Arcadia Publishing:
Telephone 843-853-2070
Fax 843-853-0044
E-mail sales@arcadiapublishing.com
For customer service and orders:
Toll-Free 1-888-313-2665

Visit us on the Internet at www.arcadiapublishing.com

This book is dedicated to the members and donors whose decades of support and generosity have created the Harrison Township Historical Society's rich and remarkable collections.

Contents

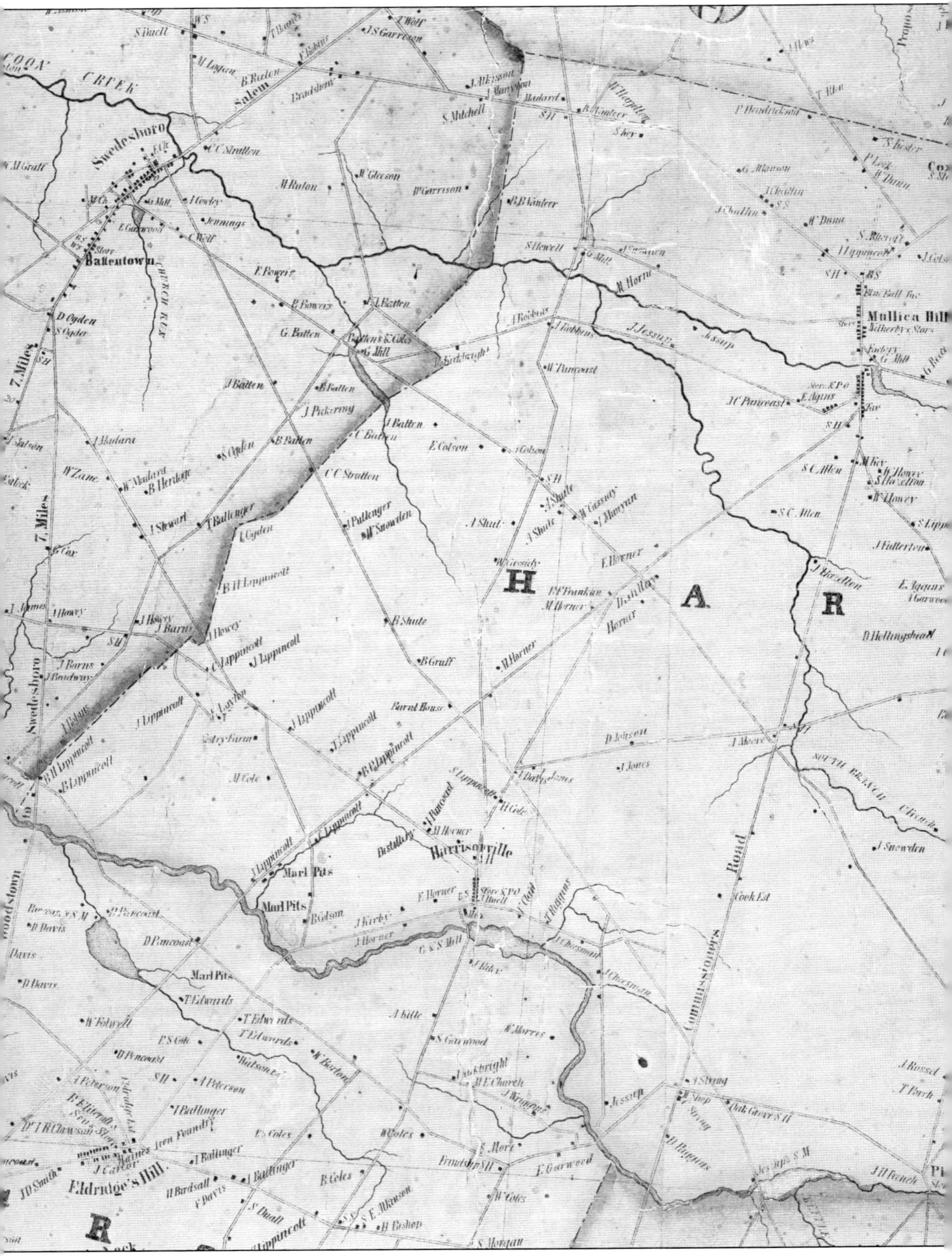
Swedesboro
Battentown
Church Run
7 Miles
Salem
Mullica Hill
Harrisonville
Marl Pits
Eldridge's Hill
Commissioners Road
South Branch
H
A
R

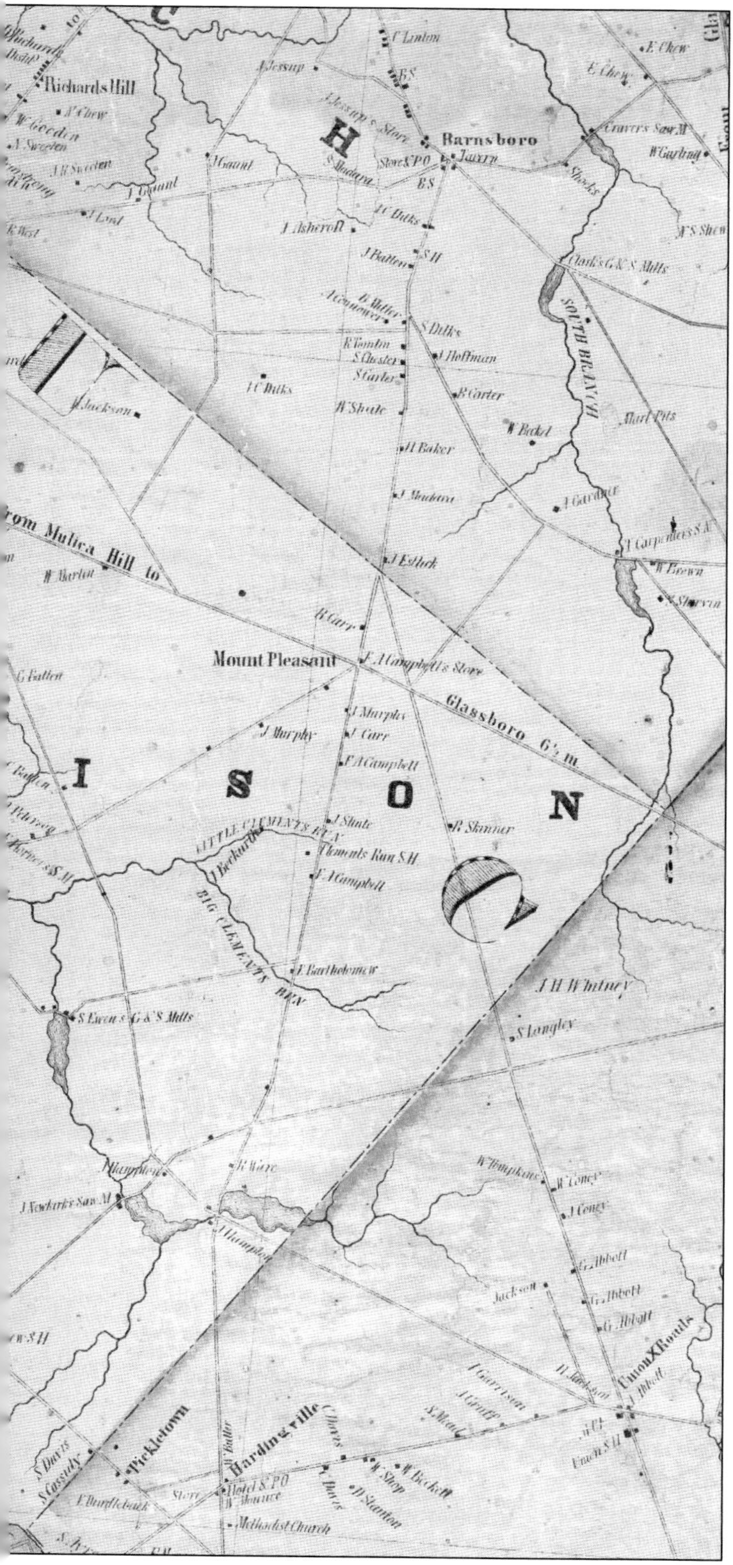

Old Harrison Township, 1849. Published only five years after the township was established, this map shows the boundaries of Old Harrison, which included present-day South Harrison and the western edge of Elk. The confluence of roads at Mullica Hill helps explain why the village grew in size and prominence in the area. This is a detail from the Stansbie, Keily, and Rea map *The Counties of Salem and Gloucester, New Jersey.* (Courtesy of the Harrison Township Historical Society.)

Acknowledgments

This book, the first pictorial history of Old Harrison Township, is a project of the Harrison Township Historical Society in Mullica Hill, New Jersey. Special thanks are extended to Richard C. Ridgway, without whose technical expertise and assistance this book would not have come to fruition. In addition, the society's collections committee provided ongoing research support throughout the project.

A number of individuals generously provided invaluable research assistance, including Brian Bartholomew, Sara A. Borden (Rowan University Archives and Special Collections), J. Harlan Buzby, Eileen Ferguson, Robert Greene, Rich Guido (Salem County Historical Society), the New Jersey State Archives staff, Lawrence Owen, Barbara Price (Gloucester County Historical Society), and Rita Reuter.

Unless indicated otherwise, all images included in this volume are from the collections of the Harrison Township Historical Society. Additional images were generously provided by:

Alabama Department of Archives and History (ADAH)
Clearview Regional Board of Education (CRBOE)
David Tinney (DT)
Ewan Fire Company (EFC)
Frank Stubbins Collection (FSC)
Ferrell United Methodist Church (FUMC)
Gloucester County Historical Society (GCHS)
Harrisonville Fire Company (HFC)
Harrison Township Board of Education (HTBOE)
Judy Ferguson (JF)
J. Harlan Buzby (JHB)
J. Richard Mood (JRM)
Judy Suplee (JS)
Kirk Horner (KH)
Lake Gilman Owners, Inc. (LGO)
Mildred Moore (MM)
New Jersey State Archives (NJSA)
Norman Schleicher (NS)
Princeton University Library (PUL)
Richwood Academy Association (RAA)
Richard and Barbara Ridgway (RBR)
Rowan University Archives and Special Collections (RUASC)
Salem County Historical Society (SCHS)
Shirley Daniels (SD)
South Harrison Township Board of Education (SHBOE)
Special Collections and University Archives, Rutgers University Libraries (SCUARUL)
Tim Hawk/South Jersey Times (SJT)
St. Stephen's Episcopal Church (SSEC)
Thomas and Stacey Holtzhauser (TSH)
Woodstown-Pilesgrove Library (WPL)
Wilbert Reed (WR)

INTRODUCTION

Old Harrison Township's story stretches back thousands of years to prehistoric times. Paleolithic stone artifacts and pottery sherds provide evidence of human habitation here as early as 8000 BC and have been prized by local farmers for decades. Local agriculture was also responsible for the discovery of even more ancient artifacts. Marl, a natural mineral containing potassium and magnesium, was formed in the sediments of the ancient ocean that once covered New Jersey and was mined in the 19th century in Ewan, Harrisonville, and Mullica Hill for agricultural use as a fertilizer. These excavations yielded fossilized remains of ancient sea creatures that attracted the attention of pioneering paleontologists. Specimens from Old Harrison can be found in the natural history collections of several major American museums. Little evidence remains of these mining operations, except a few water-filled pits and in place-names like *Marl Road* and *Marl Run* in South Harrison.

Natural history, geography, and location have shaped Old Harrison's history and development. Paleolithic settlements were located along the banks of Raccoon and Oldmans Creeks and their tributaries and an ancient Indian trail from the Delaware River to the Bayshore crossed the township through present-day Mullica Hill. This woodland pathway led Swedes, Finns, and English Quakers to the area in the late 17th and early 18th centuries and came to be known as the Cumberland Road leading south to present-day Bridgeton. The township's earliest and largest settlement, Mullica Hill, developed as a coaching town where several roads crossed Raccoon Creek. This convergence led to the establishment of taverns and blacksmith shops in the 18th century.

The rolling topography along Raccoon and Oldmans Creeks and their tributaries provided sites for grist-, saw-, and woolen mills that, in turn, spurred settlement and commerce at Mullica Hill, Ewan, Harrisonville, Lincoln, and Wright's Mill. Expanding farmlands produced both grain and timber to feed the mills and by the mid-19th century no less than 12 milling establishments were operating throughout the area. These enterprises catered largely to a local clientele; the volume of water and relatively low dams limited production.

The 19th century saw the dramatic expansion of the area's farming economy and consequently more roadways. Small villages like Richwood, Jefferson, Ferrell, and Cedar Grove sprang up at rural crossroads with a scattering of small shops and often a schoolhouse and church.

By the 1840s, the population had sufficiently increased that citizens petitioned for the creation of a new municipality carved out of Woolwich and Greenwich Townships. The Whig Party championed the movement and proposed it be called Harrison to honor the first Whig president, William Henry Harrison, who died shortly after taking office in 1841. The Democratic majority in Trenton, however, rejected this plan, and so an alternate, apolitical name was proposed resulting in the establishment of Spicer Township in 1844. The designation honored Jacob Spicer, a prominent 18th-century Quaker settler and philanthropist. In 1845, however, the Whigs won the legislative majority and promptly renamed the township Harrison. The new municipality encompassed land all the way to the Salem County line. These boundaries remained unchanged until 1883, when residents of the southern precinct successfully petitioned to create South Harrison Township. Eight years later, a small area along South Harrison's eastern boundary around Ferrell seceded to become part of the new Township of Elk.

Farming provided the foundation for the local economy from first settlement until well into the 20th century. Access to Philadelphia—and later, New York—markets was a major contributor to this prosperity and brought about the transition from grain to more diversified vegetable and fruit crops as well as livestock and poultry. Agricultural transport became more efficient with the opening of a railroad spur to Mullica Hill in 1889. The station quickly became a major produce shipping point, one of the busiest in the region. In the 20th century, improved highways expanded markets even farther afield.

Local farmers have long been noted for their innovation and adaptation to changing markets and opportunities—the first air shipment of fresh produce in the United States flew from Mullica Hill to Boston in 1922. The 20th century also saw dramatic growth of peach and apple production. Orchards proliferated and by mid-century Richwood became the center of one of the largest areas of peach production in the United States. Many farmers also opened seasonal farm markets to diversify income streams. The 21st century has seen these retail businesses increase in market sophistication and popularity.

Even as agriculture continued to dominate the landscape and local economy, the postwar period signaled the beginning of an era of change. New regional highway construction including the New Jersey Turnpike, Interstate 295, State Route 55, and the Commodore Barry Bridge all made the area much more accessible and the township's picturesque farmlands proved very attractive to builders. The first housing developments sprang up around the perimeters of Mullica Hill and gradually expanded eastward toward Richwood and Ewan and south into South Harrison. Population growth brought about the need for more classrooms and the creation of three regional school districts (Clearview, Kingsway, and Delsea) to serve Harrison, South Harrison, and Elk students.

As the number of farms declined so did the number of agriculture-based businesses that just decades earlier had dominated local commerce. At the same time, a large number of antique shops opened in Mullica Hill, and the village became known as "Antique Country." With this development came new interest in local history and historic preservation resulting in the founding of the Harrison Township Historical Society and state and national recognition of the Mullica Hill Historic District. All three municipalities marked the US bicentennial and in the 1980s and 1990s held sesquicentennial and centennial celebrations.

The 21st century finds Old Harrison Township still evolving. The population continues to grow, but farming remains a valued part of the economy, even as the crops being raised are again diversifying. Vineyards are supplanting orchards, a part of the statewide growth in wineries. In addition, thousands of acres have been permanently preserved as agricultural lands through the state and county farmland preservation programs. With careful planning, Old Harrison's rich and vibrant heritage can be preserved amidst managed growth and change.

One

MULLICA HILL

Mullica Hill is a well-preserved country village reflecting over 300 years of history. Swedes, ethnic Finns, and Quakers began settling here in the first decade of the 18th century, forming two clusters of houses on both sides of Raccoon Creek. Quakers initially dominated settlement on the south bank, which was informally known as Spicerville after prominent landowner Jacob Spicer. Originally only the settlement on the north bank was known as "Mullica's Hill," where Eric, John, and William Mullica purchased lands starting in 1705. Finnish/Swedish cultural traditions survived there for a few decades, but by the late 18th century, they had all but disappeared. By then, only the place-name *Mullica Hill* reflected that heritage, but it did come to designate the entire settlement on both sides of the creek.

The town's first real period of growth began at the end of the Revolution around 1780 and continued until about 1830. Most of this activity took place on South Main Street, which became the commercial center. By contrast, North Main Street was dominated by farmsteads that were not developed as town lots until the mid-19th century and later.

Mullica Hill's historic and architectural significance was recognized in 1991 when the entire village was placed in the prestigious National and New Jersey Registers of Historic Places. The following year, Harrison Township designated the village as a local historic district. Mullica Hill has been cited as one of New Jersey's most impressive and unspoiled village enclaves, an assertion increasingly recognized by residents and visitors alike.

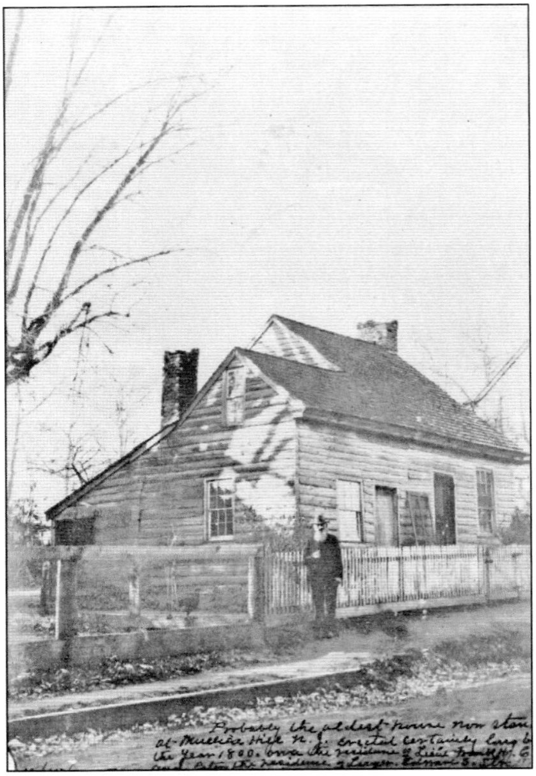

Mullica House. In 1705, brothers William, Eric, and John Mullica began acquiring property on the north bank of Raccoon Creek, which came to be known as "Mullica's Hill." The little house William Mullica built in the early 18th century still stands on North Main Street and is believed to be Old Harrison's oldest building. (GCHS.)

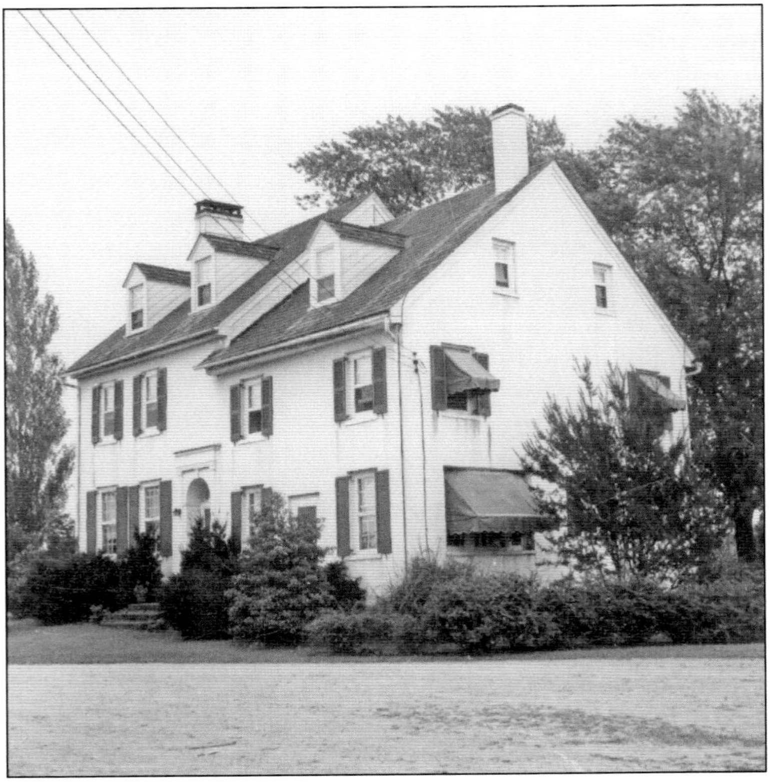

Spicer-Folwell Homestead. Quaker Jacob Spicer is believed to have built the lower section of this house in the mid-18th century. Spicer was a highly regarded citizen with extensive landholdings on the south side of Raccoon Creek. A generous philanthropist, he provided land for the first school and bequeathed property to the Quakers for a burial ground. Nathan and Rebecca Folwell added the larger half of the house, one of the area's oldest homes.

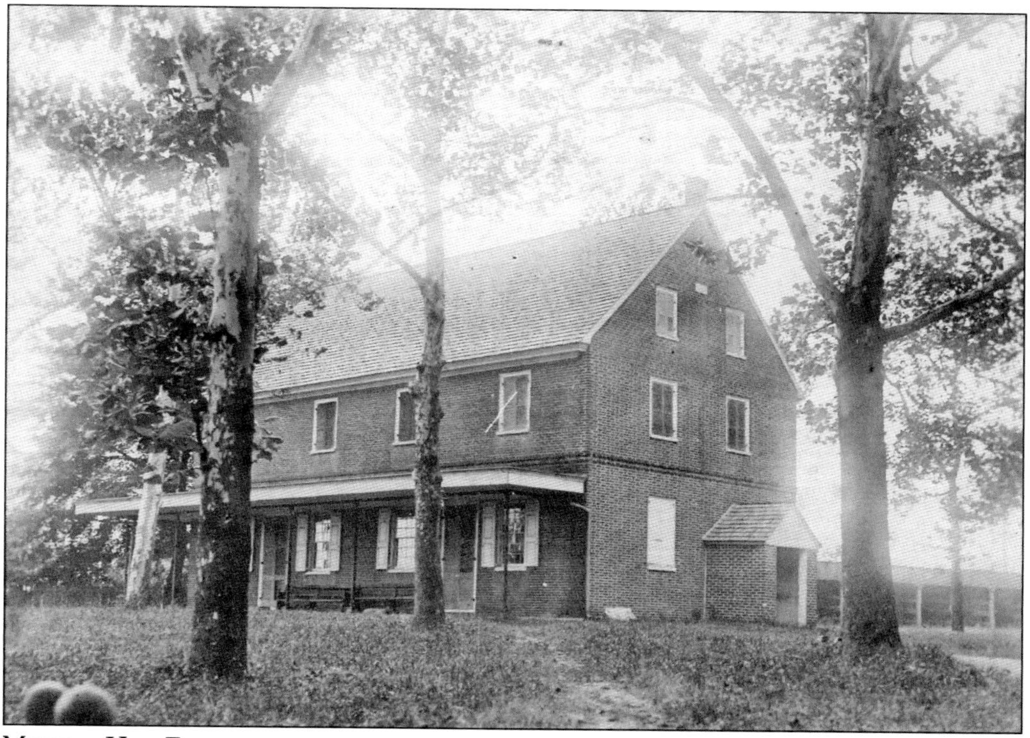

MULLICA HILL FRIENDS MEETINGHOUSE. Quakers settled primarily on the south side of Raccoon Creek early in the 18th century, but they did not establish a separate meetinghouse until 1797. The meetinghouse was built in 1808 on property that Jacob Spicer willed to Friends in 1779 and is the oldest house of worship in the township. Quakers played a prominent role in Harrison Township's early history and culture.

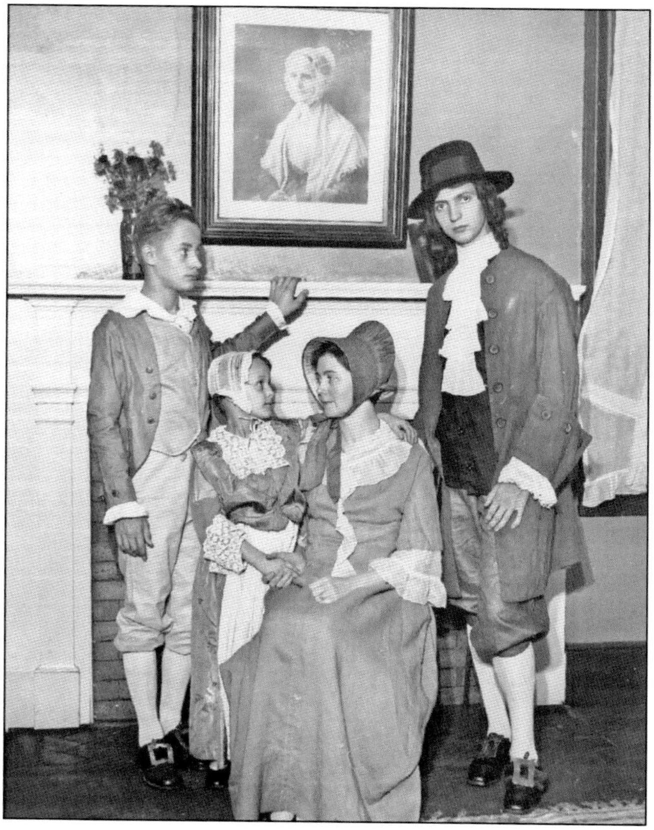

THE WILLIAM PENN PAGEANT. From left to right, Norman Skinner, Beryl Skinner, Florence Kester, and Paul Colson portrayed the William Penn family in a play presented at the Mullica Hill Friends First-Day School Union in 1932. Coincidentally, the Penn family once owned the land on which the meetinghouse was built.

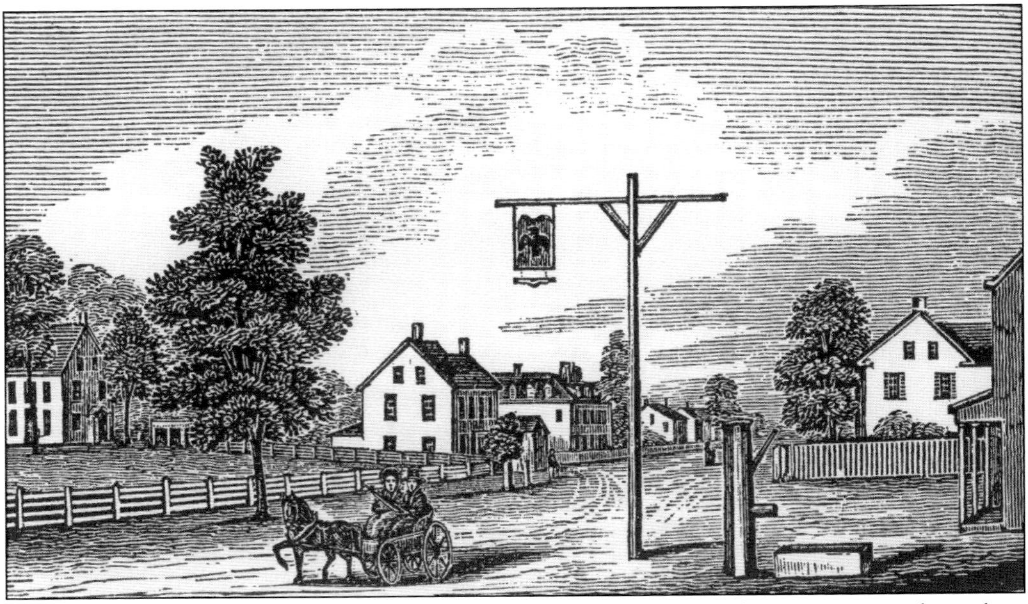

CENTRAL VIEW AT MULLICA HILL, 1844. This wood engraving of South Main Street is the earliest known view of Mullica Hill. The south side of Raccoon Creek became the center of commercial activity and at one time was informally called Spicerville. The Friends Meetinghouse is visible at the far left, as is the row of brick townhouses north of High Street in the center.

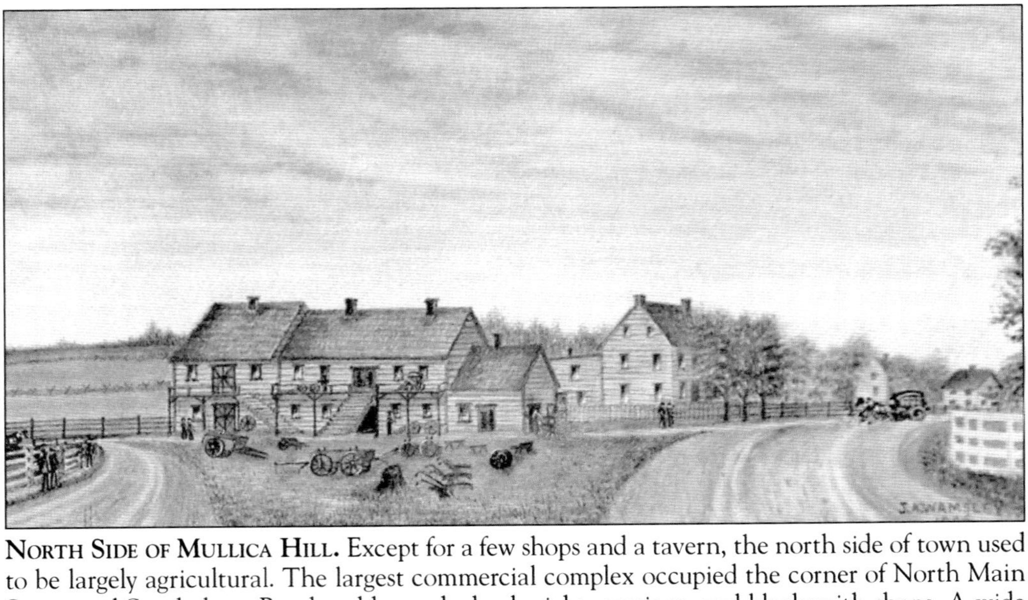

NORTH SIDE OF MULLICA HILL. Except for a few shops and a tavern, the north side of town used to be largely agricultural. The largest commercial complex occupied the corner of North Main Street and Swedesboro Road and housed wheelwright, carriage, and blacksmith shops. A wide variety of vehicles and farm implements were manufactured here from 1844 to 1866, when mass-manufactured goods made the business unprofitable. The buildings came down in 1886.

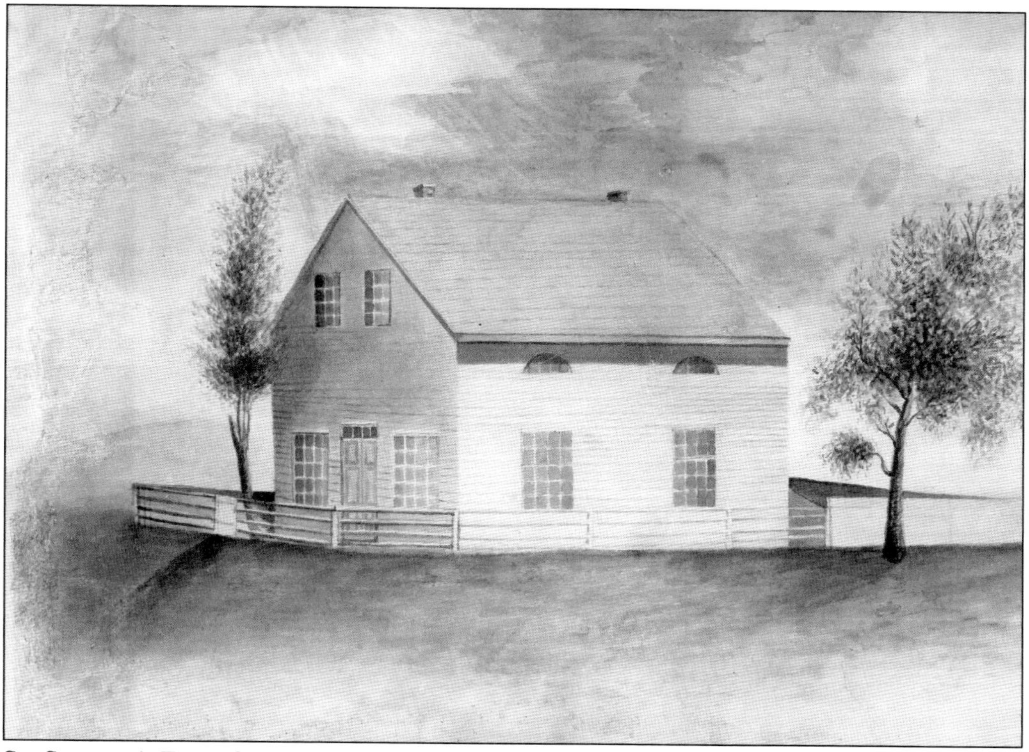

St. Stephen's First Church. Tradition maintains that Episcopalians first held services in the gristmill around 1800. In 1813, the congregation built this church, the township's second house of worship, on the north corner of South Main and East Church Streets. When the present church was built in 1853, this building was deconsecrated and sold, serving first as a private school and later as a piggery, after which it was demolished. (SSEC.)

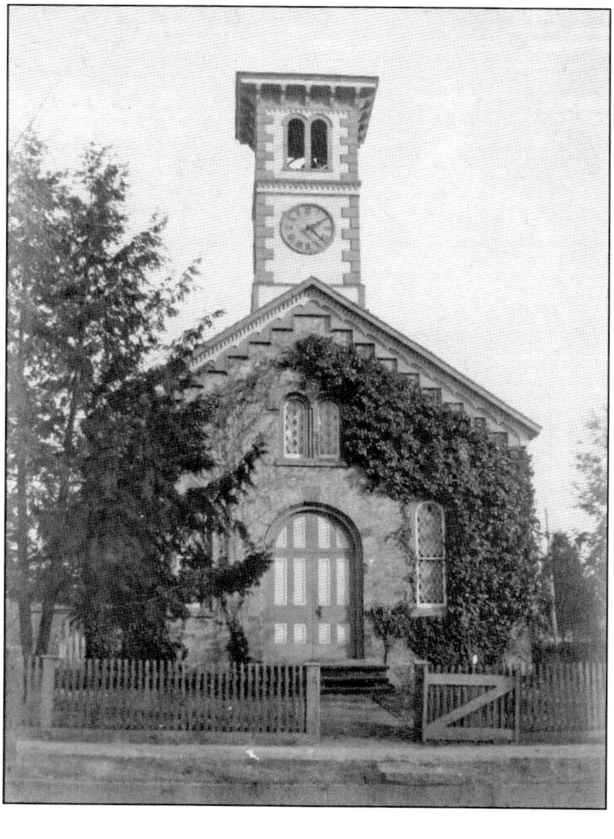

St. Stephen's Episcopal Church. In 1853, St. Stephen's celebrated completion of its elegant new stone church. As it was customary to have the cemetery adjacent to the church, burials at the old church were disinterred and removed to the new location. In that process, several of the bodies were found to be in a perfect state of preservation, causing a local sensation. The clock tower was added in 1879.

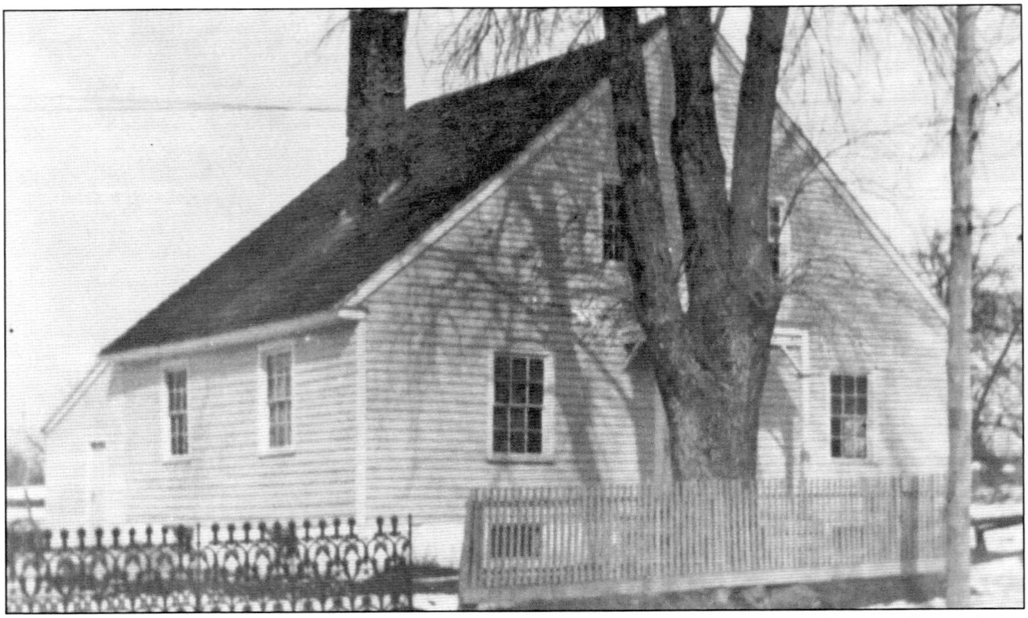

TRINITY METHODIST CHURCH, 1827. Local Methodists first met in home gatherings for perhaps 20 years prior to building this their first sanctuary on High Street in 1827, which became a private house after the new church was built on South Main Street. It was razed in the mid-20th century, and all that remains is the cemetery located west of the old building.

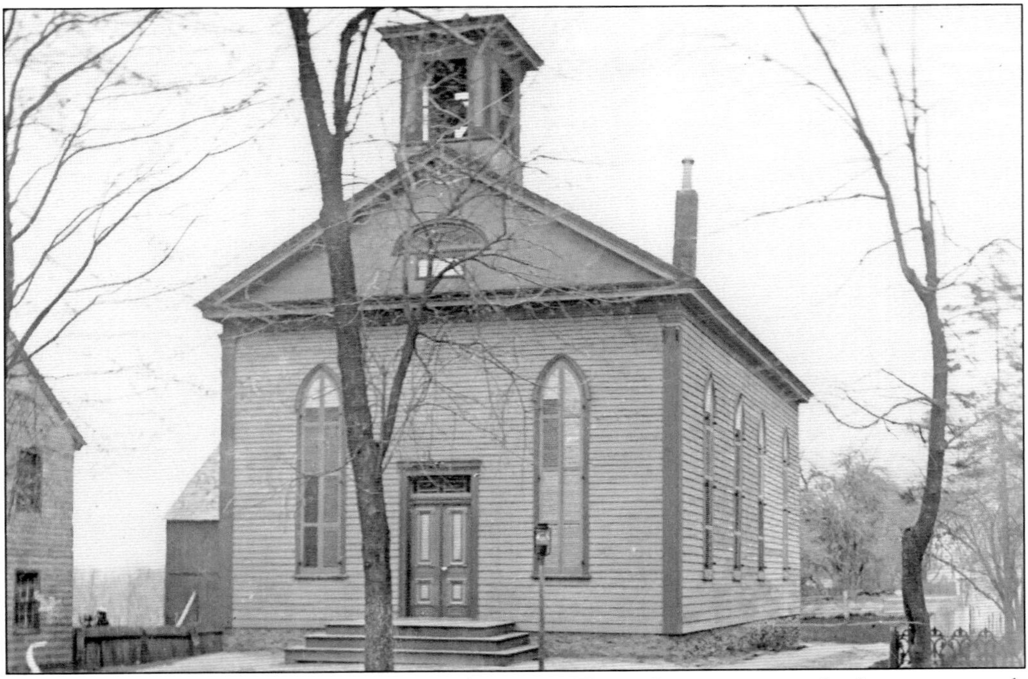

TRINITY METHODIST CHURCH, 1848. By the 1840s, Trinity's congregation had grown to such an extent that a larger and more prominently located sanctuary was deemed necessary. During the next century, the building was enlarged to provide rooms for a growing Sunday school. In 2003, a new sanctuary on Cedar Road in Jefferson replaced the historic church, which became a commercial building.

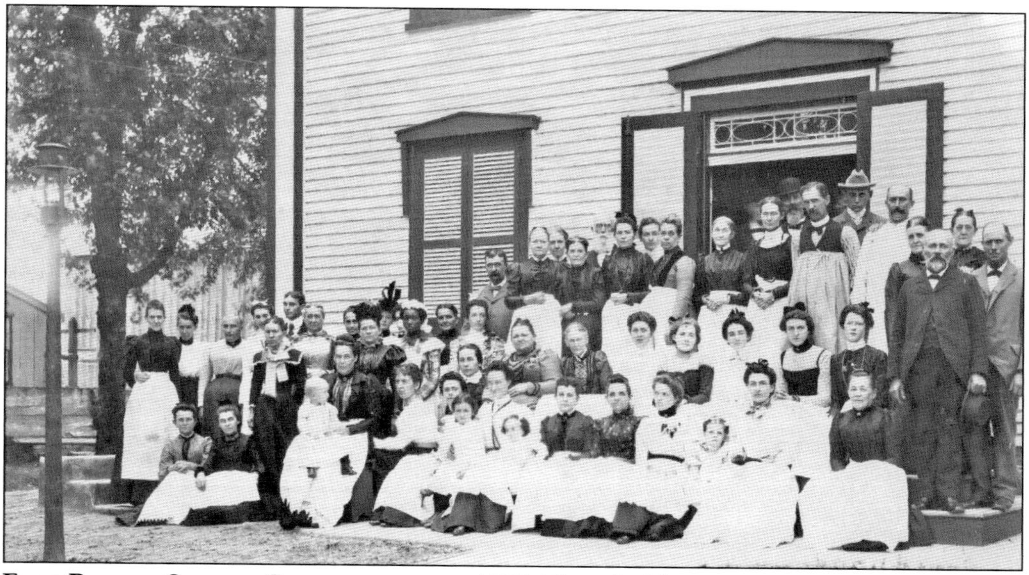

First Baptist Church Congregation, c. 1895. There had been Baptist preaching in Mullica Hill long before the founding of the church, but it was not until 1845 that 18 people united to establish a congregation, which afterward grew and flourished. The church's name is especially appropriate, as it was the first Baptist church established in Gloucester County.

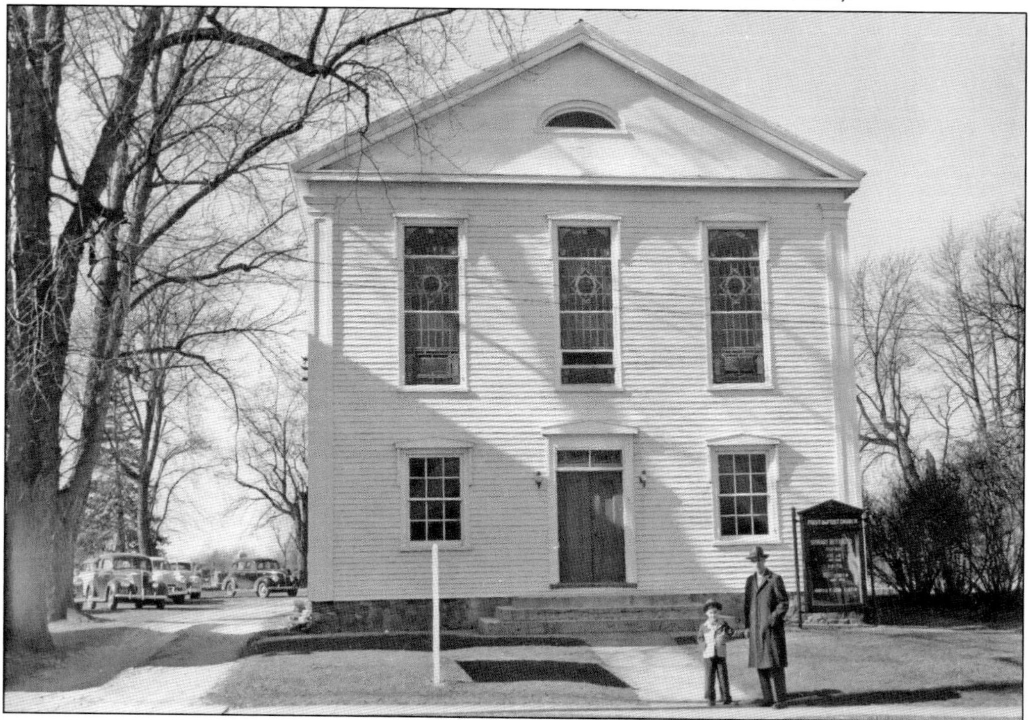

First Baptist Church. First Baptist's sanctuary was built on land donated by Deacon John and Abigail Mulford very shortly after its founding. Charles Kain was called as the first pastor and served the congregation for 20 years. Although additions have been made to accommodate growth, the original building's exterior remains largely unchanged and is a landmark on South Main Street.

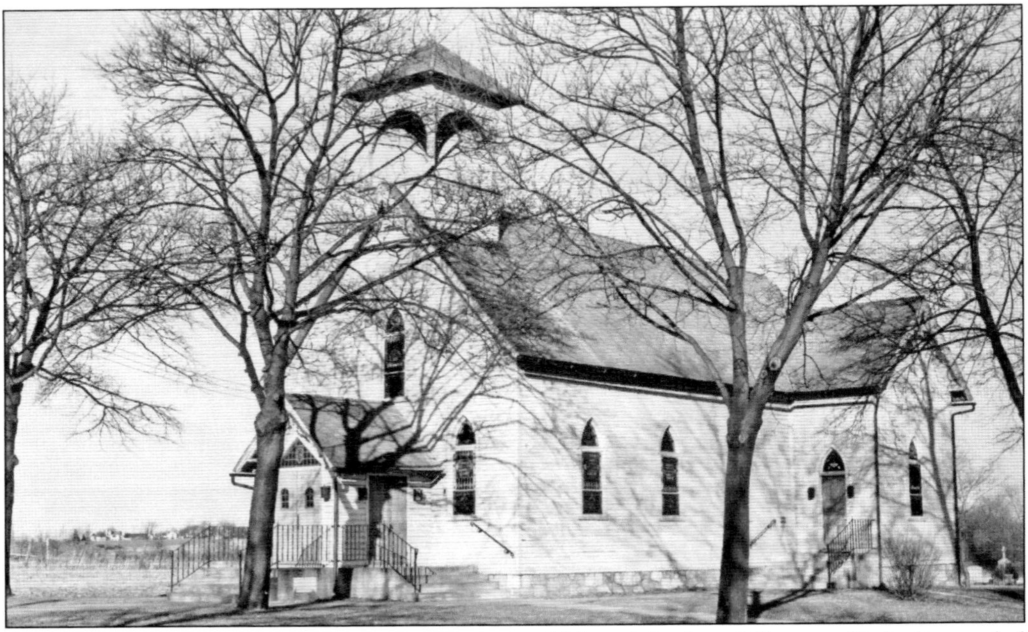

HOLY NAME OF JESUS ROMAN CATHOLIC CHURCH. Although Irish and German Catholics settled in Old Harrison throughout the 19th century, Holy Name Parish was not established until 1901. The parish has merged with St. Joseph's, Woodstown, and St. Ann's, Elmer, to form the Catholic Community of the Holy Spirit. A new church has been built nearby, but the original sanctuary still stands on Earlington Avenue.

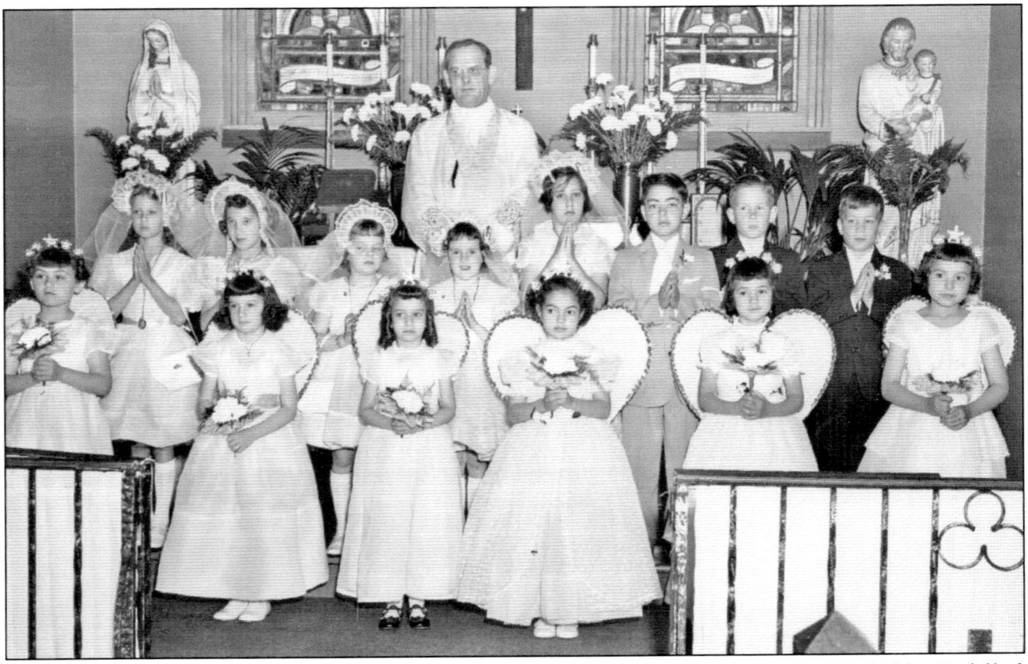

FIRST COMMUNION AT HOLY NAME. Children from the Alestra, Caltabiano, Childs, Dahllof, Dalton, Dougherty, Gallagher, O'Reilly, Schaefer, and Sheehan families gathered under the watchful eye of the Reverend Jerome Piontkowski at the altar in Holy Name Church for their First Communion photograph in 1954.

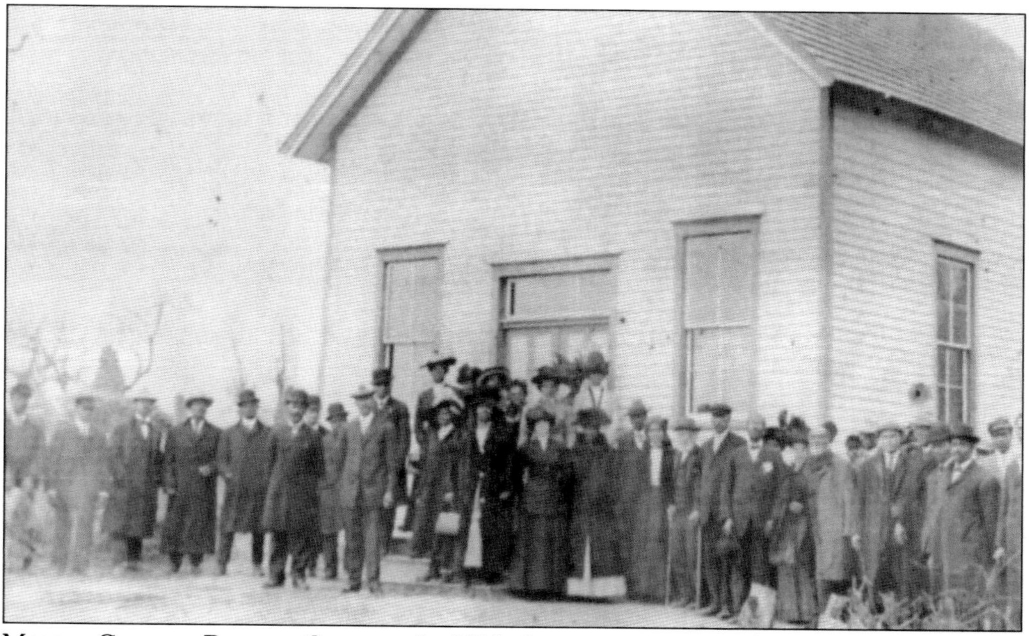

Mount Calvary Baptist Church. In 1905, the cornerstone was laid for the first African American church in Mullica Hill on High Street. The small church on a hill reminded the members of Calvary, so they named it Mount Calvary. The congregation first met for services in members' homes and then in Old Town Hall. This sanctuary served the congregation until 1976, when the present building was erected.

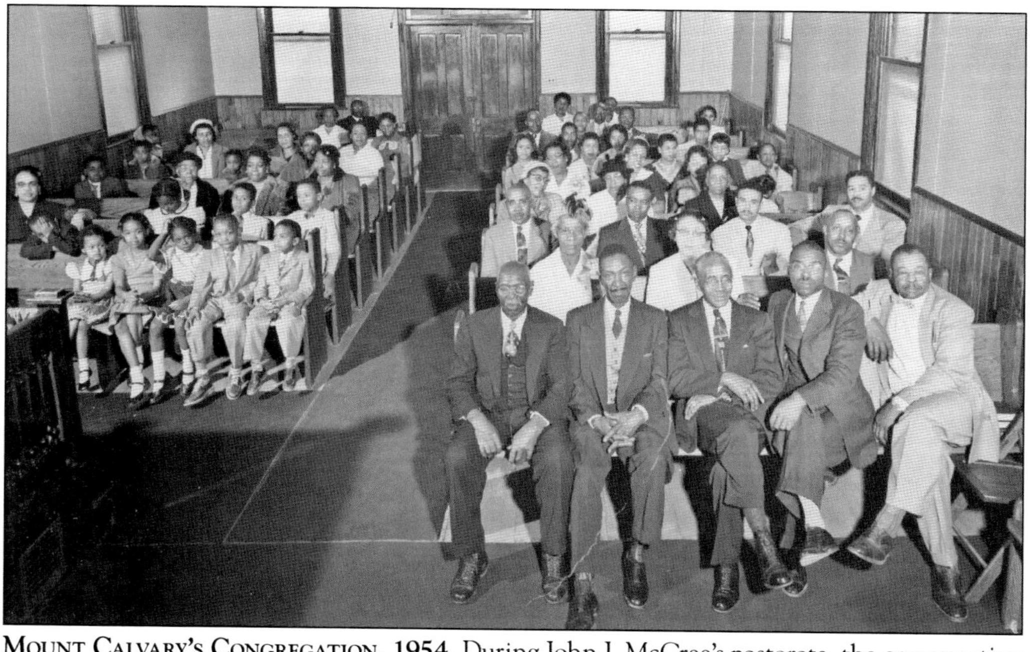

Mount Calvary's Congregation, 1954. During John J. McCree's pastorate, the congregation gathered in the church for a group photograph. Congregants present include members of the Banks, Bosdale, Bowens, Clark, Coleman, Combs, Gaines, Greene, Hall, Harris, Higgins, Hill, Holmes, Hynson, Jackson, Lane, McCree, Ratcliff, Robins, Thompson, Tyson, and Washington families—some of whom were involved in the church's founding.

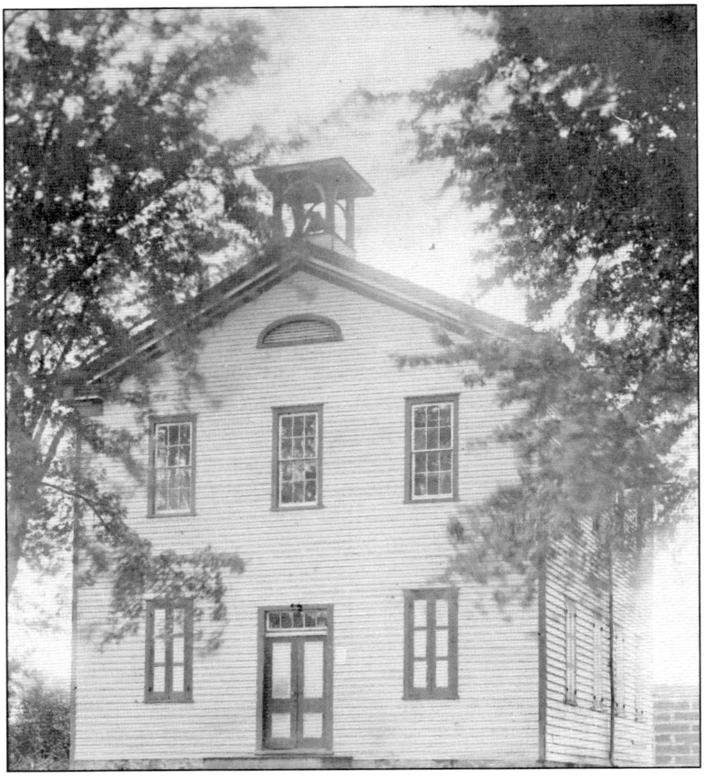

Union Academy. Quakers established the area's first schoolhouse, certainly one of earliest in Gloucester County, at this location on Woodstown Road around 1720. The log building was replaced twice before Union Academy, a public school, took its place in 1824. It was superseded by this two-story schoolhouse in 1855. In 1908, this building was moved to 24–26 Woodstown Road and converted into a double house to make way for the new Union Academy.

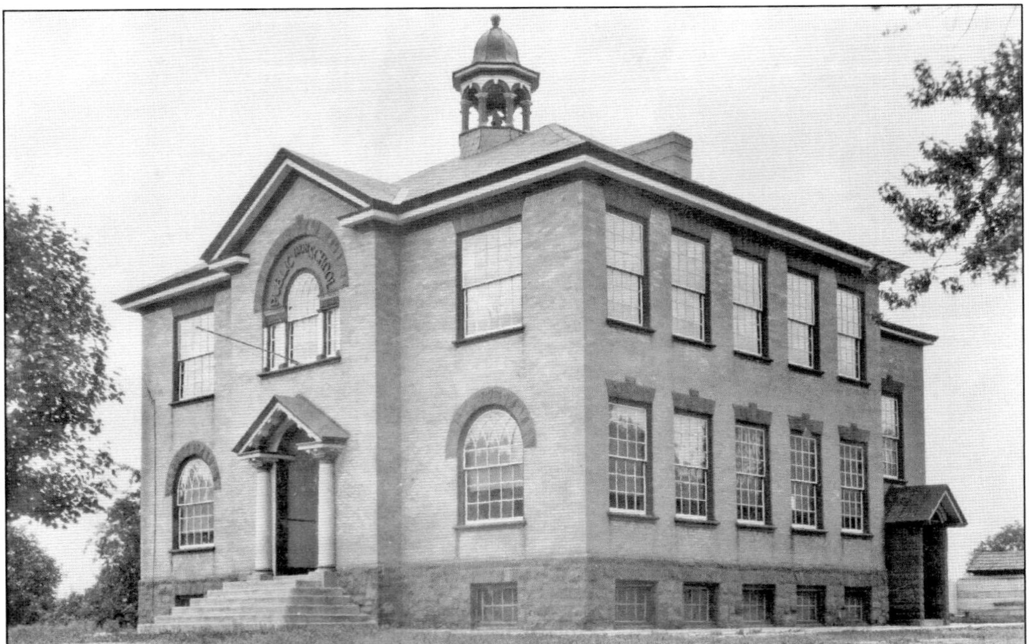

The New Union Academy. This handsome Colonial Revival building, the sixth and largest schoolhouse to occupy this location, opened in 1908. After the consolidated school opened in 1950, this building was used as a lodge hall, warehouse, sewing factory, and boat works until Friends School of Mullica Hill returned it to its original purpose in 1969.

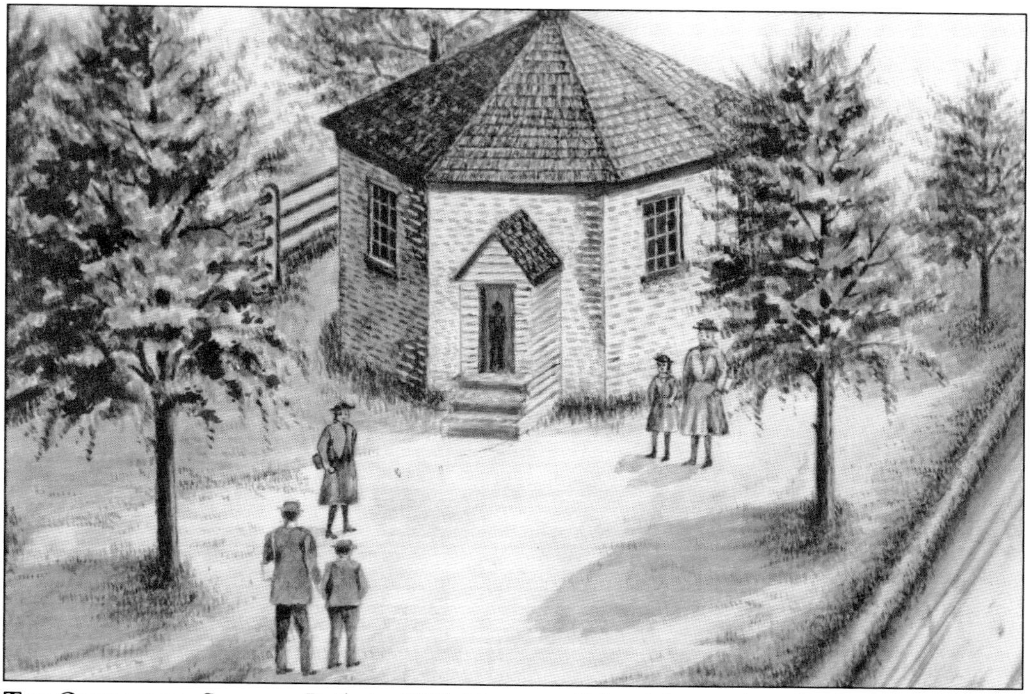

The Octagonal School. Built in 1805, Harmony School featured an "eight-square" design popular in the 19th century. The configuration was intended to provide equal light, ventilation and heat, and the windows were placed high in the wall to eliminate distractions. It also placed the schoolmaster in proximity to practically every student. It was replaced by a larger frame building in 1888.

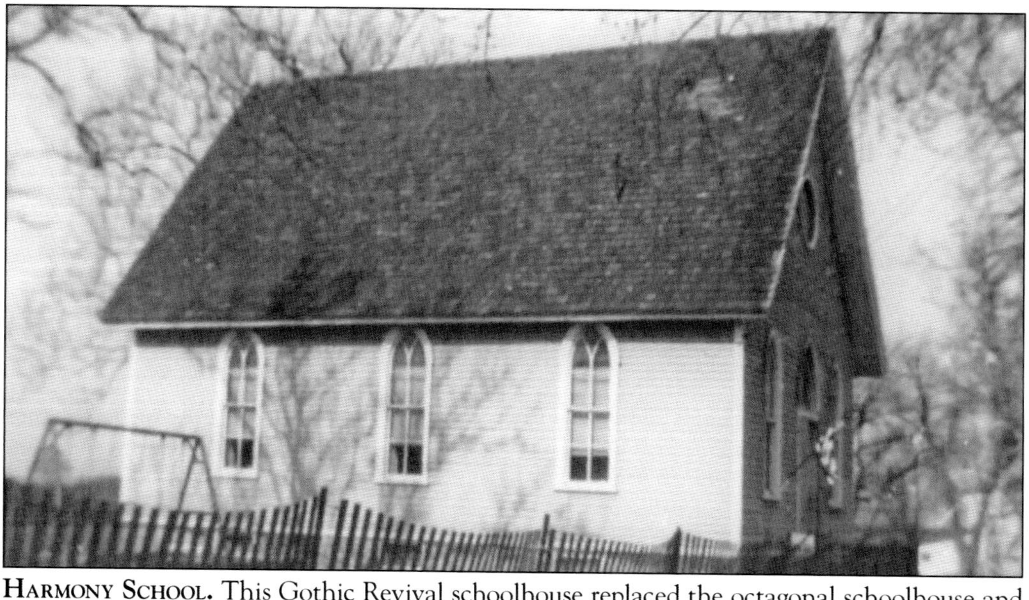

Harmony School. This Gothic Revival schoolhouse replaced the octagonal schoolhouse and served the community until the new consolidated school opened in 1950. All five of the small schoolhouses were subsequently sold. Harmony was used as a farm building until a hurricane twisted the structure off its foundation, rendering it unsafe. Harmony Fire Company was called upon to burn the building as a firefighting exercise in 1973.

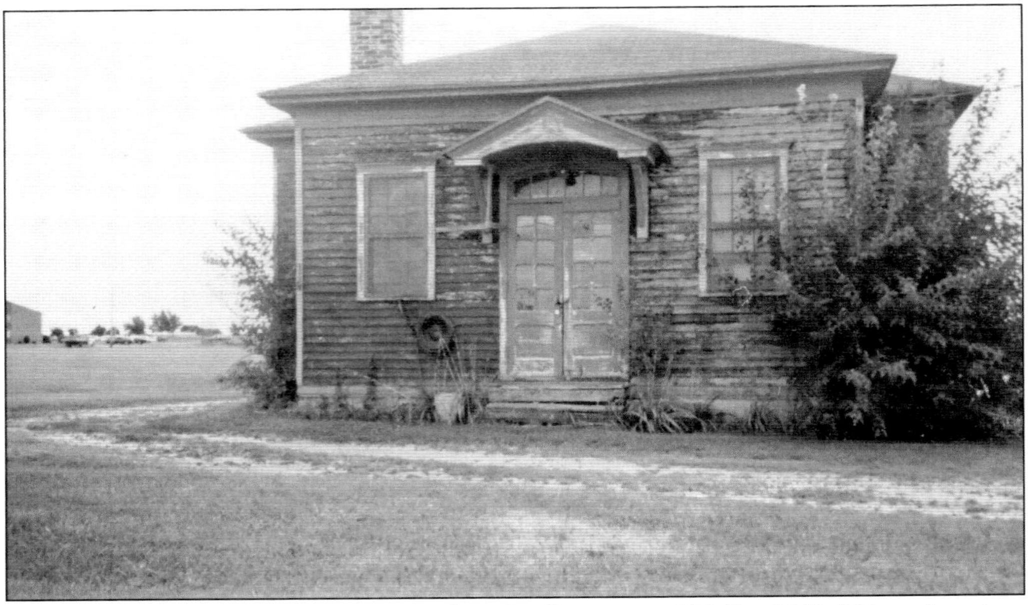

High Street School. From 1919 to 1950, this schoolhouse served Mullica Hill's African American community. Tradition maintains that the black citizenry here requested creation of a neighborhood school in order to provide employment opportunities for black teachers. The area's outlying schools, however, remained integrated. This photograph was taken after the schoolhouse was sold and, like Harmony School, was being used as a farm building. It was razed in the 1990s.

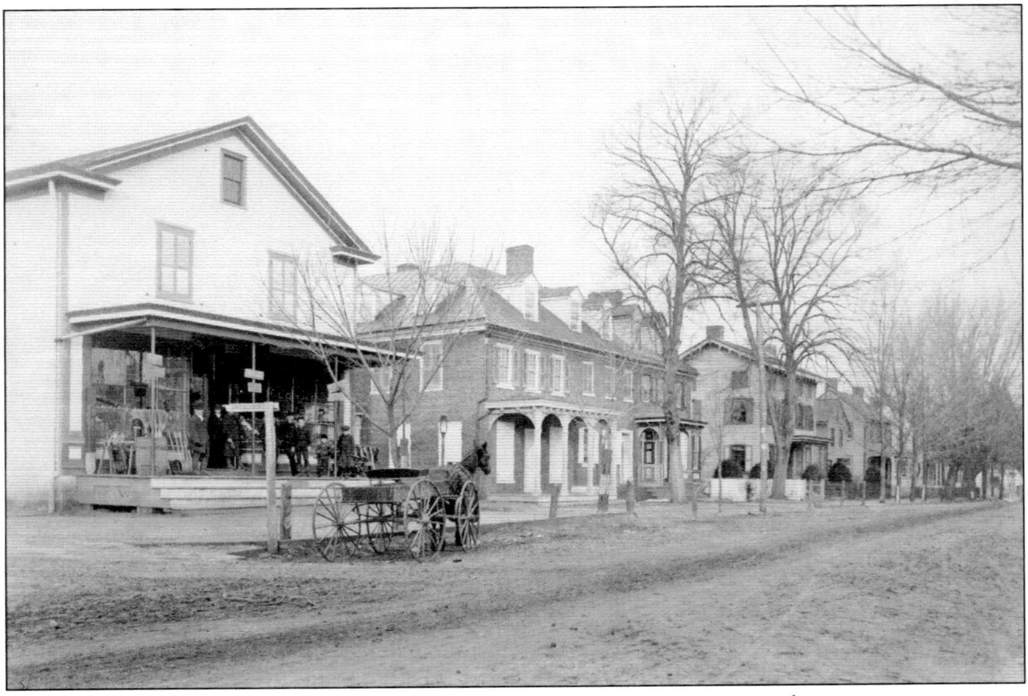

South Main and High Streets. Although taken over a century ago, this view remains very recognizable today. The row of brick townhouses, the center section of which was built in 1771, remains virtually unchanged and is a landmark building in the historic district. As in the past, the neighborhood remains a mix of residences and businesses.

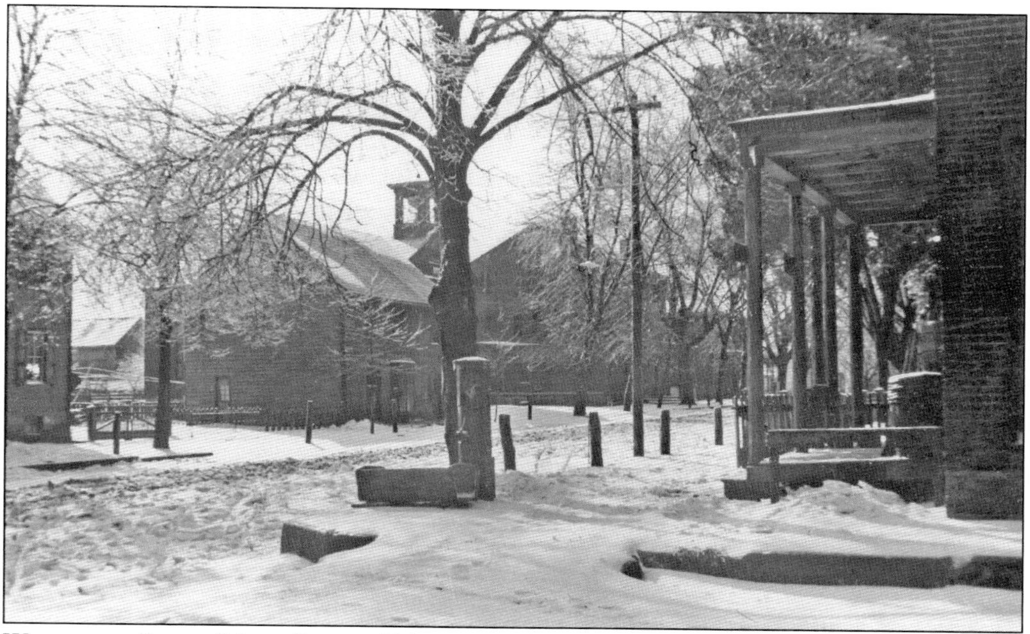

WINTER ON SOUTH MAIN STREET. Taken around 1905, this view of South Main Street centers around Trinity Methodist Church. The large building to the right of the church was Kier's Tin Shop. Joseph P. Stratton tore down the shop to build his new house, which later became the church's parsonage. Stratton owned Mullica Hill's first automobile dealership.

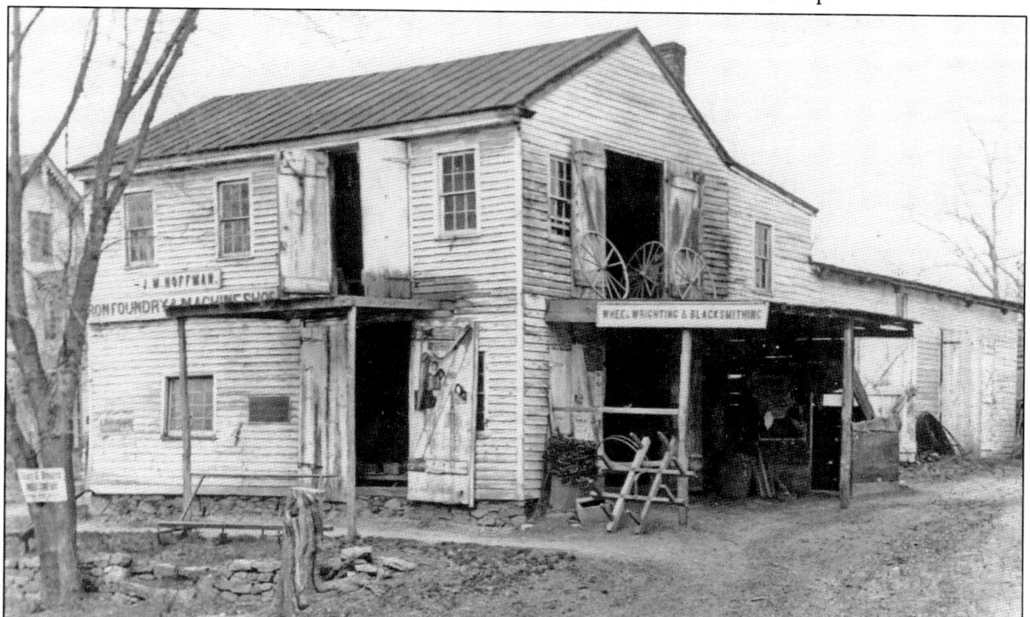

JACOB HOFFMAN IRON FOUNDRY AND MACHINE SHOP. Located on the corner of South Main and East Church Streets, the foundry was built in 1857 by Jacob Stratton and John Reece. Hoffman purchased Stratton's interest and took over the business after Reece retired. Reece and Hoffman manufactured wagons, farming implements, small castings, and ornamental iron fences. The building was later moved to the rear of the lot and turned to face Church Street, where it remains today.

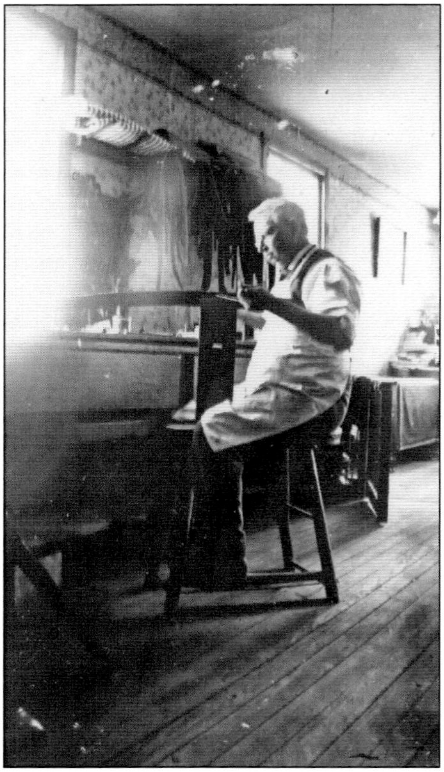

William F. Iredell, Harness Maker. In addition to operating his harness shop, William F. Iredell was also Mullica Hill's postmaster from 1897 to 1910. The store and post office were located in the north end of his home at 26 South Main Street. This photograph was taken by his son, Edward, who succeeded him as postmaster. Mullica Hill's post office was established in 1802.

French Lodge No. 89, Independent Order of Odd Fellows. French Lodge was instituted in 1849 and named in honor of Capt. Samuel Gibbs French, hailed at the time as a local Mexican-American War hero. In 1853, members dedicated their first lodge hall, located on the third floor of a building that once stood on South Main Street, south of First Baptist Church. Today, the lodge meets in Richwood Academy and is the township's oldest civic organization.

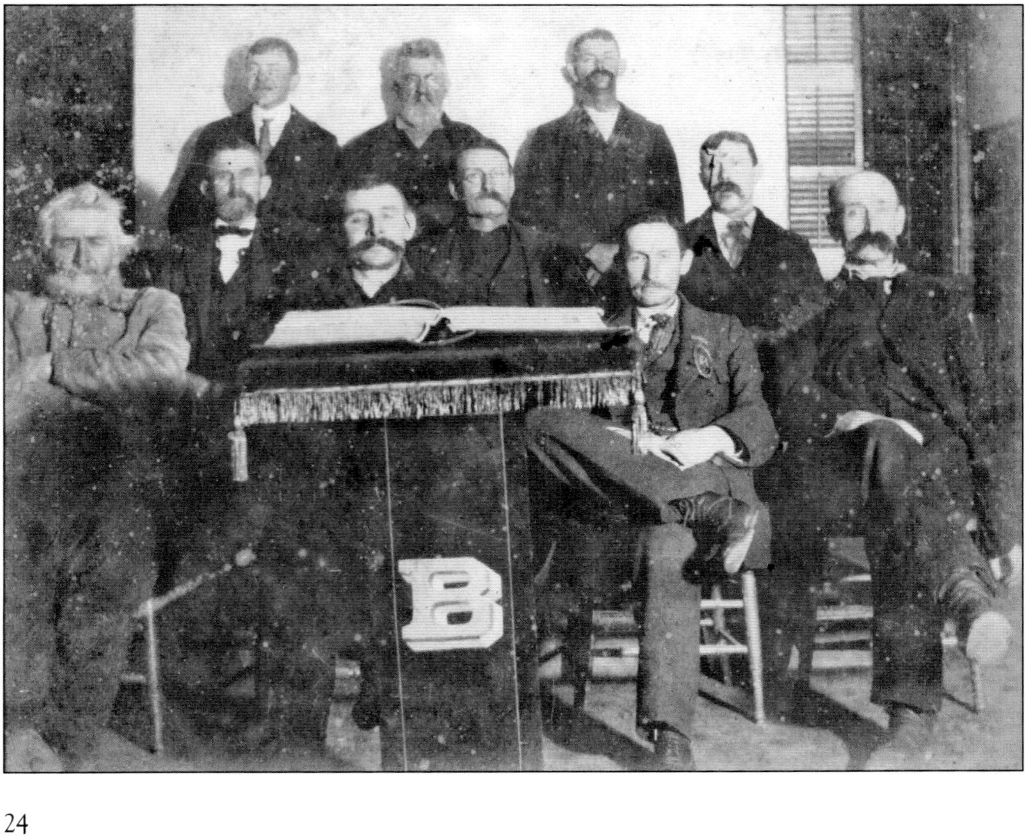

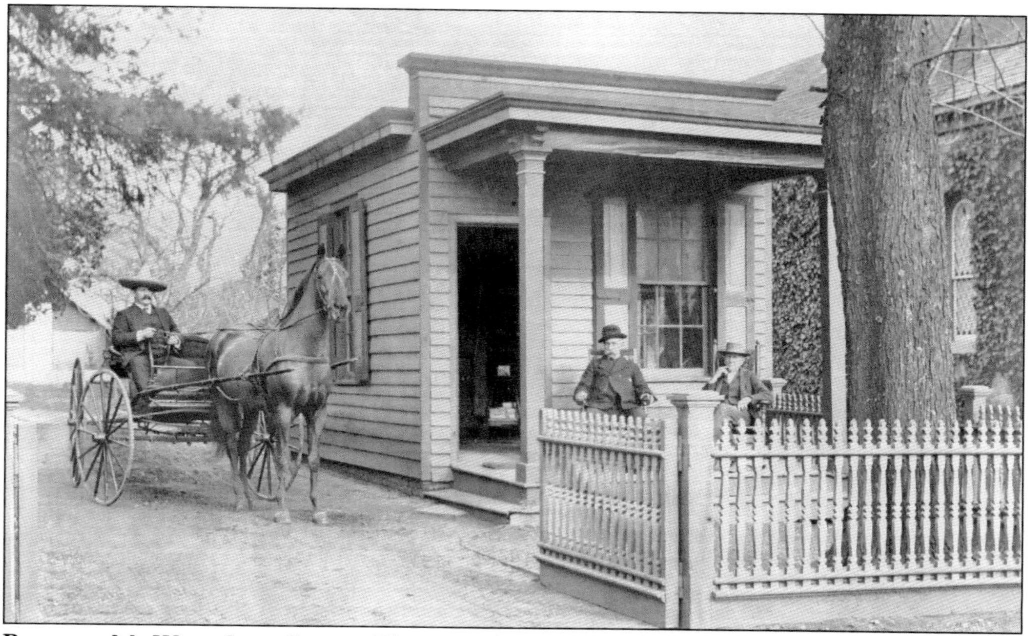

RICHARD M. WARE LAW OFFICE. The seventh son of well-known chair-maker Maskell Ware, Richard M. Ware practiced law instead of following the family business. He moved to Mullica Hill in 1842 and in 1850 built his home and office to become the town's first lawyer. His office was turned into a cottage in the late 19th century and moved behind his house at 53 North Main Street, where it remains today.

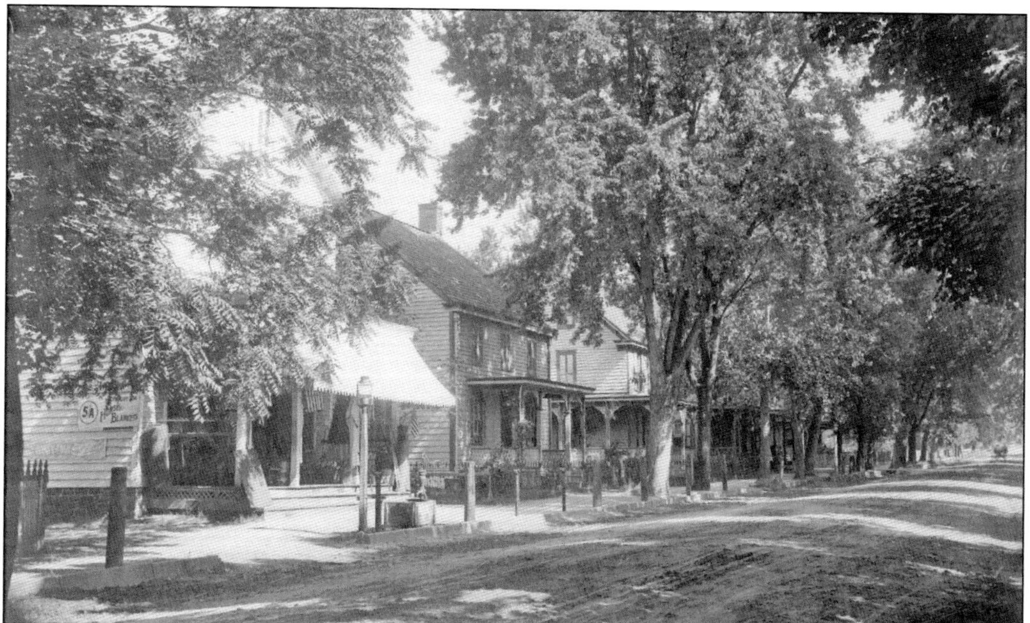

NORTH MAIN STREET, C. 1900. The Union Store Company commenced business in 1866 at the corner of North Main Street and Woodland Avenue. Shortly thereafter, it opened a new and more commodious building at 46 North Main Street and became one of the principal merchants of Mullica Hill, although the surrounding neighborhood remained largely residential. The Union Store remains a well-preserved 19th-century commercial building.

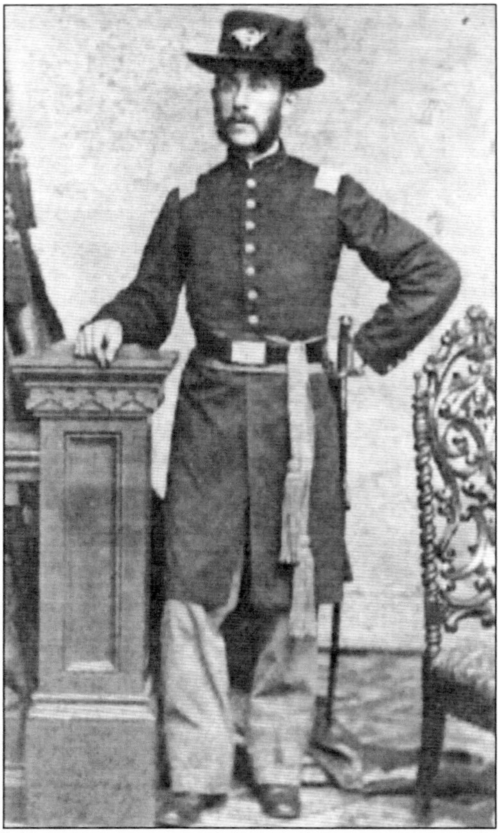

Capt. Edward L. Stratton. Commissioned as captain, 12th New Jersey Volunteers, in 1862, Edward was the elder son of Congressman Nathan T. Stratton. In 1863, he was severely wounded at Chancellorsville resulting in the amputation of his right leg. In 1865, he was brevetted major and lieutenant colonel for gallant and meritorious service. The war took its toll on his family—his brother James lost his life at Ream's Station in 1864. (DT.)

Edward Stratton House. Stratton resided in this elegant house after the war until his death in 1915. Stratton kept the minié ball that caused the amputation of his leg. He was remembered in later years sitting on the porch and showing this grim souvenir of his brush with death to the town's children.

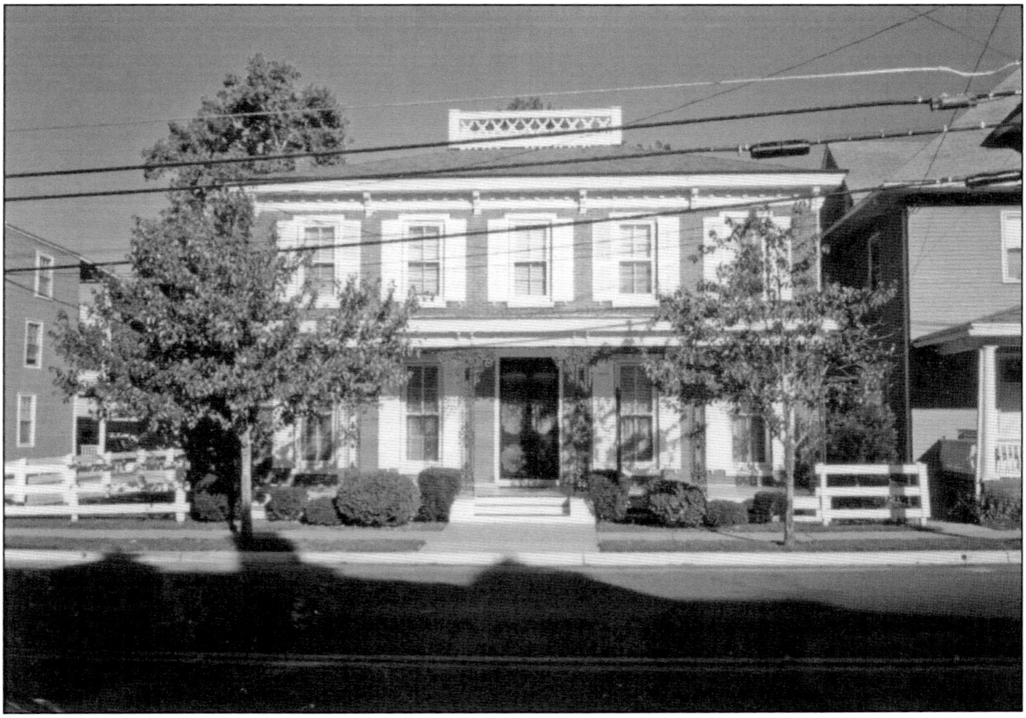

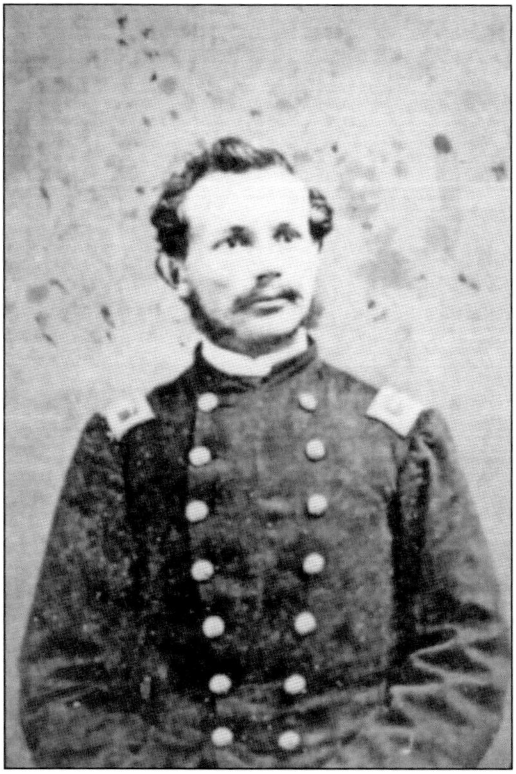

Brig. Gen. Charles G. Harker. Born in Swedesboro in 1835, Harker moved to Mullica Hill to clerk in Nathan Stratton's store in 1848. He received an appointment to West Point through Congressman Stratton. During the Civil War, Harker distinguished himself at Stones River and Chickamauga. At Kennesaw Mountain, however, he was shot from his horse and died June 27, 1864. Funeral services were held at his brother's home in Mullica Hill. (DT.)

Decoration Day, First Baptist Cemetery, c. 1900. The tradition of decorating military graves with flowers in May began in the aftermath of the Civil War. Several Union soldiers, including James and Edward Stratton, are buried in the cemetery behind the First Baptist Church. In recent years, a Civil War reenactment encampment has been held there annually in the fall.

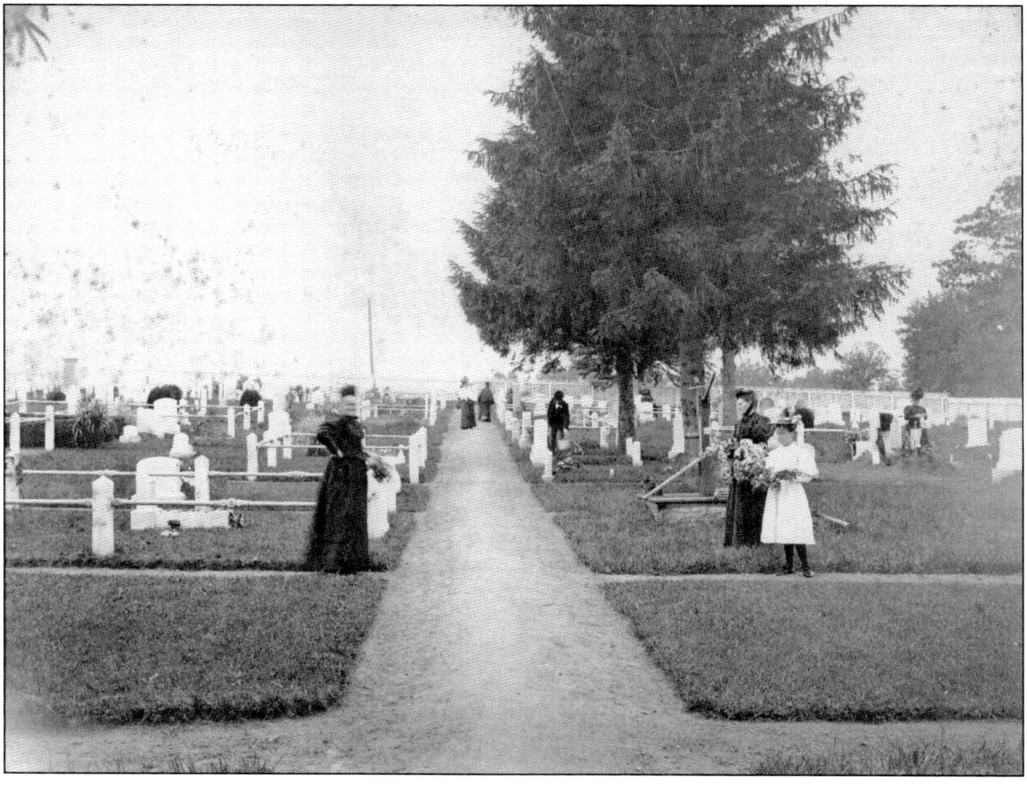

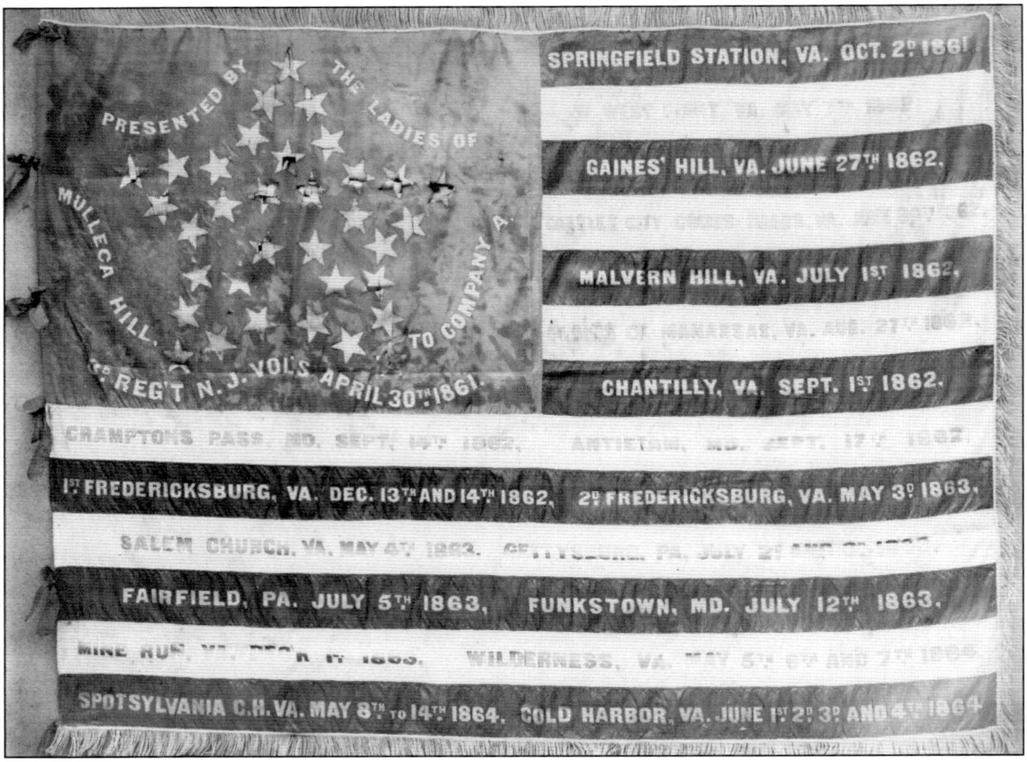

FLAG, COMPANY A, 3RD REGIMENT, FIRST NEW JERSEY VOLUNTEERS. The men of Company A were the first from Gloucester County to join the Union army. On April 30, 1861, the company marched from Woodbury to a reception at the Union Academy in Mullica Hill. That afternoon Lucretia Stratton, daughter of former congressman, Nathan T. Stratton, Helen Coats, and Sue Batten presented this flag made for the company by the women of the town.

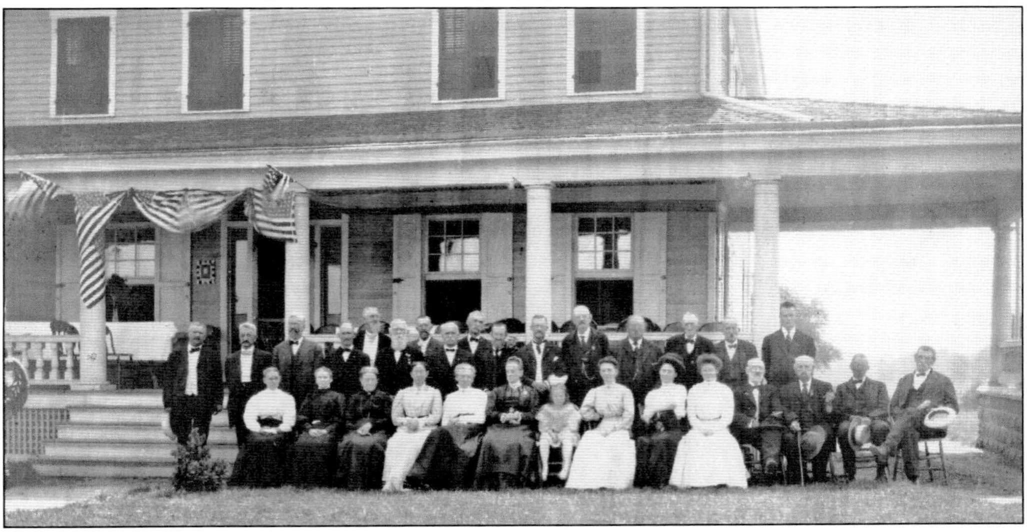

COMPANY A REUNION, 3RD REGIMENT, FIRST NEW JERSEY VOLUNTEERS. On September 14, 1909, veterans of Company A and their wives gathered at the home of Dr. James Wamsley on Folwell Lane 48 years after their enlistment. The men had survived many of the major battles of the Civil War and had witnessed the surrender at Appomattox.

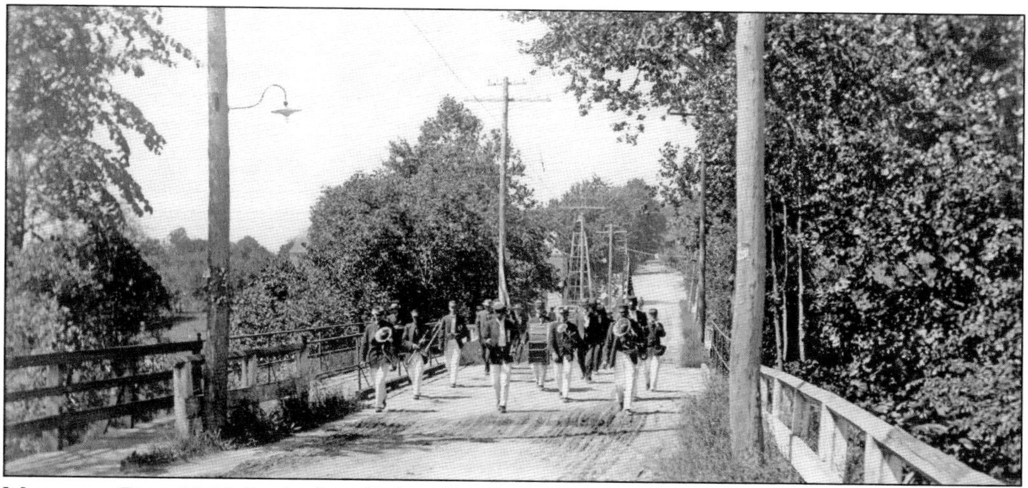

Memorial Day, 1906. In the late 19th and early 20th centuries, Memorial or Decoration Day was a solemn occasion. In the morning, children collected wildflowers to place on graves throughout the town. Patriotic speeches and a picnic followed in the afternoon. Music was also provided by the Mullica Hill Concert Band, seen here crossing the bridge to the south end of town. (WPL.)

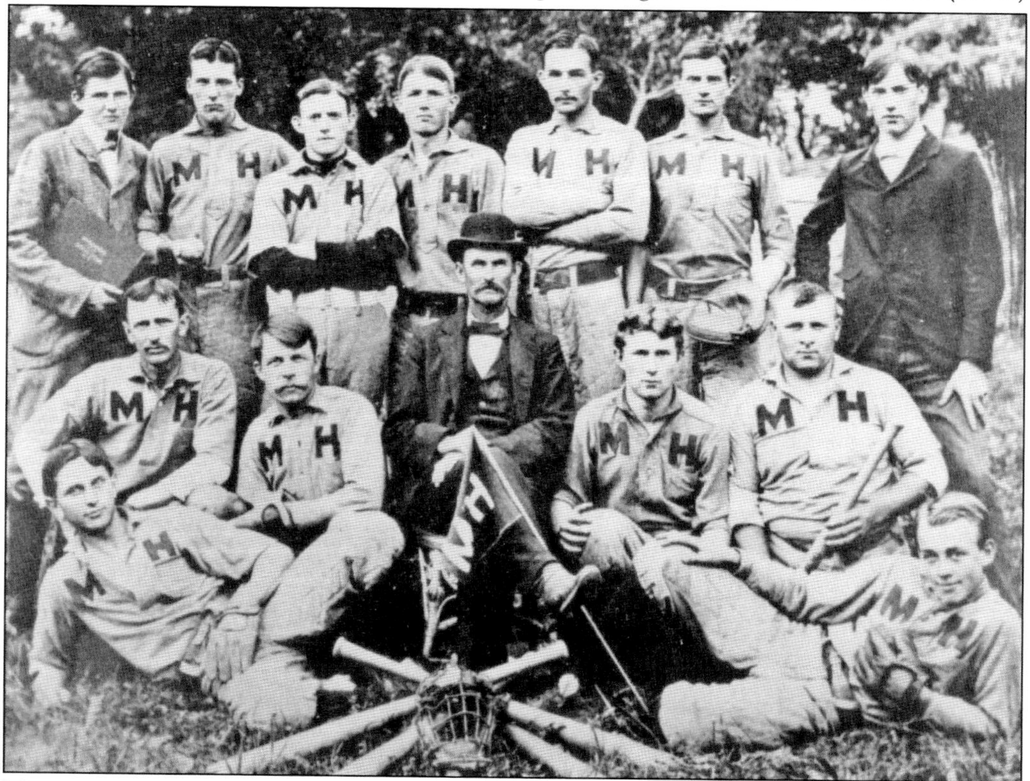

Mullica Hill Baseball Team, 1902. Small-town baseball games were very popular in the 19th and early 20th centuries. Pictured from left to right are (first row) Wash Warner and Walter Bunning; (second row) George Shea, Thomas Thompson, Isaac White, Matt Firman, and George Madara; (third row) Tom Folwell, Bill Streeper, Ward Davies, Charles Folwell, Sam White, Joe White, and Ira Fox. On July 4, 1918, members of this team soundly defeated the local team of younger players.

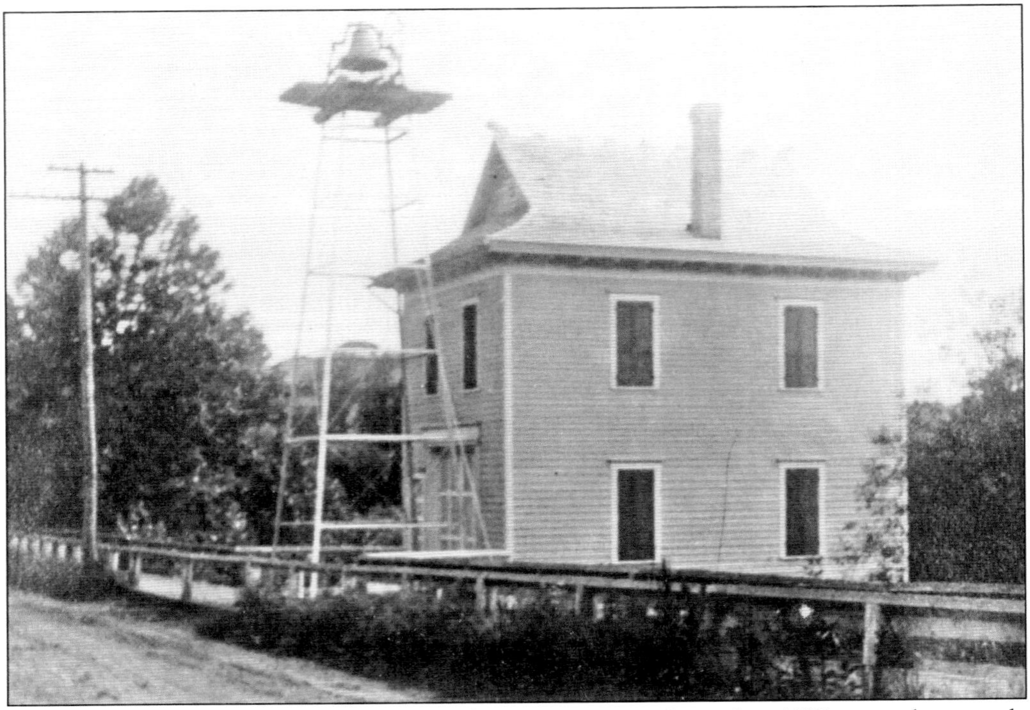

Harmony Firehouse. Mullica Hill's first fire company was formed in 1827 as much to evade military service as to fight fires; fire company members were exempt from serving in the local militia. A small building on the Friends Meeting property housed a 1790 hand pumper, still in the company's possession. In the early 20th century, the company reorganized and built this, its second firehouse, in 1905 at 14 North Main Street.

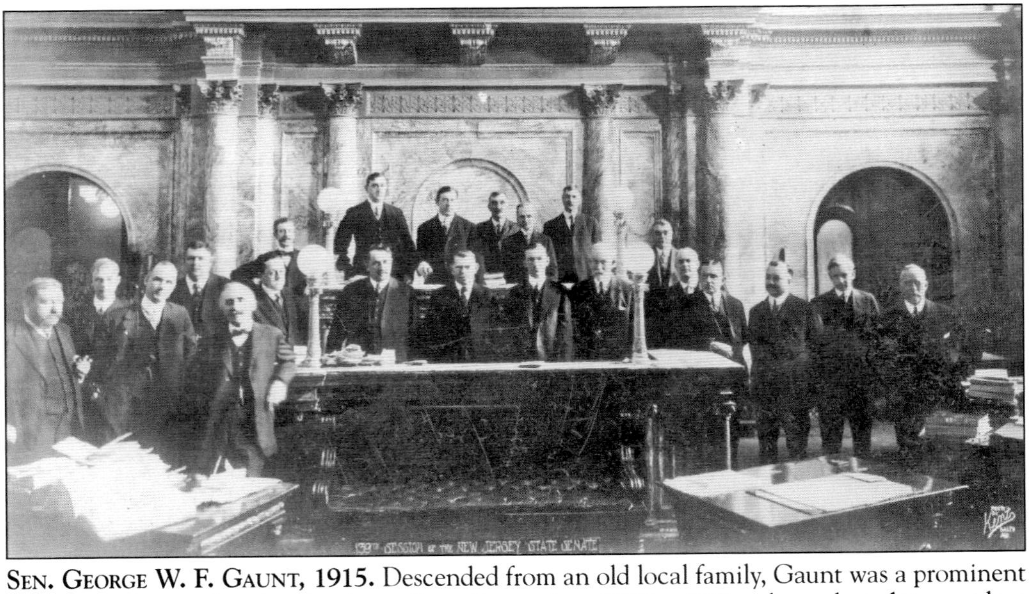

Sen. George W. F. Gaunt, 1915. Descended from an old local family, Gaunt was a prominent politician. He served in the New Jersey State Senate from 1909 to 1917 and was elected its president in 1916–1917. In that capacity, he briefly served as acting governor. He is pictured here in the senate chamber, second from the left behind the front desk. He died tragically on September 18, 1918, of injuries sustained fighting a local fire.

PVT. ELMER MORGAN. Of the 30 local men who served in World War I, Elmer Morgan was the only serviceman who lost his life. He was a member of Company E, 303rd Ammunition Train, 78th Division, US Army. He died in France on February 5, 1919. He was 27 years of age. (NJSA.)

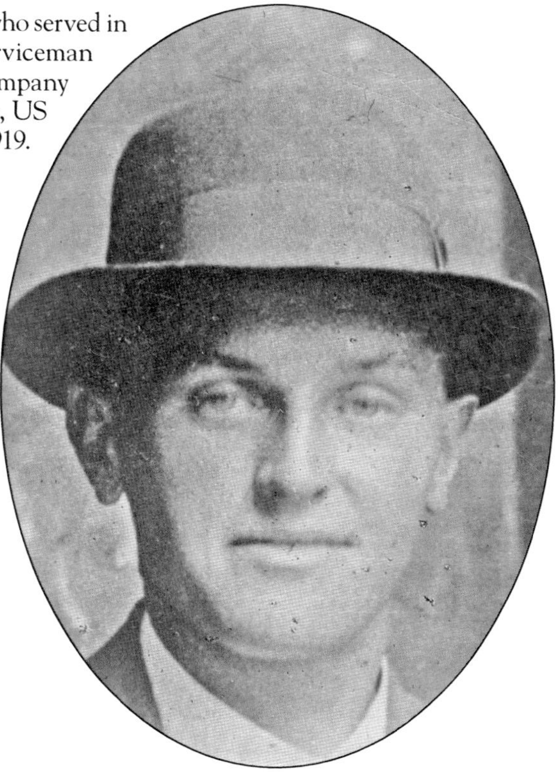

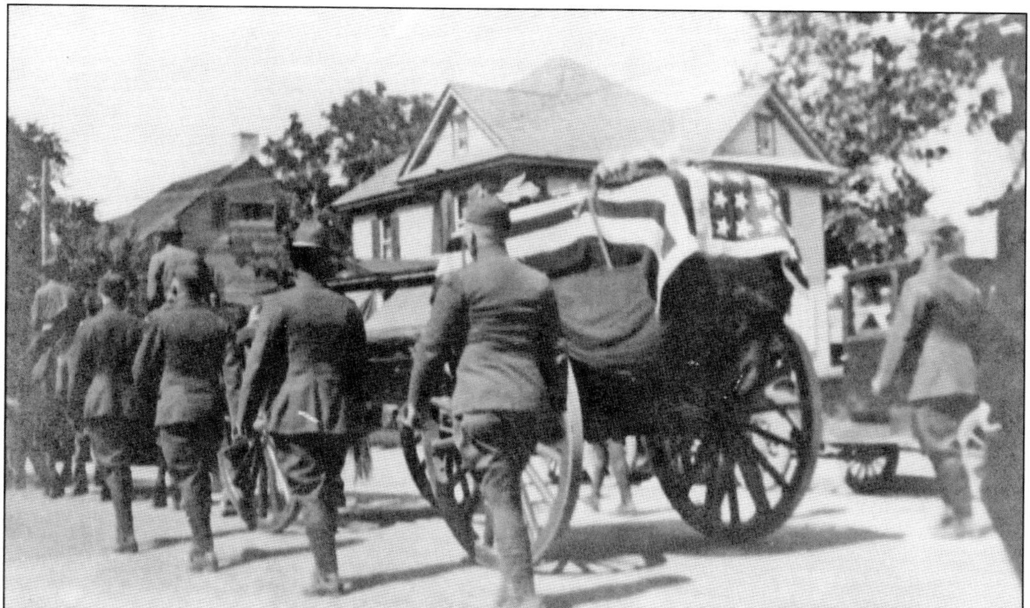

ELMER MORGAN'S FUNERAL PROCESSION. Morgan's remains were laid to rest in the First Baptist Cemetery on June 19, 1921. Woodbury's American Legion Bonsal Post organized a full military funeral with firing squad and horse-drawn caisson, which was attended by a huge crowd. Swedesboro Band provided music. The previous year, a monument honoring Morgan and all those who served in the World War I had been erected in front of Old Town Hall.

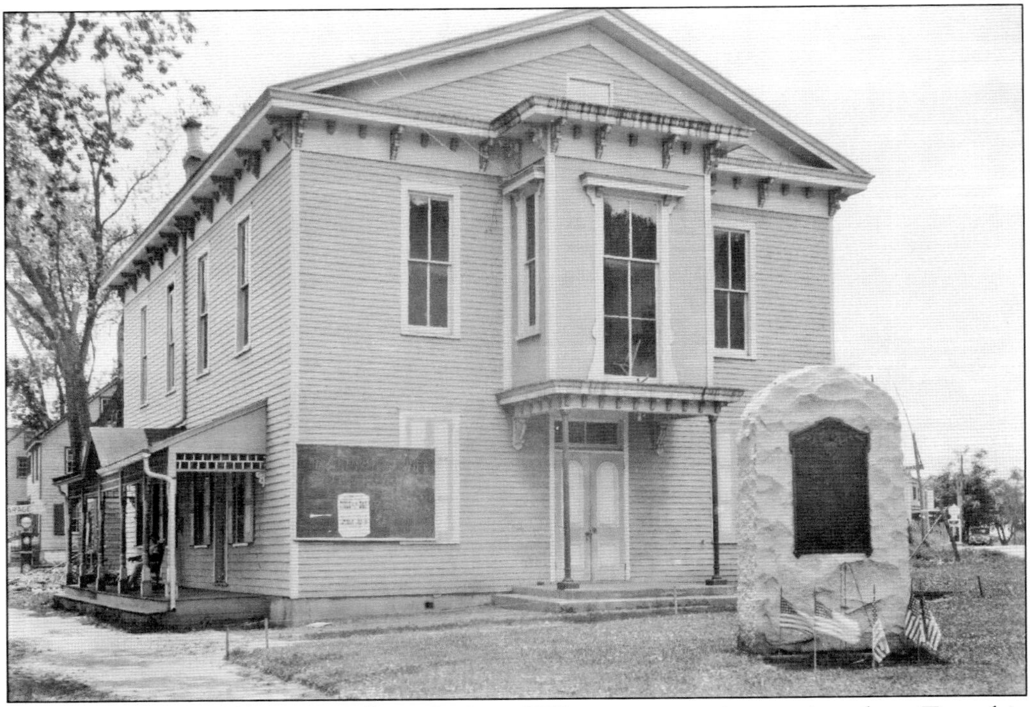

OLD TOWN HALL. Old Town Hall was built in 1871 as a community meeting place. Township business was conducted here, along with entertainments, small businesses, a Friends School, and the first meetings of Mount Calvary Baptist Church. By 1971, the landmark was no longer used by the township and became the Harrison Township Historical Society's museum and research library. The society has won state and national awards for its exhibitions, programs and publications.

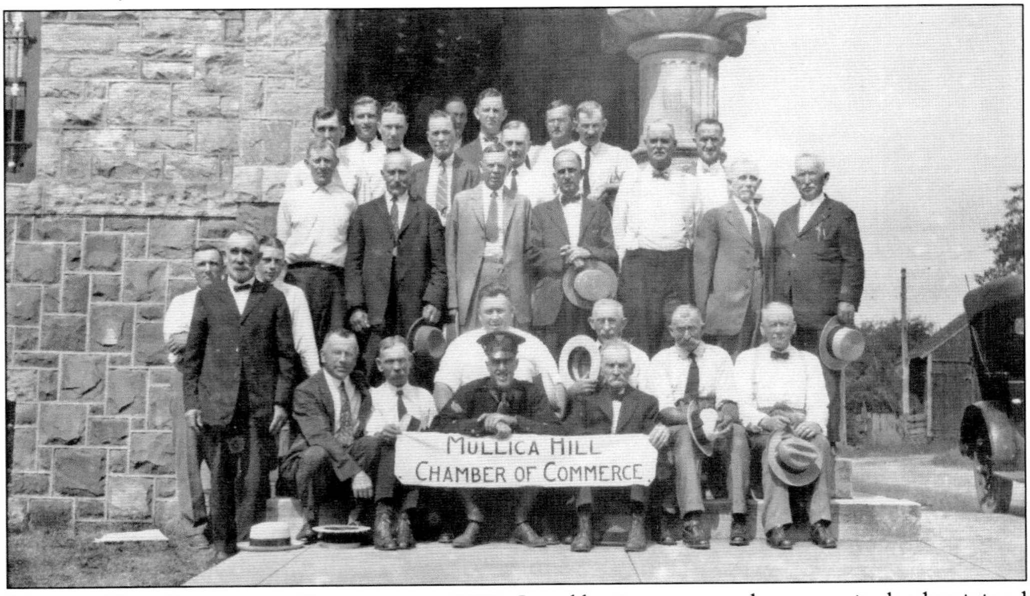

MULLICA HILL CHAMBER OF COMMERCE, C. 1920. Local businessmen and community leaders joined together in the 1920s to encourage investment and economic growth. Touting its advantageous location, they promoted Mullica Hill as "Beautiful, High, Healthful in every sense of the word." Their efforts proved short-lived when the Depression gripped the nation at the end of the decade.

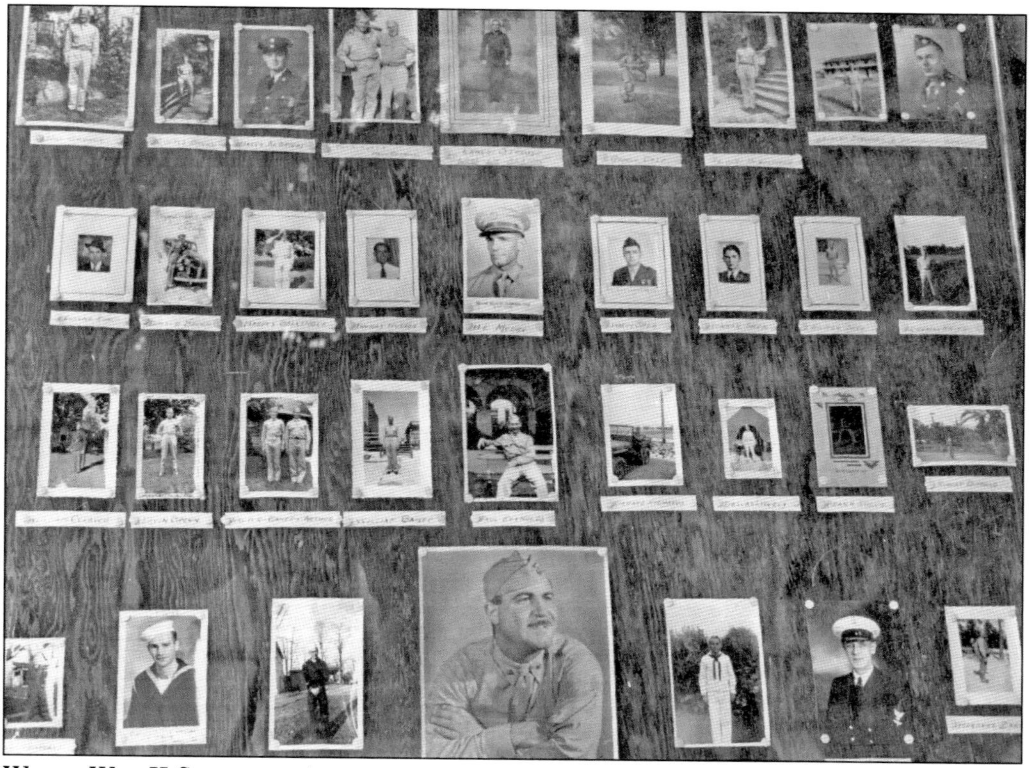

World War II Servicemen's Display, Estilow's Store. Wanting to honor the men of Mullica Hill serving in the military, C. C. Estilow gathered photographs from family members to create this patriotic collage in the front window of his grocery, the former Union Store Company on North Main Street. The display remained on view until the end of the war. (GCHS.)

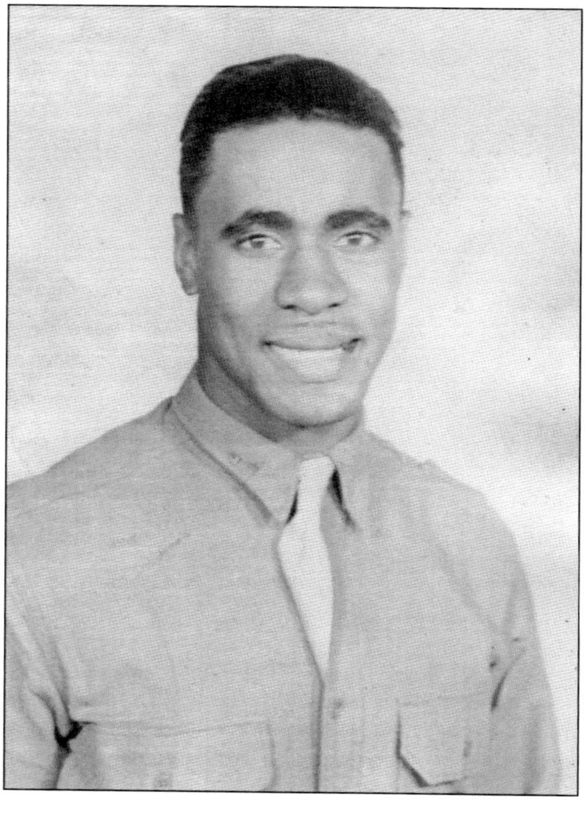

2nd Lt. James C. Johnson (1920–1945). The eldest son of William Johnson and Mary Seeney of Mullica Hill, James "Billy" Johnson enlisted as a private in the US Army in October 1941 and later received an officer commission. In 1944, he was assigned to the Italian theater, where he was killed in action in 1945. He was one of two men from Mullica Hill who died during World War II. The Mullica Hill Post Office was named in his honor in 2018.

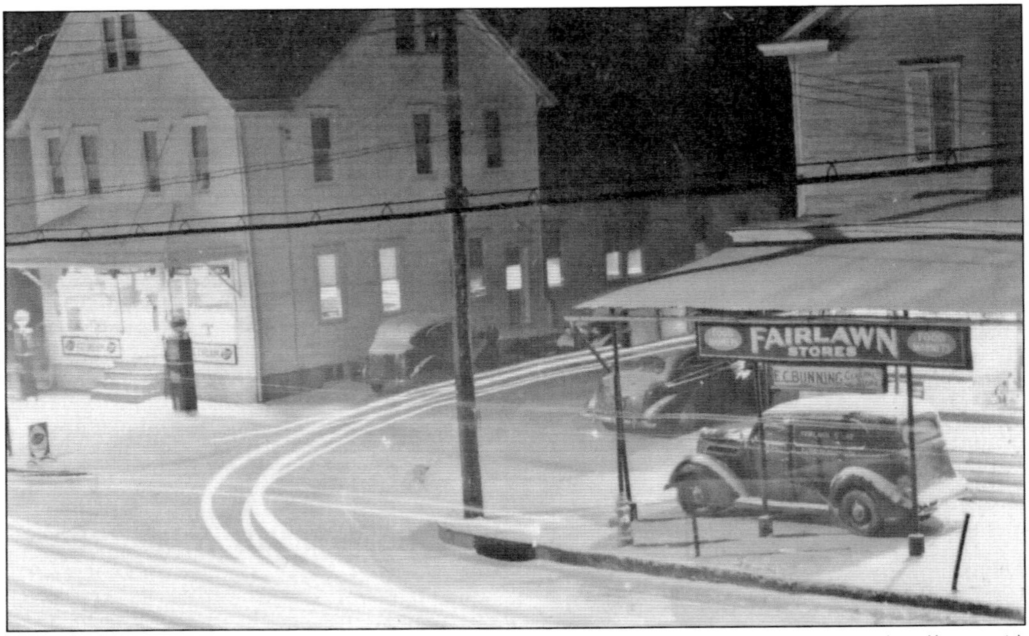

Winter Evening at South Main and High Streets. E. C. Bunning's (formerly Elkinton's) Store and Bowe's Restaurant (later Mullica Hill's post office) were centers of activity on the south side of town. Like C. C. Estilow on the north side of town, Bunning continued to operate a traditional country store, and the two competitors had an informal agreement not to encroach on each other's territory.

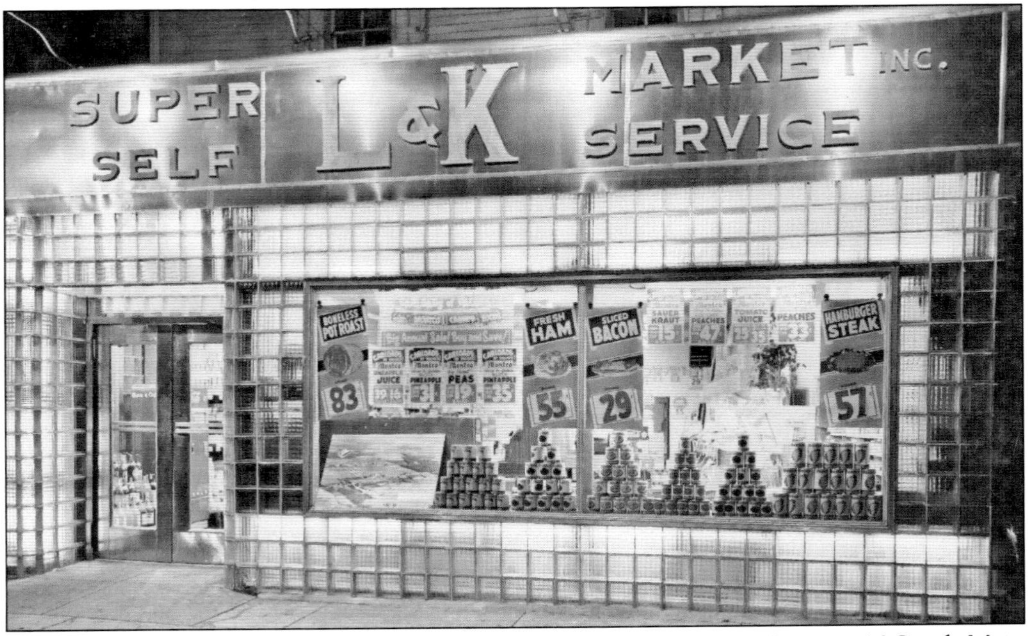

L&K Market. "Izzy" Lees and "Smiles" Kaplan purchased Bunning's Store at 46 South Main Street in the late 1940s and shortly thereafter undertook a major remodeling. L&K was the town's first self-service market and the glass block facade and stainless steel signage, unlike anything else in the township, conveyed modernity. It signaled the demise of old-style country stores, although it, too, would be supplanted by larger supermarkets.

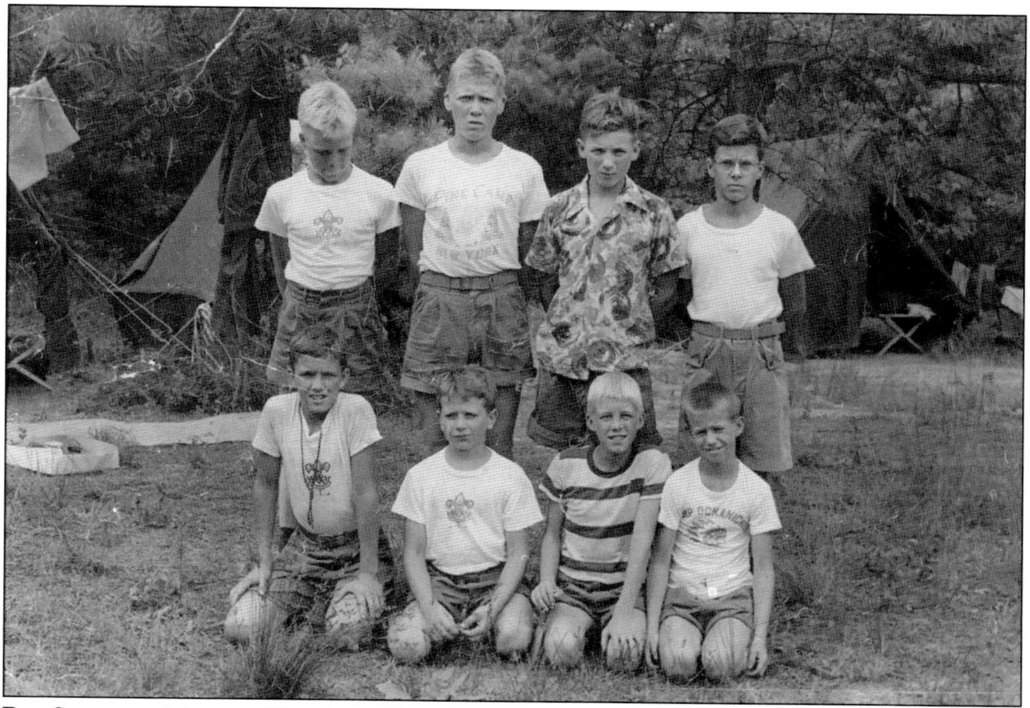

Boy Scouts in Mullica Hill. Local boys have long been involved with Scouting, however, it was not until 1951 that Troop 44 received its official charter at St. Stephen's Episcopal Church. Pictured from left to right at Camp Roosevelt near Alloway are (front row) Scouts Walter Jones, Richard Lippincott, David Rope, and Allen Thompson; (back row) Scouts J. B. Rope, Jim Wigglesworth, Phil Ashcraft, and Roy Duffield. The troop celebrated its 60th anniversary in 2011.

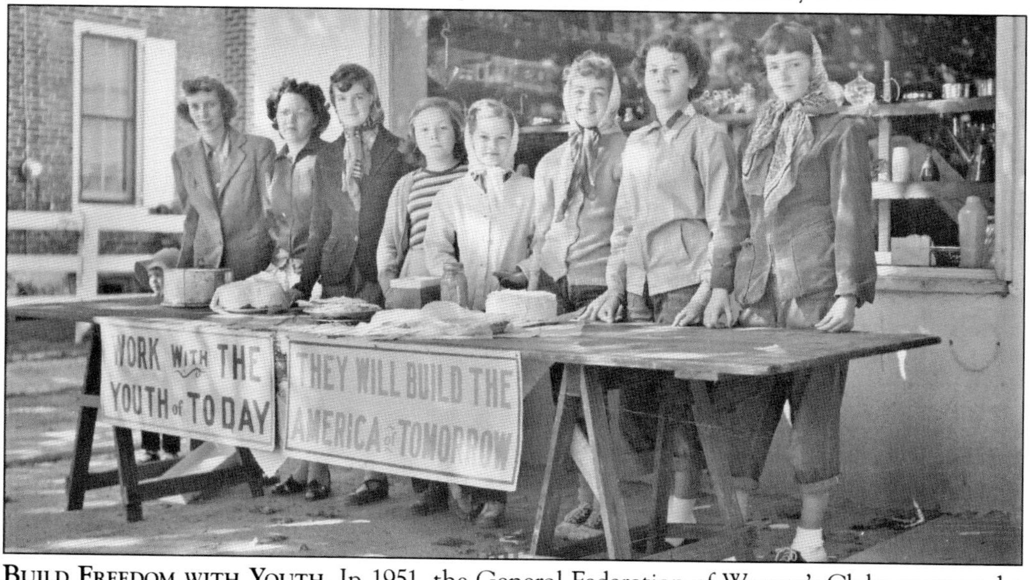

Build Freedom with Youth. In 1951, the General Federation of Women's Clubs sponsored a national contest to encourage development of programs for young people with a $10,000 first prize. Mullica Hill Women's Club decided to reorganize Girl Scout Troop 51, which had disbanded in 1949. The troop's first fundraiser was a cake sale at Dosch's Market, 38 South Main Street. A dictionary stand for the school library was purchased with the proceeds.

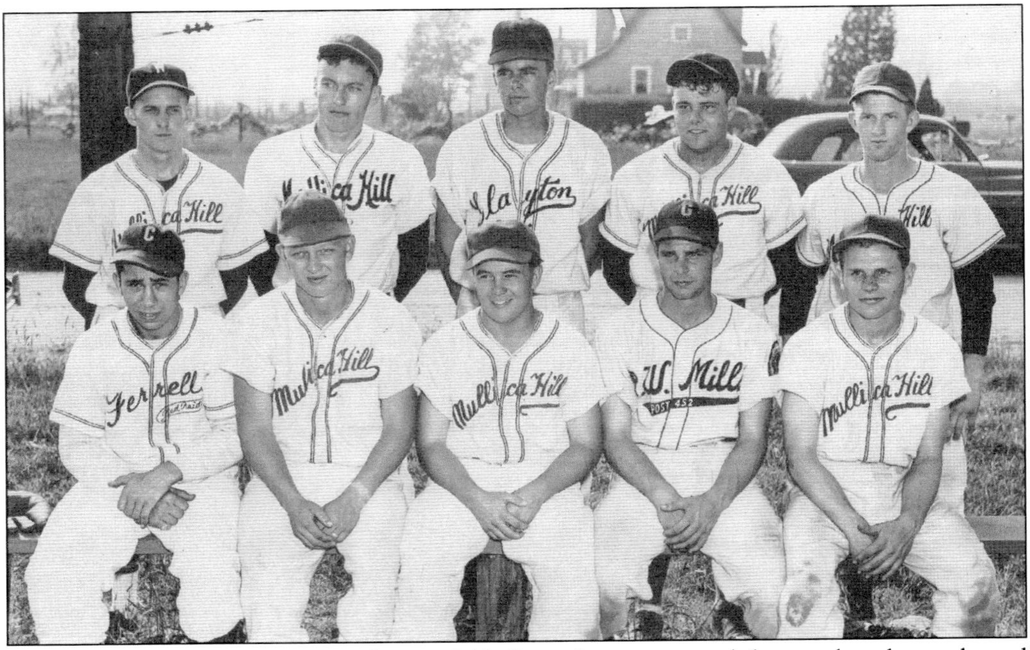

MULLICA HILL JUNIOR BASEBALL CLUB, 1948. By mid-century, youth leagues largely supplanted the local men's teams. The 1948 team included a number of talented players. William Wilt, for example, was a stand-out athlete and was scouted by the Yankees, but he enlisted in the Marines. Pictured from left to right are (first row) Joseph Razze, Leon Kincaid, Kenneth Steffen, William Wilt, and Walter Heritage; (second row) Roger Lee, George Knapp, Sidney Moore, Thomas Holtzhauser, and William Datz.

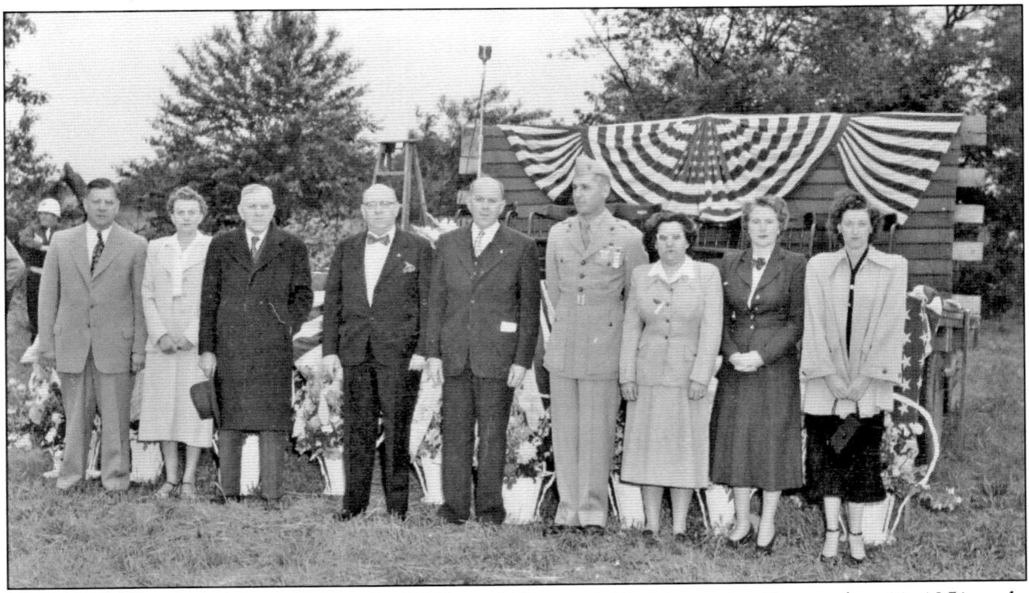

WILT MEMORIAL DEDICATION, 1952. William Wilt was killed in action September 11, 1951, only six months after his enlistment. He was the only local casualty of the Korean War. Less than a year later, it was decided to name the athletic field and erect a monument behind Harrison Township School in his honor. In 2008, the monument was moved to the new soccer complex, which was dedicated to his memory.

Two

Along Raccoon Creek

The Raccoon Creek watershed was the site of the first European settlement in Old Harrison Township.

It is said that the creek was navigable by small boats to Mullica Hill in the early 18th century. Intensive clearing for farming and the timber trade caused the channel to silt in, making such navigation difficult to imagine today. The waterway's principal value, however, came from the waterpower it could supply. The ravine through which the creek travels offered several potential millsites, and the number and types of mills proliferated into the 19th century. Communities subsequently developed around the mills at Mullica Hill and Ewan.

The gristmills and sawmills at Ewan were established around the time of the American Revolution, and the gristmill continued operating into the 1920s. Ewan, however, lacked Mullica Hill's advantageous location on a major roadway and so remained a small country village throughout its history. Still, the town was once able to boast of a church and school, several stores, hotel, blacksmith, and wheelwright shops, a distillery, bicycle manufacturer, and a large livestock auction in addition to the mills.

The sawmill and pond at present-day Lake Gilman had long disappeared when work commenced to create a lakeside park and summer cottage community in the 1920s. Instead of powering a mill, the lake development was part of an emerging leisure economy. Although no longer a public park, Lake Gilman remains true to its recreational origins. Raccoon Creek's string of lakes are today scenic and recreational assets, not drivers of industry.

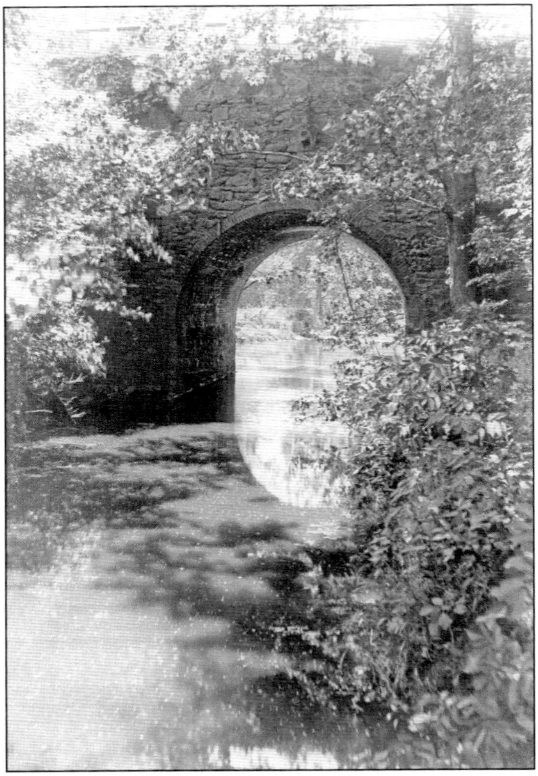

The Stone Arch Bridge. Mullica Hill's picturesque masonry arch bridge over Raccoon Creek was a Main Street landmark for over a century. When Bridgeton Pike was paved in 1919–1920, the bridge was replaced and the piers buried beneath the new structure. (WPL.)

Mullica Hill Gristmill. For 200 years, milling played a vital role in Mullica Hill's industrial history. Christopher Knisell built this building in 1809, replacing a mid-18th-century mill that was located across Mill Road. A lengthy raceway from the millpond increased the height of the spillway. The equipment was updated several times, but ultimately, the business could not compete with mass-manufactured brands of flour and feed.

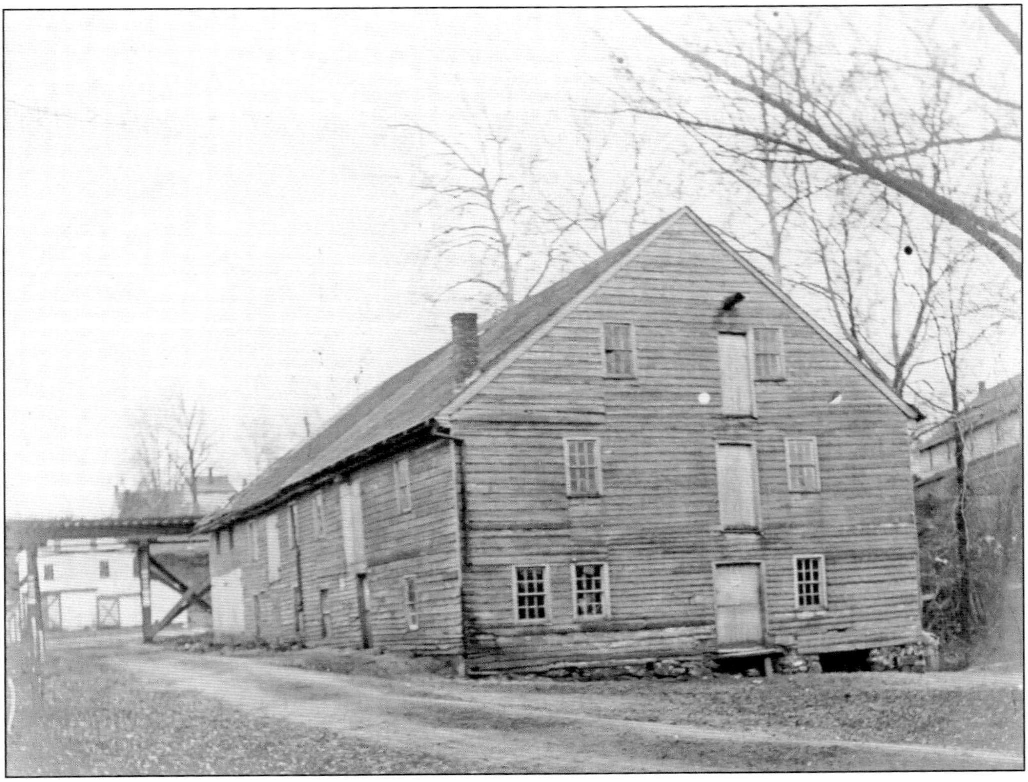

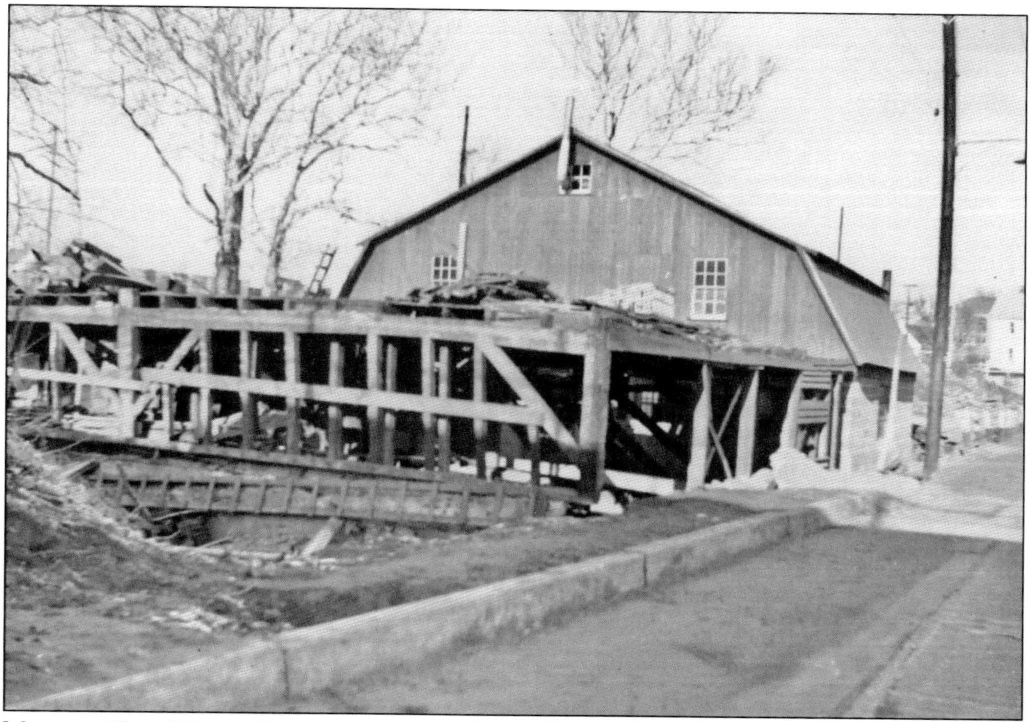

Mullica Hill Water Company, 1940. After milling operations ceased, the building became a pumping station for the newly formed water company. When fire destroyed the second story, the building was remodeled. The September 1940 flood resulted in yet another major alteration. Finally, after floodwaters in 2011 submerged the entire first floor, the building was razed. The site, however, continues to provide water from two deep wells.

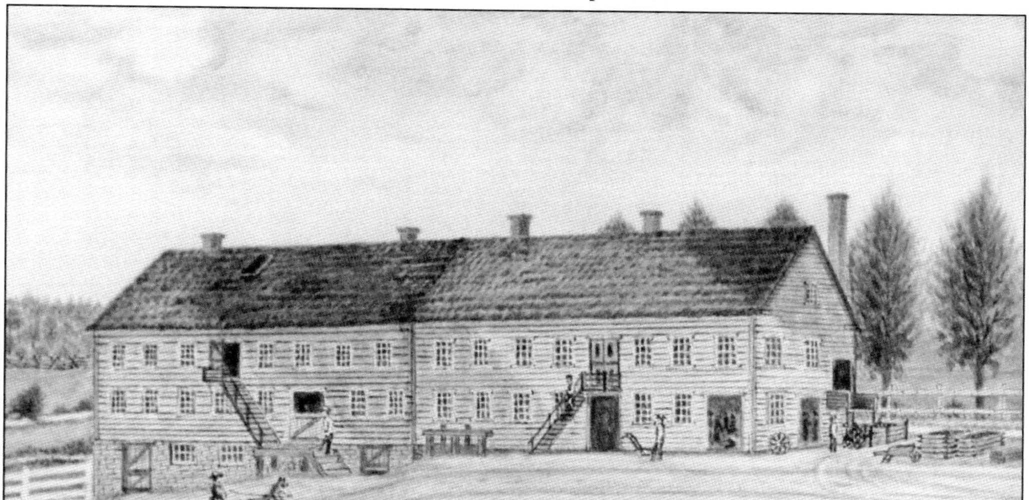

Mullica Hill Woolen Mill & Foundry. Mill Road was a hub of industrial activity during the first half of the 19th century. A woolen mill making blankets and fabric moved into the former gristmill around 1810. Forty-four years later, an iron foundry was added to the north side. In 1862, the woolen mill operation ceased when it went into bankruptcy; five years later, a foundry fire destroyed the entire complex.

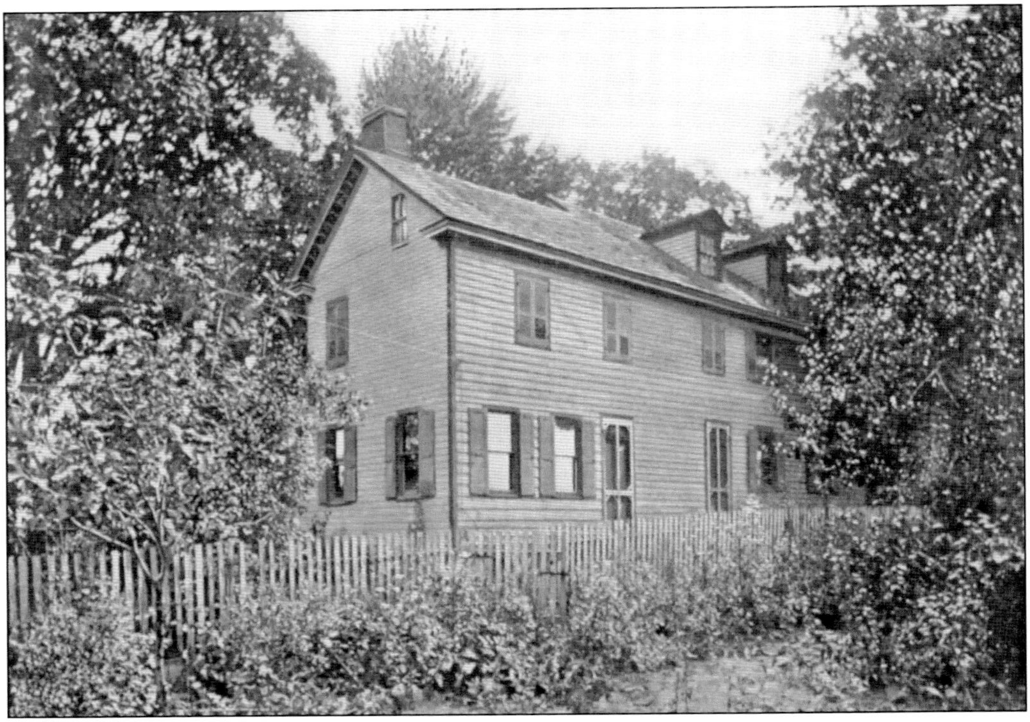

SAMUEL AND MARY FRENCH HOMESTEAD. Samuel French, a prominent Quaker and member of the state assembly, purchased 1,000 acres at the confluence of Raccoon Creek and Clems Run in 1771 and shortly thereafter built this house, which stood on Clems Run Road. He also established a sawmill on Raccoon Creek near Harrisonville Road, which continued operating until 1875. Fire destroyed the house in the late 20th century.

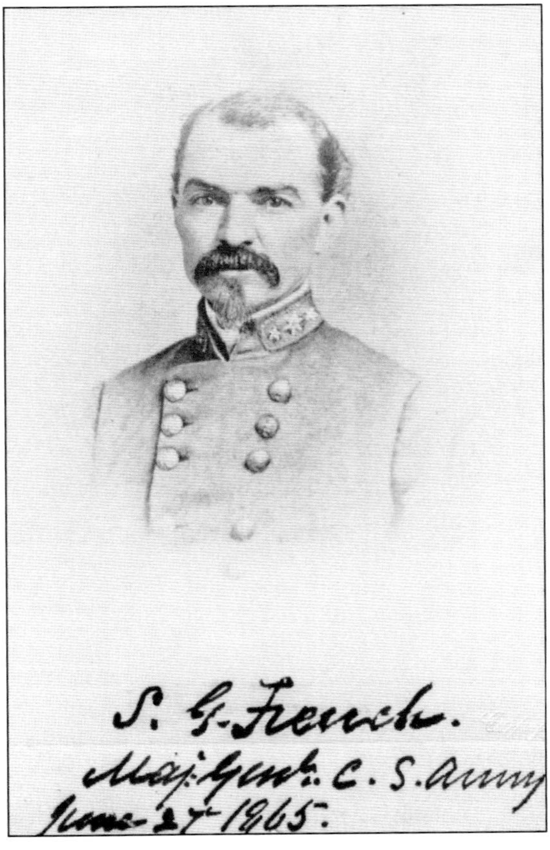

SAMUEL GIBBS FRENCH (1818–1910). The grandson of Samuel and Mary French, Samuel French was attracted to the military, despite his local Quaker upbringing. He attended West Point and served with distinction in the Mexican-American War. He married Eliza Roberts from Natchez, Mississippi, and acquired a plantation near Greenville. During the Civil War, he served as a brigadier general in the Confederate army. In his 1904 memoir, *Two Wars*, he continued to defend the Southern cause. (ADAH.)

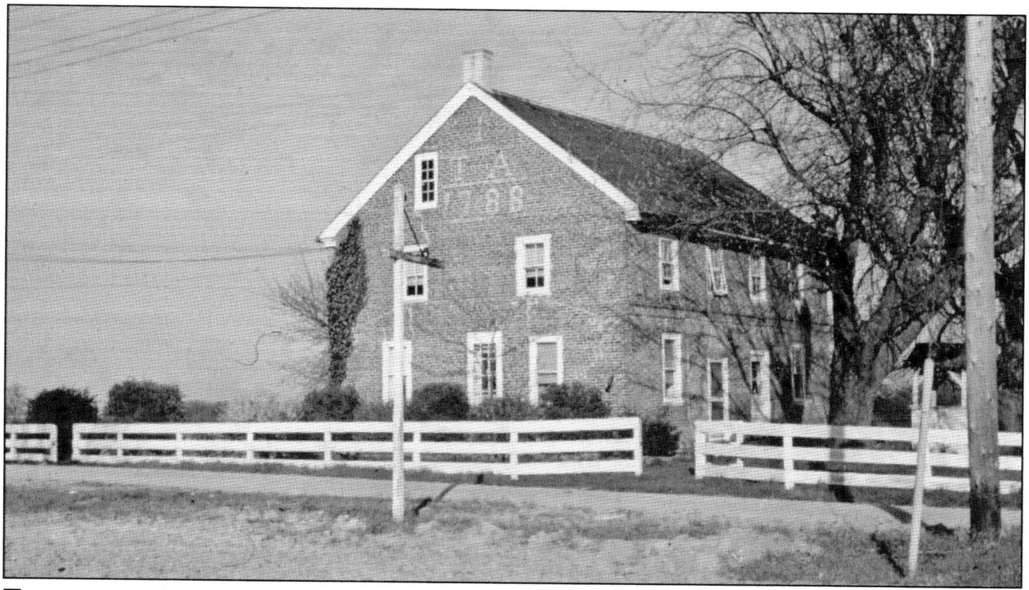

Thomas and Ann Iredell House. The Iredells acquired much of the land that would become Ewan around 1772. He built this house in 1788, proudly incorporating the date and their initials into the gable design. Their home remains a prominent landmark on Moods Road and is the oldest example of pattern brickwork in Old Harrison.

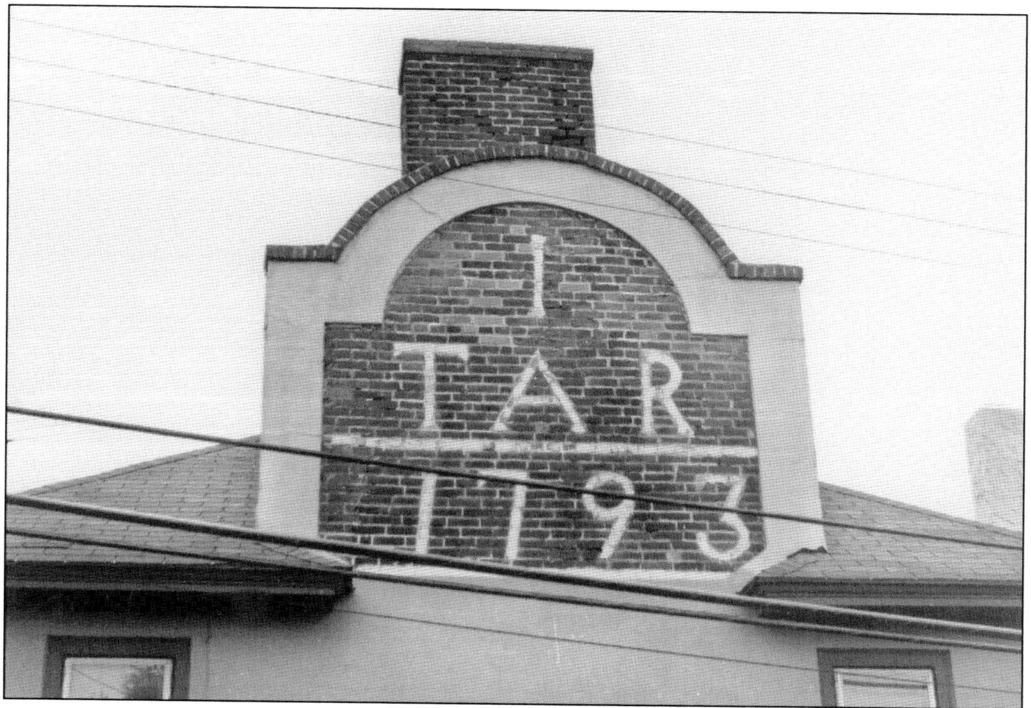

Thomas and Rebecca Iredell House. After Ann Iredell's death, Thomas remarried and built a new house on the other side of Raccoon Creek that included his new wife's initials. Originally, the building resembled the 1788 house. Daniel Brown undertook an extensive remodeling in 1908 but preserved the 18th-century brickwork through this distinctive chimney design. Only three examples of dated pattern brickwork survive in Old Harrison, all around Ewan.

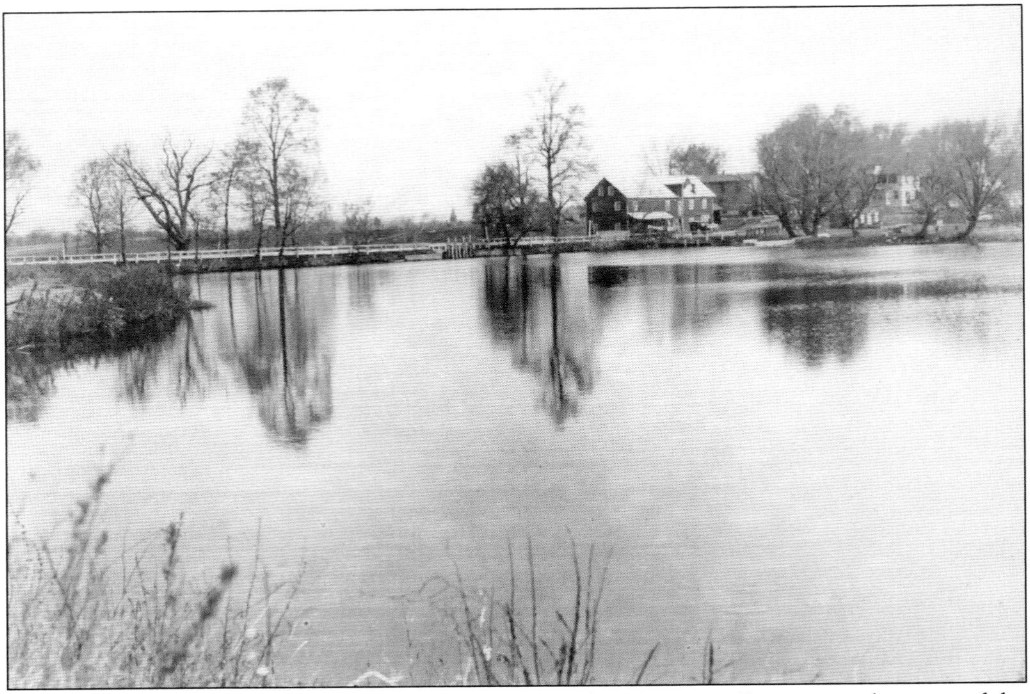

EWAN LAKE. Raccoon Creek flows through a narrow, deep ravine at Ewan, providing one of the area's best millsites. Thomas Iredell is credited with building a dam here to power a gristmill. The mill and the 1793 house are visible in this view taken from the Elk Township shore.

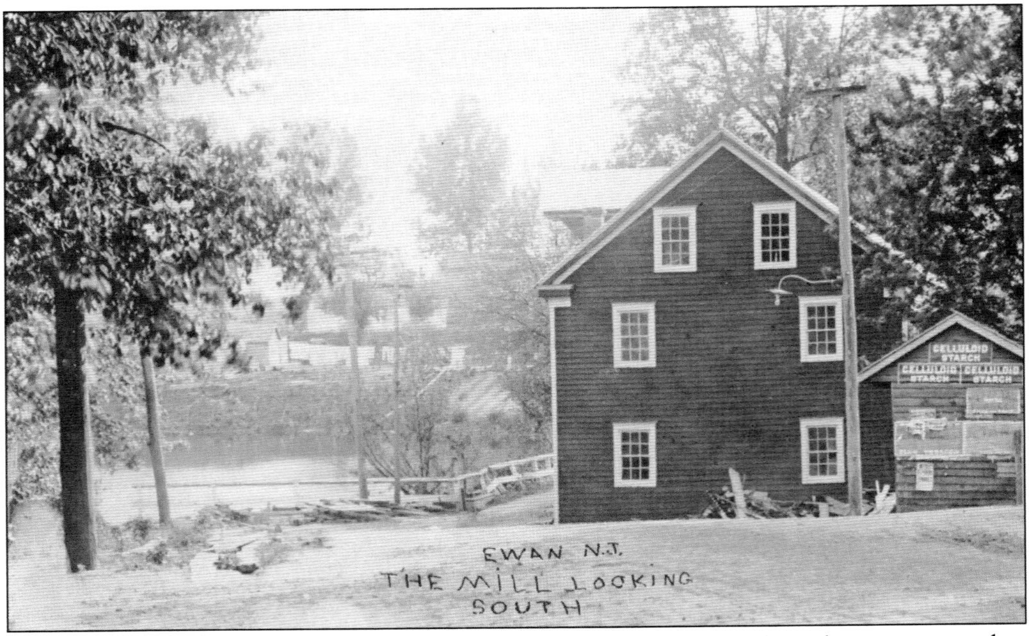

EWAN GRISTMILL. The mill at Ewan was likely the oldest in the township when it was razed in the 1930s. Thomas Iredell is believed to have established the enterprise shortly after acquiring this property around 1772. From 1847 to 1877, the Ewan family operated the mill and expanded their holdings to include a sawmill, store, and blacksmith and wheelwright shop. Not surprisingly, the village became known as Ewan's Mills.

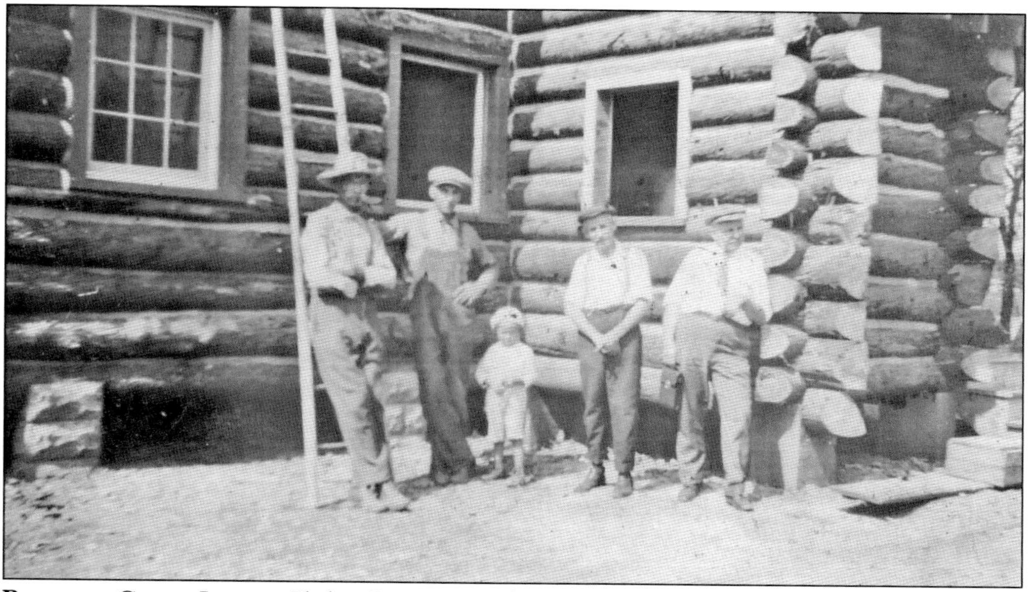

BUILDING CEDAR LODGE. Philip Cass acquired Ewan Lake in 1921 and had a large log cabin built on the Harrison Township shoreline as a summer retreat. David Ebner (left)—posing with, from left to right, his son Harry, grandson Walter, Harry's father-in-law Andy Keifer, and a Mr. Holtzman from Jersey City—was a local carpenter who also built two Craftsman-style bungalows in Ewan. Fire destroyed this locally unique residence.

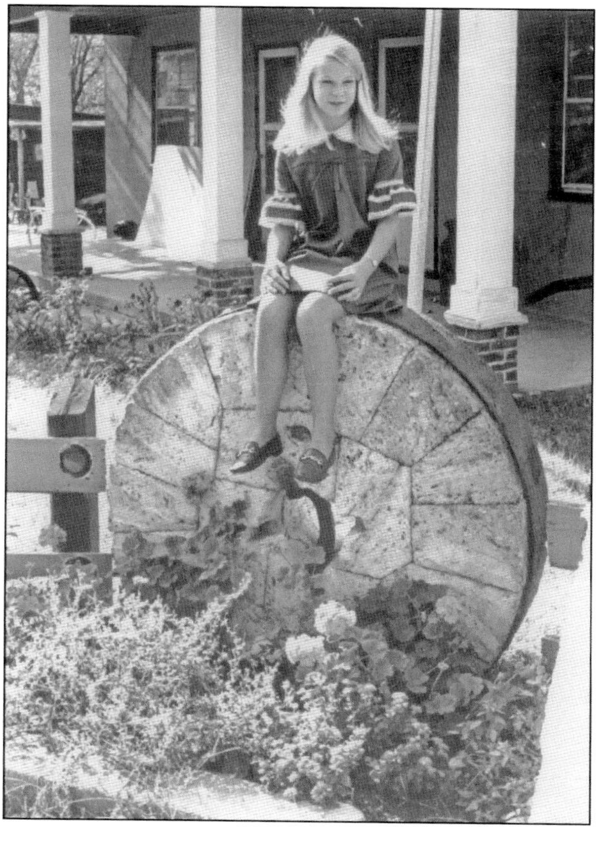

THE MILLSTONE FROM EWAN'S MILL. The gristmill was torn down in 1938 when the dam and bridge were rebuilt and the roadway straightened. One of the millstones was rescued and placed at the corner of Ewan Road and New Street by the 1793 house, where Sheryl Powell Schenkel poses for a photograph. The stone is now preserved at the Harrison Township Historical Society.

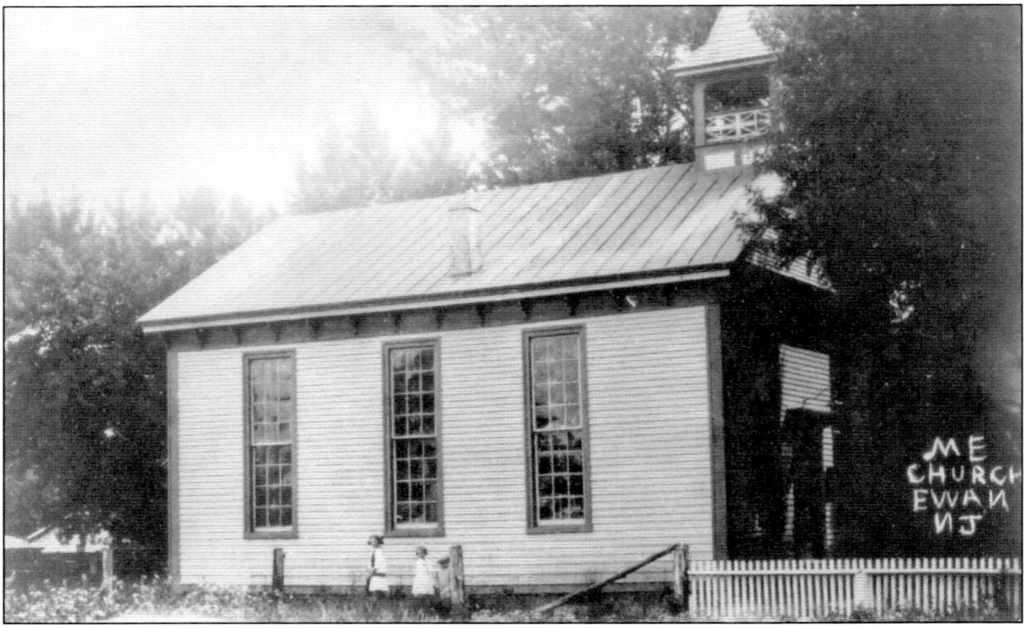

Ewan Methodist Church. Methodists first met here in the 1820s but did not organize until 1865, with Josiah and Israel Ewan as leaders. Two factions promoted building sites on both the east and west edges of the village. A compromise to locate midway between the two resolved the conflict. By Christmas 1865, the building was completed and dedicated at a cost of $4,000. The church remains a prominent Ewan landmark.

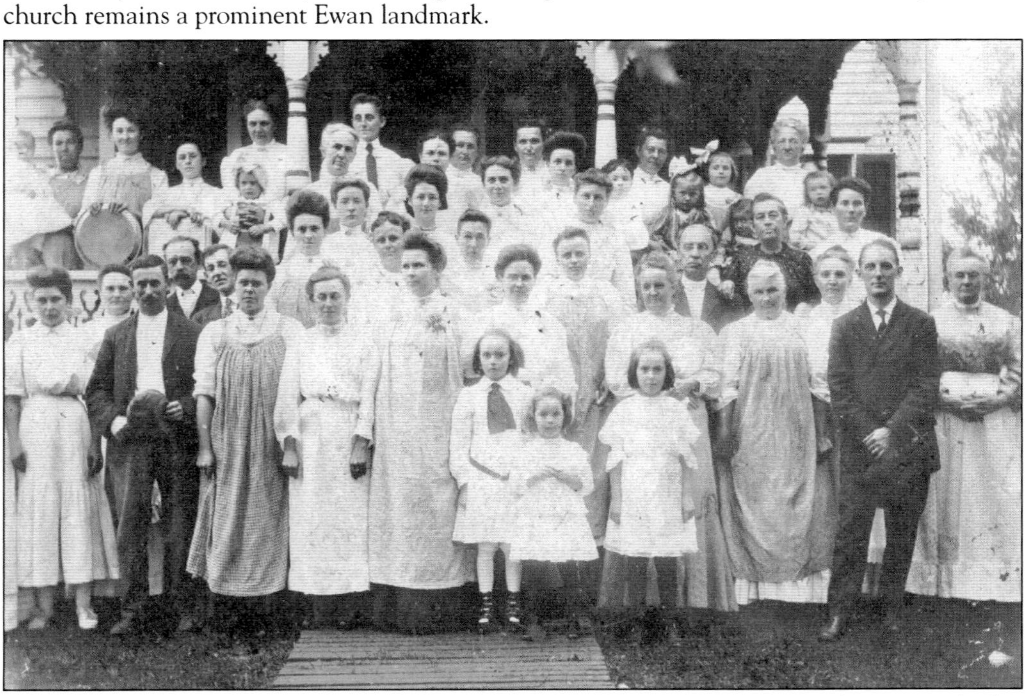

Harvest Home, Ewan. Every summer in the early 20th century, the women of Ewan Methodist Church set up woodstoves in the carriage shed to prepare traditional chicken pot pie to raise funds for the church. Dinners were served in the community building behind the church and attracted large crowds, including summer cottagers from Pitman Grove Camp Meeting.

EWAN SCHOOL. This two-room schoolhouse was built on Clems Run Road in 1874 to replace an earlier building that stood near the church on New Street. Originally, four grades were housed in each of the two classrooms. After the consolidated school in Mullica Hill opened in 1950, the schoolhouse was sold and converted into a residence.

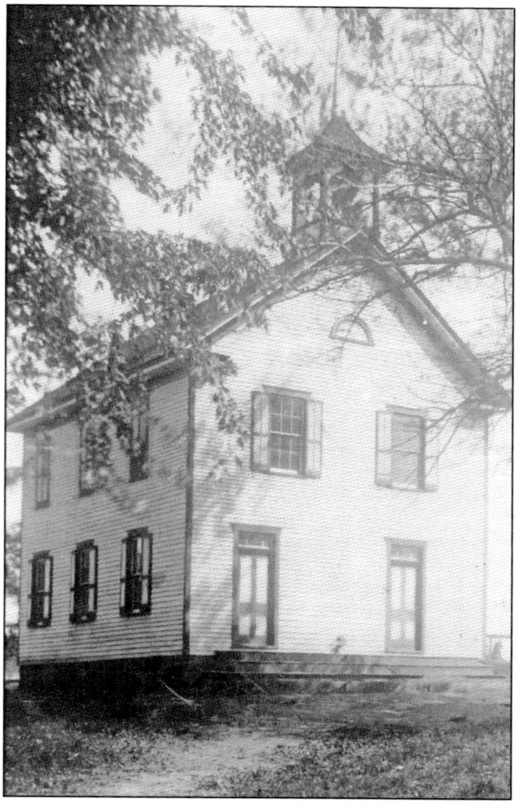

EWAN SCHOOL, 1926. Mabel Nutt taught first through fourth grades in the downstairs classroom to children from the Bartholomew, Boyd, Bowers, Carr, Cassaday, Ebner, Hand, Johnson, Kier, Langley, Pritchett, Souder, and Turk families.

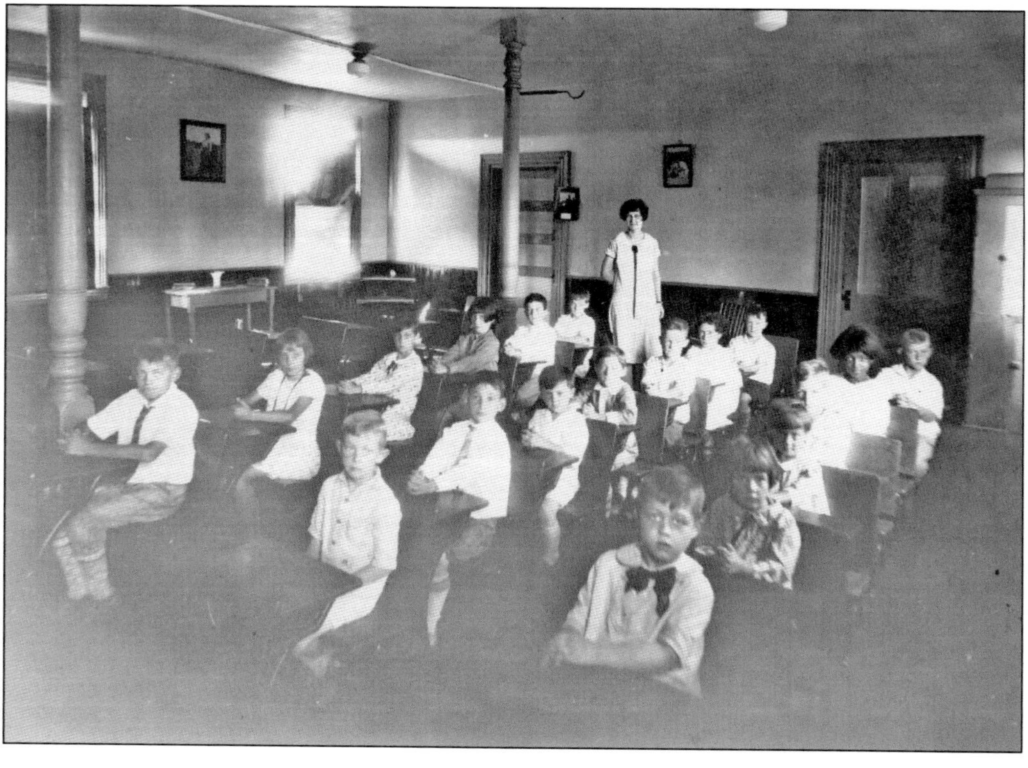

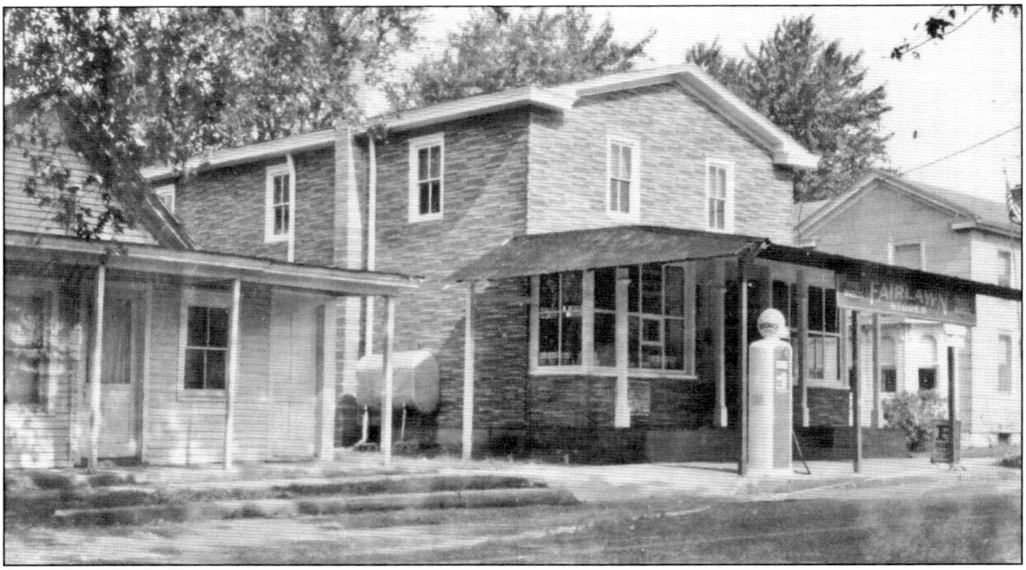

ALLEN CLARK'S GENERAL STORE. Allen Clark built this store nearly opposite the church in 1884. After Clark relocated to Pitman, the business continued to be operated by a number of owners including the Smalleys and Walkers, until closing in the late 20th century. For most of its history, the store also housed the Ewan Post Office and was a community gathering place. A devastating fire ultimately destroyed this landmark.

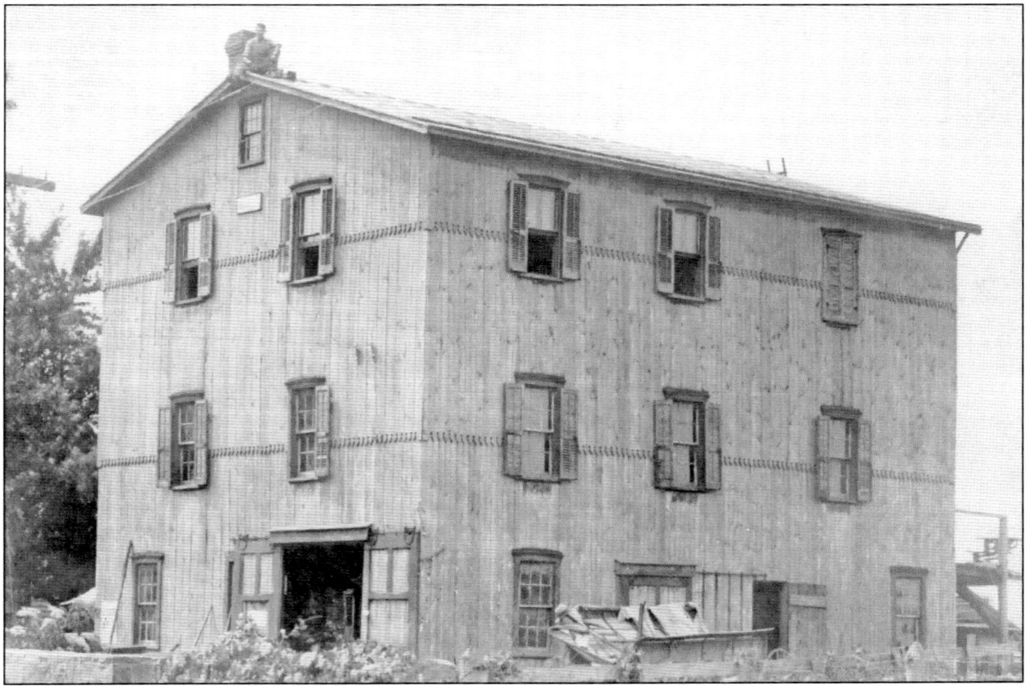

ELLIOTT'S/STRATTON'S HALL. Once located in the center of the village at the bend, this large building housed blacksmith and wheelwright shops. It originally had only two stories and was enlarged by raising the top floor to add a second story in between. The third floor served as a community hall where entertainments were held and the local Red Men's Lodge met. It later housed John Elliott's Garage and Automobile Agency.

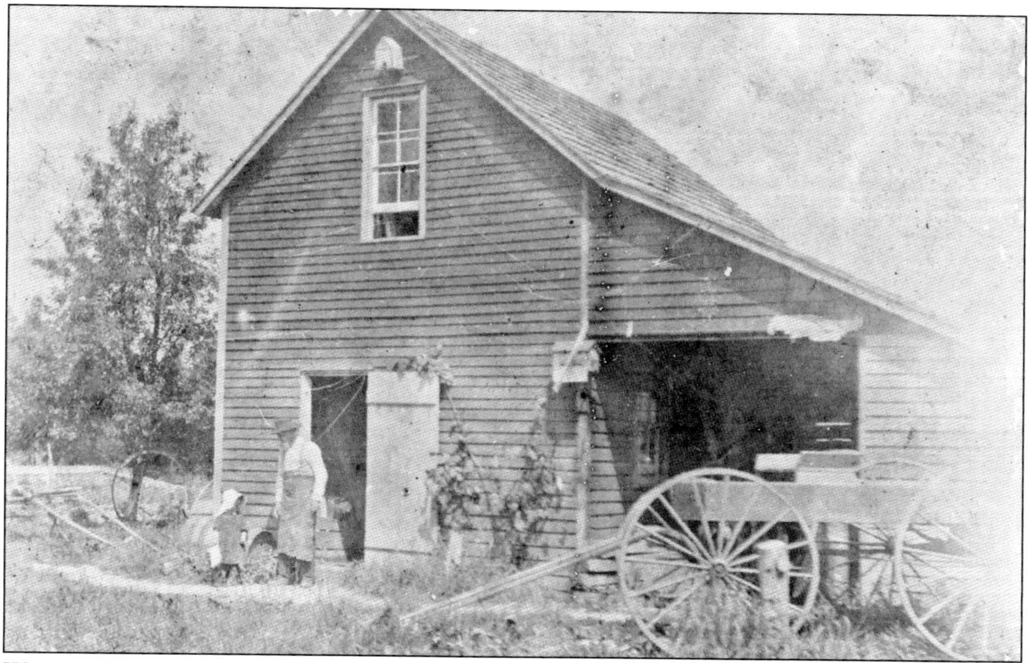

William Nolte's Paint Shop. Two generations of Noltes operated a wagon body paint shop on New Street in the late 19th and early 20th centuries. William Nolte Jr. studied law but never practiced, preferring to follow his father's trade. The Harrison Township Historical Society owns a side table that he decorated.

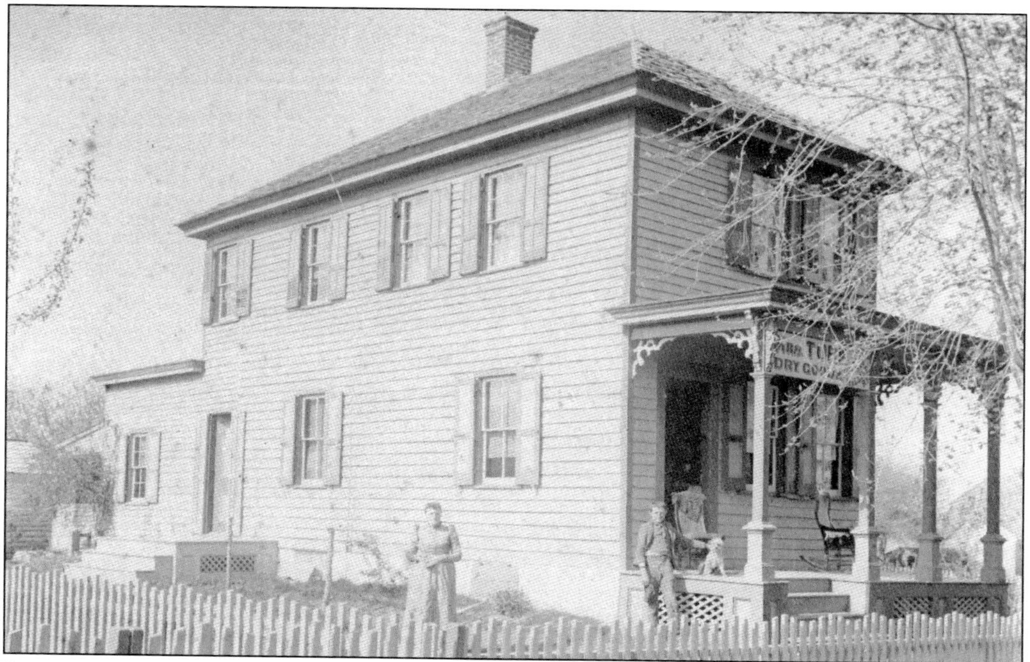

Barbara Turk's Dry Goods Store and Millinery. Barbara Binder Turk and her husband, Daniel, were among a large number of German immigrants who settled around Ewan and Richwood in the second half of the 19th century. Barbara, seen here with her youngest son, Walter, opened a store in the front room of her home around 1880. She may have been Ewan's first businesswoman.

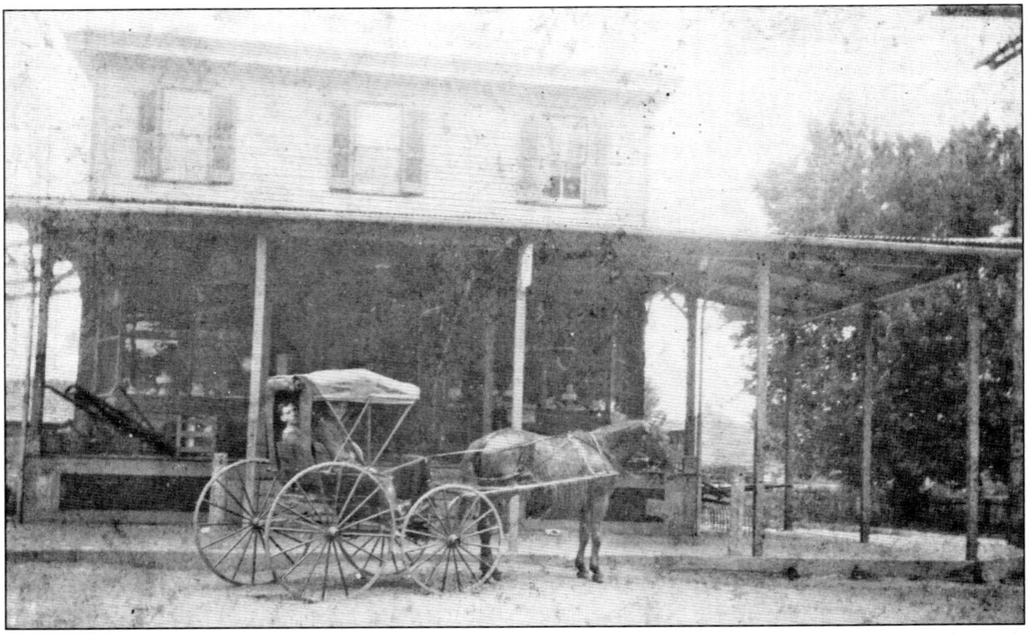

FRANKLIN TURK'S GENERAL STORE. Franklin Turk built Ewan's "uptown" store in the early 20th century at the corner of Ewan and Clems Run Roads. In addition to offering groceries, Turk also sold farm implements and supplies at this location for over 40 years. The business continued in operation as the last traditional general store in the township until converted to other uses in the 21st century.

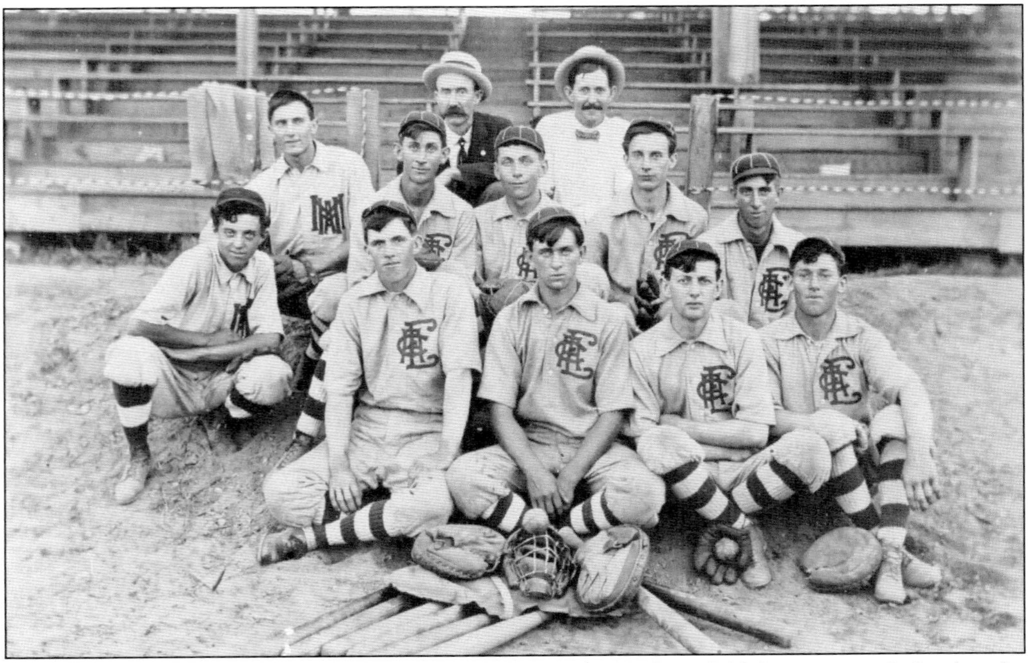

EWAN ATHLETIC CLUB, C. 1900. Amateur teams in the 19th and 20th centuries helped make baseball the national pastime. Even small villages like Ewan proudly supported their home teams, and local rivalries were popular forms of entertainment. This photograph of Ewan's team may have been taken at a game in Pitman.

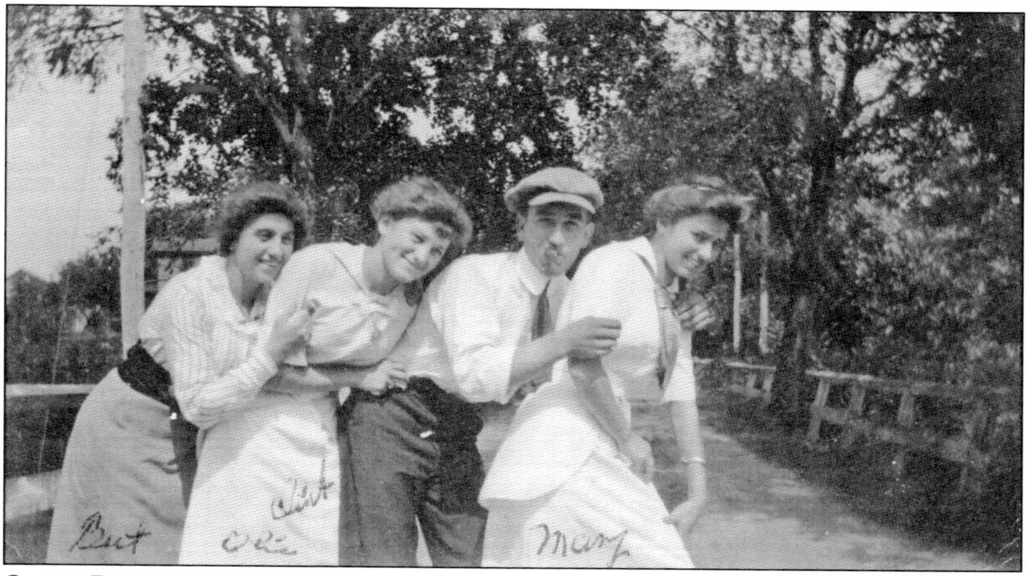

On the Bridge in Ewan. From left to right, Alberta Stratton, Viola Emerich, Clint Stratton, and Mary Emerich strike a humorous pose by the lake. The Strattons operated a livestock business in a large auction barn on New Street in the early 20th century. Clint Stratton conducted a much smaller general auction into the mid-20th century. The Emerichs owned farms east of Ewan on Ewan and Clems Run Roads.

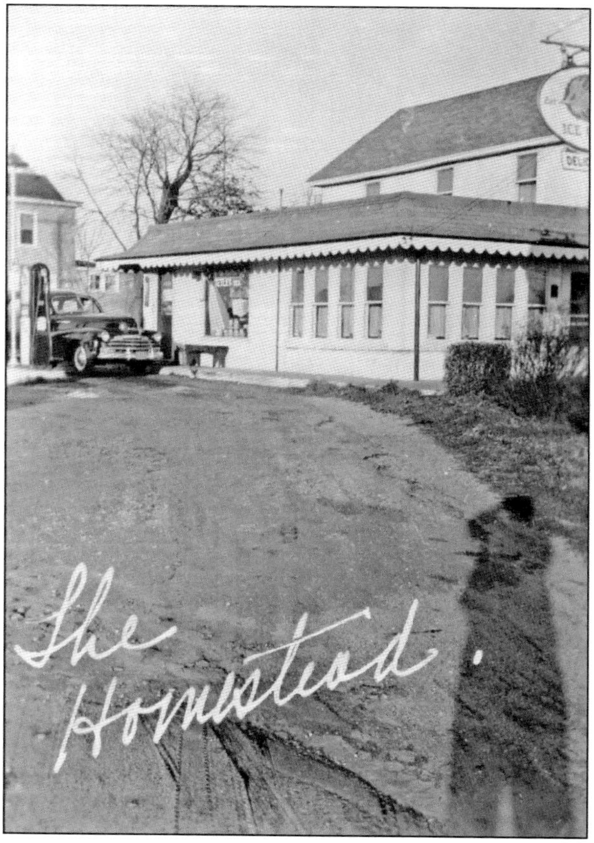

Bartholomew's General Store. The Bartholomew family first acquired property at the intersection of Ewan and Richwood Roads in 1828. In 1865, they purchased the farm across Richwood Road, where descendants still reside today. Joseph and Rena Bartholomew opened their general store and gas station in the 1930s. In the summer, they also sold produce from their farm.

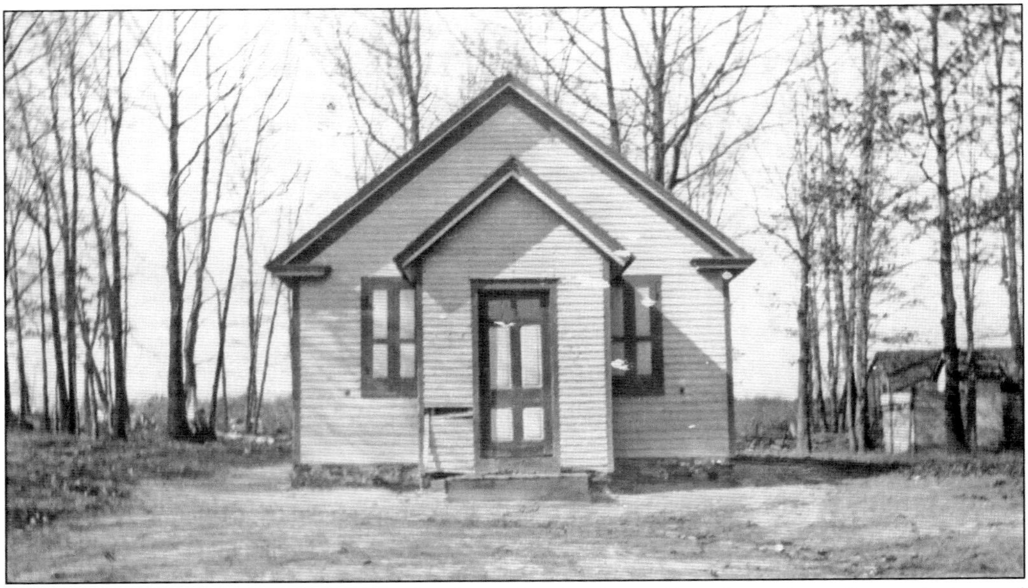

CLEMS RUN SCHOOL. This one-room school stood on Richwood Road near Deer Haven Drive and was the first schoolhouse in this part of the township. Built around 1830, Clems Run School served students from both Richwood and Ewan until it closed in 1918. It was torn down in 1949.

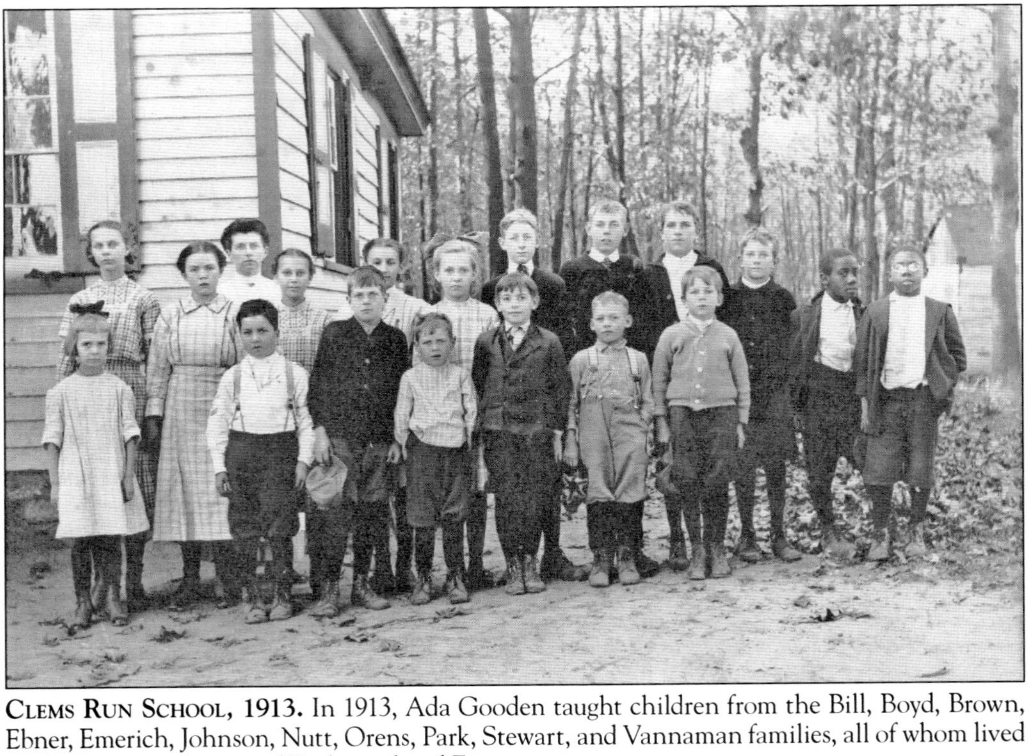

CLEMS RUN SCHOOL, 1913. In 1913, Ada Gooden taught children from the Bill, Boyd, Brown, Ebner, Emerich, Johnson, Nutt, Orens, Park, Stewart, and Vannaman families, all of whom lived in the countryside around Richwood and Ewan.

Ewan Fire Company. The first meeting to discuss organizing a fire company in Ewan took place in Stratton Hall on September 3, 1946. The first fire engine was purchased later that year. Funds were raised through raffles, carnivals, and a fried oyster and ham supper that began in 1948 and continues to this day. The first alarm was sounded in August 1947 to extinguish a grass fire at the Oland farm. (EFC.)

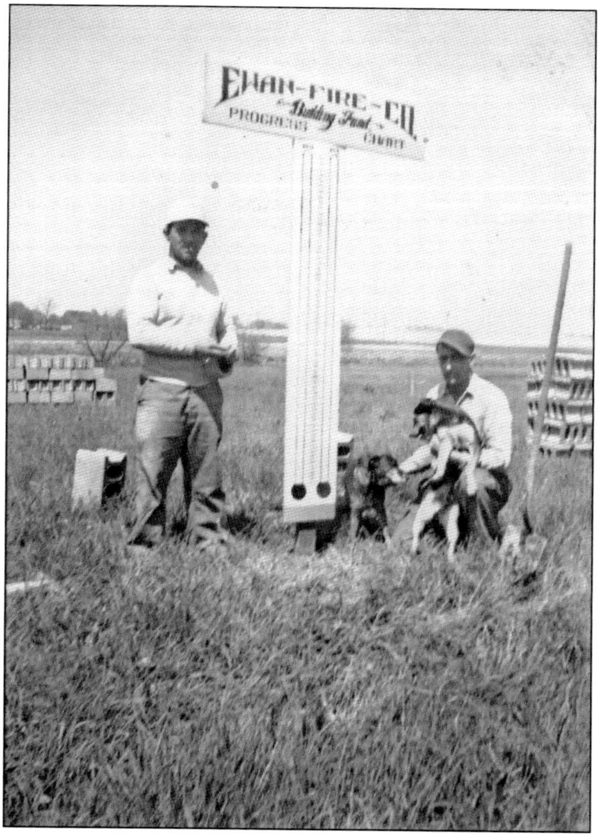

Dedication of Ewan Fire Hall. The cornerstone for the new building was laid on June 4, 1949, and the building was dedicated later that year. Since then, the structure has been enlarged and remodeled several times. (EFC.)

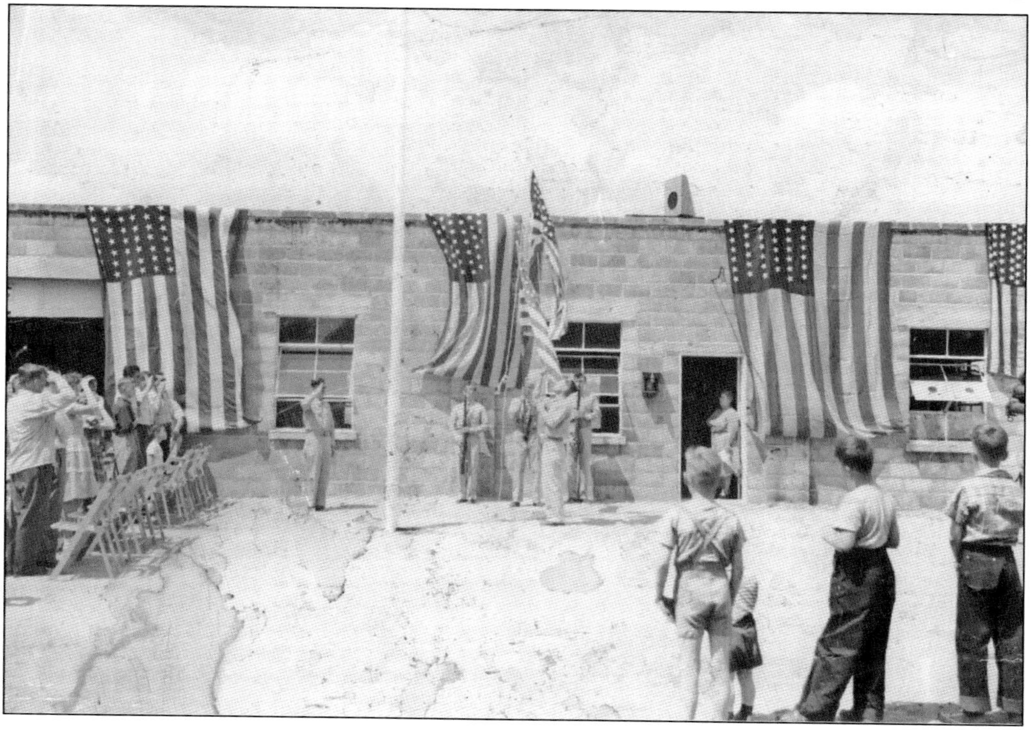

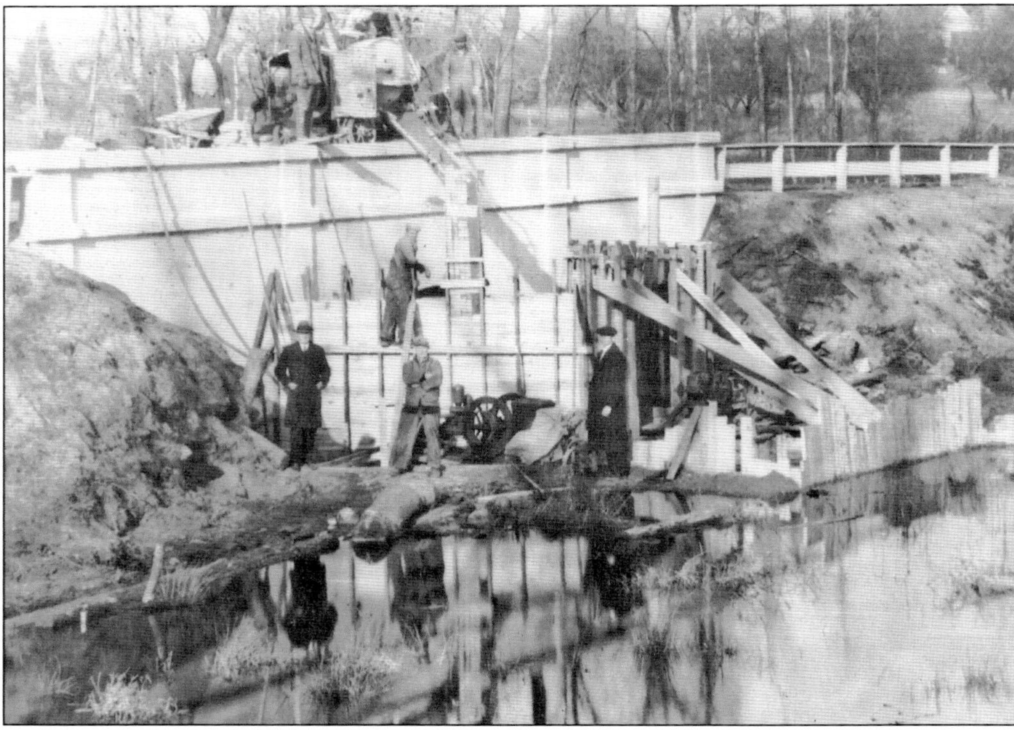

Building the Dam at Lake Gilman. Miles Gilman was looking for a site to build a lake and park when he had a flat tire on the Ferrell Road Bridge over Raccoon Creek and found the perfect spot. He acquired the farm and began clearing the land by hand. He claimed to have cut 4,000 trees and used five axes. Water first went over the dam in August 1928. (LGO.)

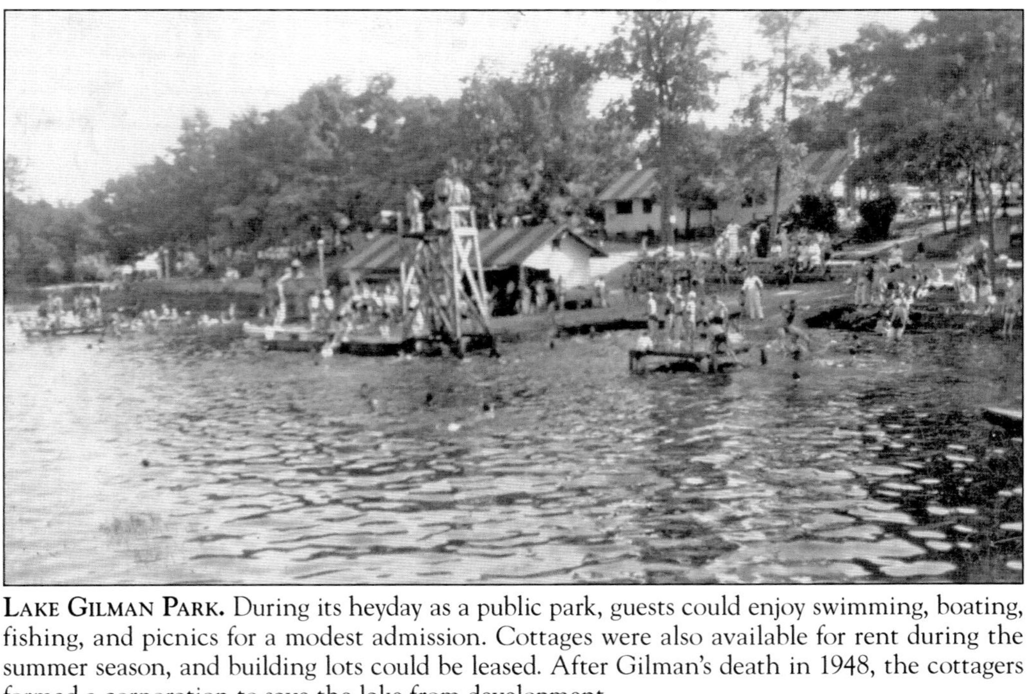

Lake Gilman Park. During its heyday as a public park, guests could enjoy swimming, boating, fishing, and picnics for a modest admission. Cottages were also available for rent during the summer season, and building lots could be leased. After Gilman's death in 1948, the cottagers formed a corporation to save the lake from development.

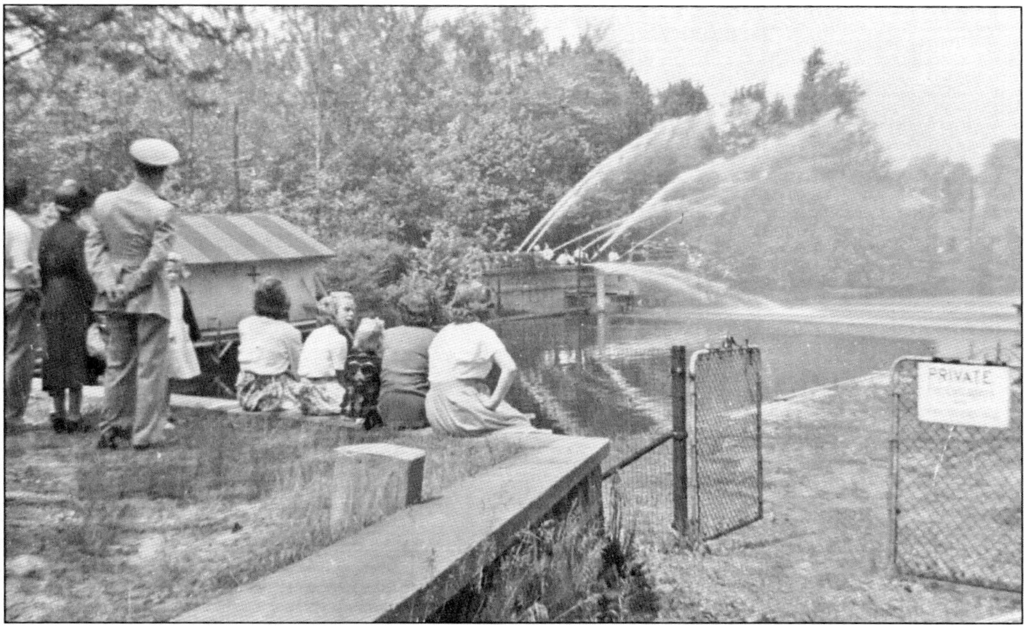

MEMORIAL DAY AT LAKE GILMAN, 1950. Miles Gilman was a World War I Navy veteran and led the effort to install the Rock of Ages monument on Ferrell Road honoring the veterans of World War II from Lake Gilman. Memorial Day ceremonies centered around the monument and in 1950 included Ewan Fire Company's pumper demonstration. Gilman died in 1948 and was interred behind the monument. (EFC.)

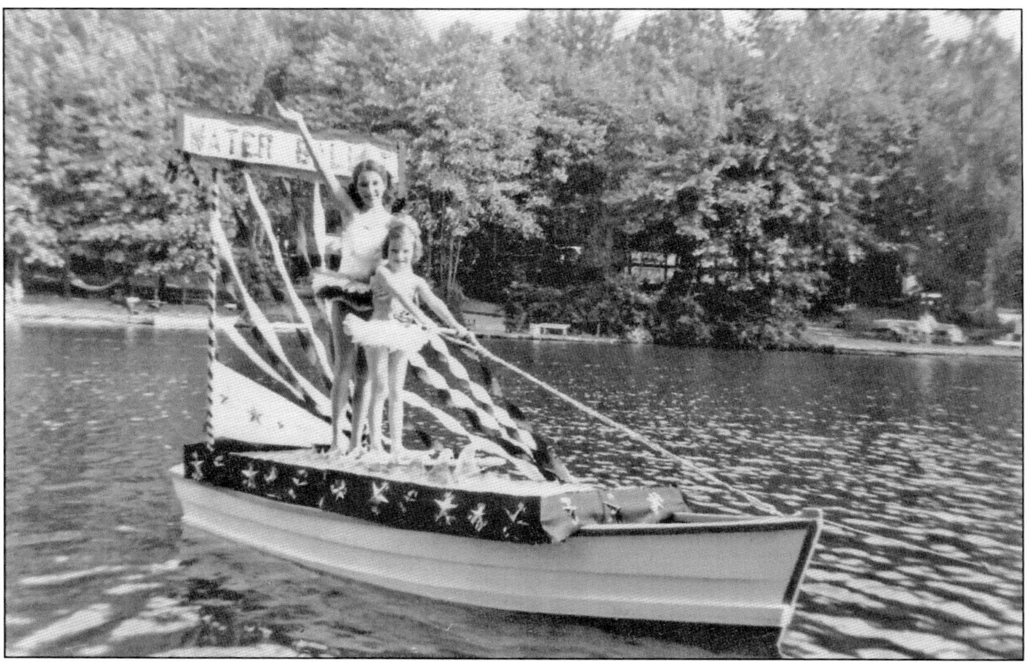

LAKE GILMAN DAY. Lake Gilman Day began as a birthday surprise for Miles Gilman in 1936 and became official in 1939. Festivities included games, a pie-eating contest, and the water pageant, a flotilla of decorated canoes and rowboats like the Albinson family's 1954 entry featuring daughters Eileen and Shirley. The Lake Gilman Day tradition continues annually every summer. (SD.)

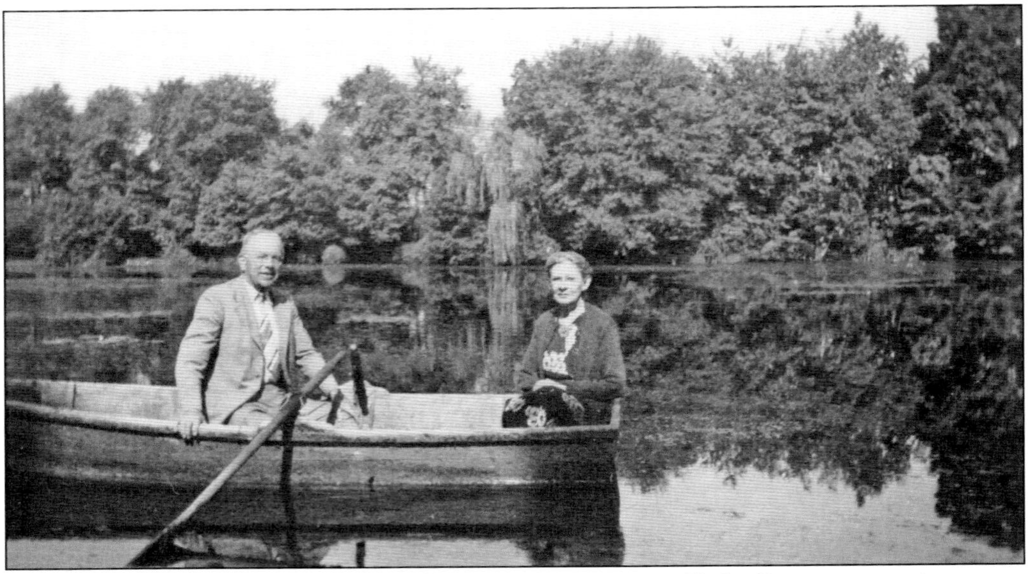

Lake Omary. Mullica Hill's J. Omar and Mary J. Heritage created Lake Omary as a rustic getaway for family and friends around 1925. Omar was proprietor of Heritage and Brother Lumber Company and a prominent local businessman. The lake featured a boat dock, arched wooden bridges, an island, "See Saw Park" (a playground), and a primitive cabin. The lake is located on a Raccoon Creek tributary between Moods and Elk Roads. (JS.)

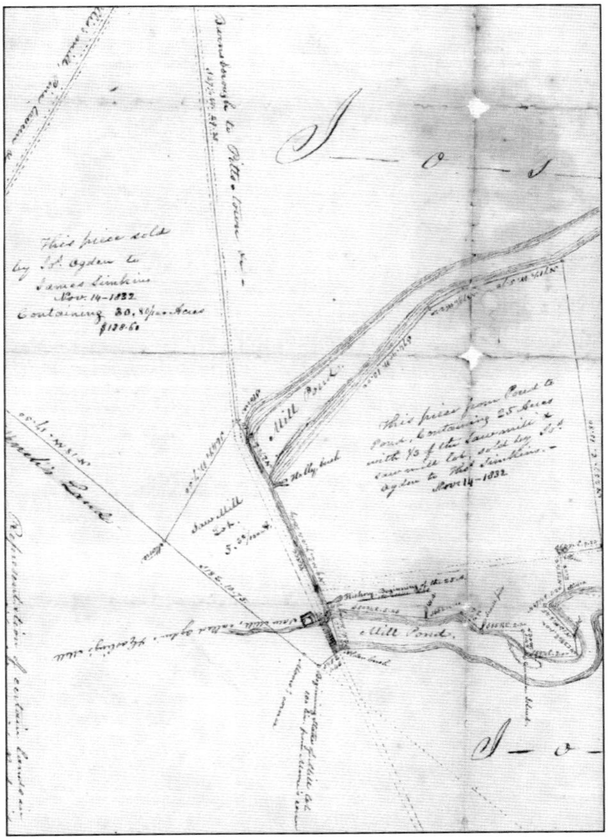

Ogden's Sawmill. This c. 1830 map of what is now called Wright's Mill illustrates the extensive engineering that was undertaken to increase the volume of water available to power the mill. The raceway along Richwood Road diverted all the water of Raccoon Creek to Cartwheel Run, where there was a deeper natural ravine more suitable as a millsite. Joseph Ogden sold the mill to Thomas Simkins in 1832.

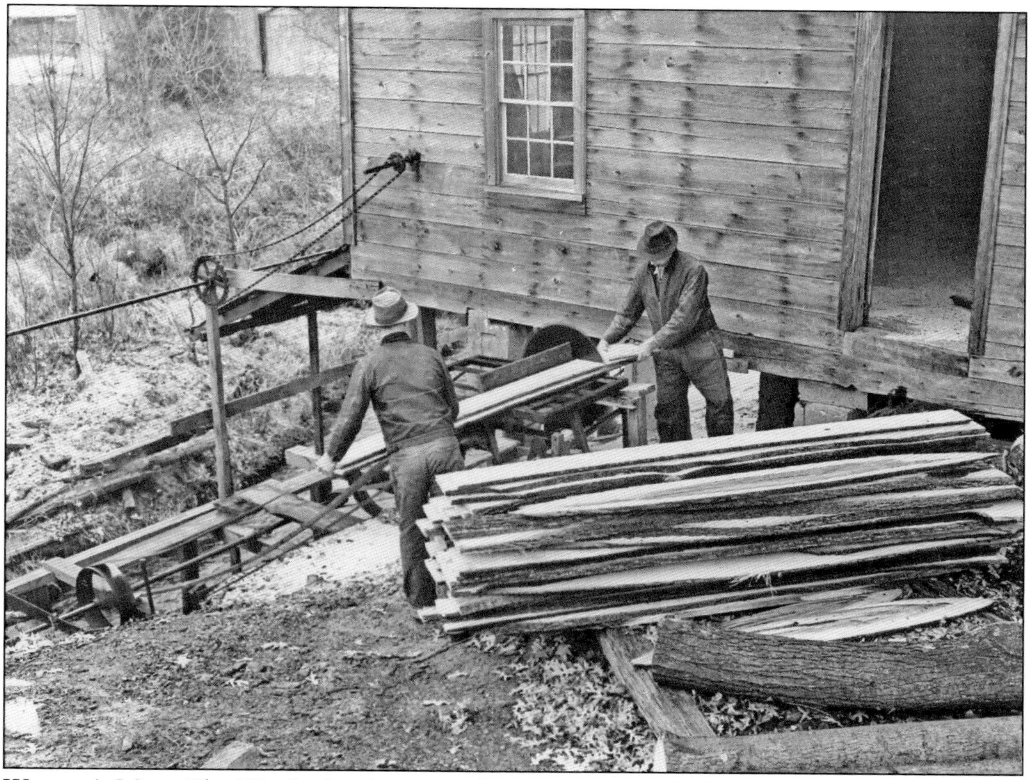

Wright's Mill. The Wright family acquired Simkins Mill around 1880 and operated it well into the 20th century. The mill building was rebuilt after a fire destroyed the original structure. In addition to making stave baskets for produce, strawberry, and asparagus crates, the Wrights also made toys and wooden stands for Christmas trees. In the early 1940s, they produced as many as 3,000 stands a week. (SCUARUL.)

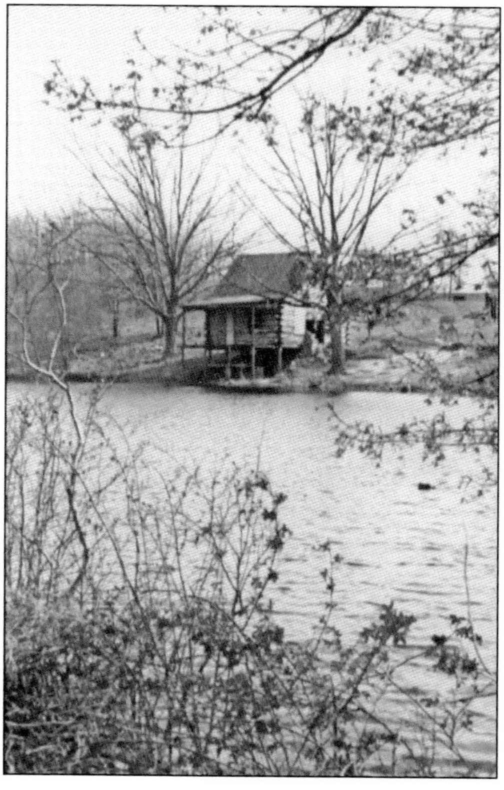

Wright's Log Cabin. The Wrights built this rustic cabin around 1930 for weekend gatherings and parties. Perched on the high south bank, the cabin was a picturesque landmark on Wright's Mill Pond. Recently, however, the dam was deemed a high risk for flooding, and the pond was drained. The cabin now overlooks woods instead of water.

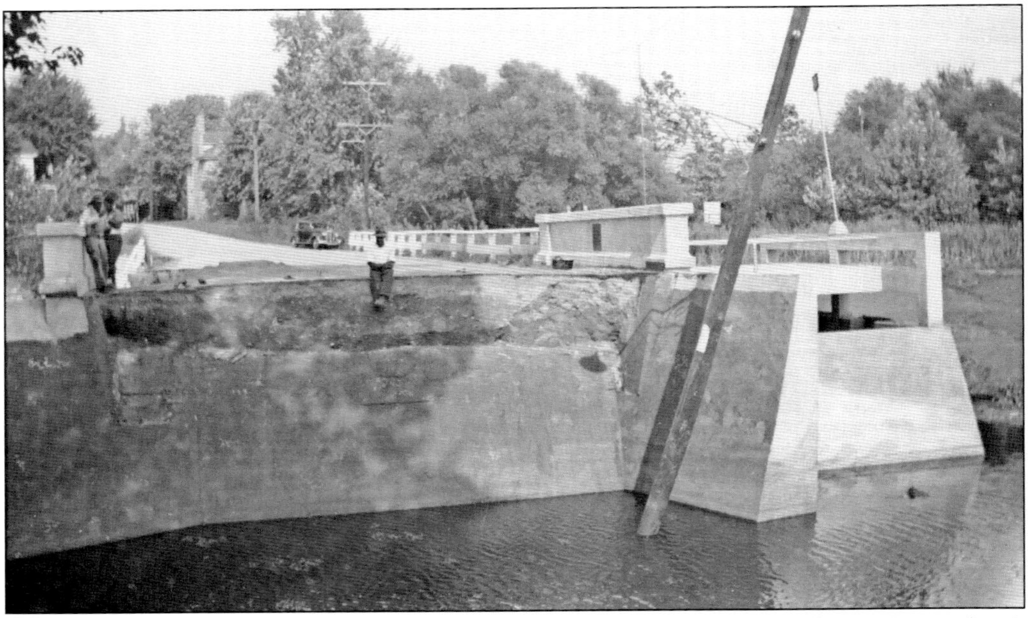

FLOOD DAMAGE AT EWAN LAKE. Normally Raccoon Creek is a placid stream, but on September 1, 1940, a tropical storm hit the western part of South Jersey and 22.4 inches of rain fell at Ewan in 24 hours. Dams gave way all along the Raccoon Creek from Wright's Mill to Mullica Hill. Small bridges on all the roads leading to Ewan washed out, isolating the village.

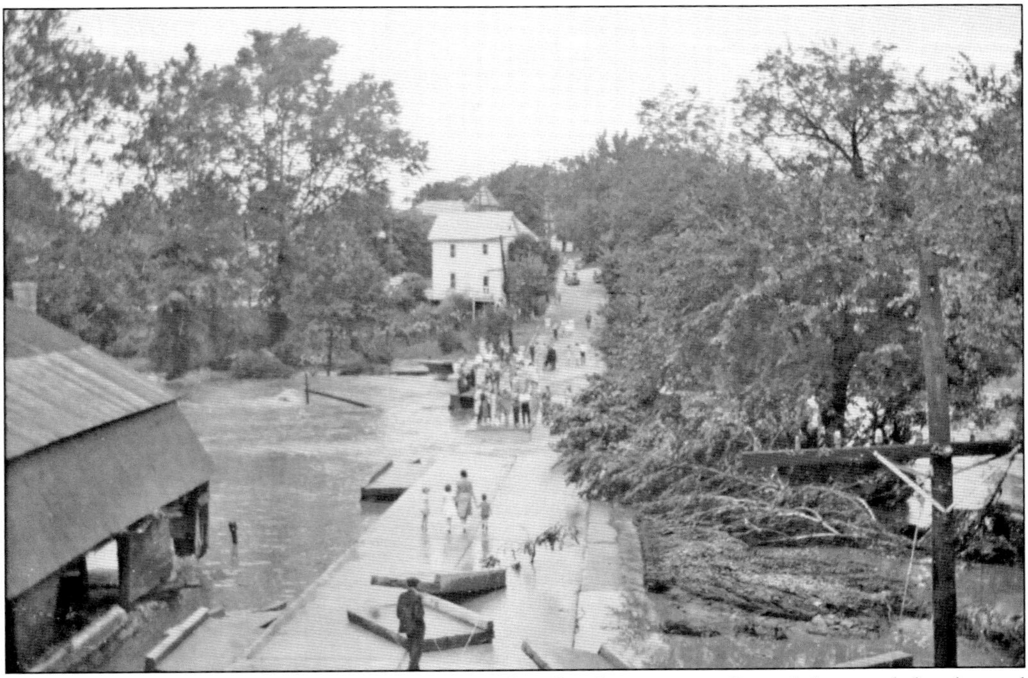

FLOOD AT MULLICA HILL, 1940. At their height, floodwaters overflowed the creek banks and filled the valley. The high bridge on Main Street collapsed and the bridges on Mill Road and Mullica Hill Road washed out entirely. The waterworks (the old gristmill) was severely damaged and had to be rebuilt. The Federal Emergency Management Agency later declared it to be a 500-year flood.

Three

Along Oldmans Creek

Oldmans Creek forms the boundary between Gloucester and Salem Counties; only a very low ridge near Ferrell separates its headwaters from Raccoon Creek. Both watercourses powered mills in the 18th and 19th centuries, but settlement along Oldmans was less robust, and the two villages along its north bank in Old Harrison were fairly small.

Like Ewan, Harrisonville traces its origins to the establishment of a gristmill in the latter part of the 18th century and did not experience very much growth until the mid-1800s. By the 1870s, the present-day town plan was in place and a church, school, town hall, Odd Fellows Hall, numerous shops, a physician's office, distillery, and several stores were interspersed among the residences. It became the seat of government when South Harrison Township was created in 1883.

Two more mills were once located upstream from Harrisonville. Only the sawyer's house and foundation ruins of the mill remain at Jessup's Mill on Swedesboro-Monroeville Road; the dam and pond have entirely disappeared. There is no evidence of the gristmill at Lincoln, and very little survives from the 19th-century village that once included a schoolhouse, blacksmith, and wheelwright shops.

Algonkin Lake, like Lake Gilman, was created for recreational purposes on the site of the pond that once powered Lincoln's mill. The Algonkin Club was a private sportsmen's retreat modeled after an Adirondack camp. Today, it is the site of Bancroft School's Lakeside Community, a national leader in providing self-sufficiency programs for special needs adults.

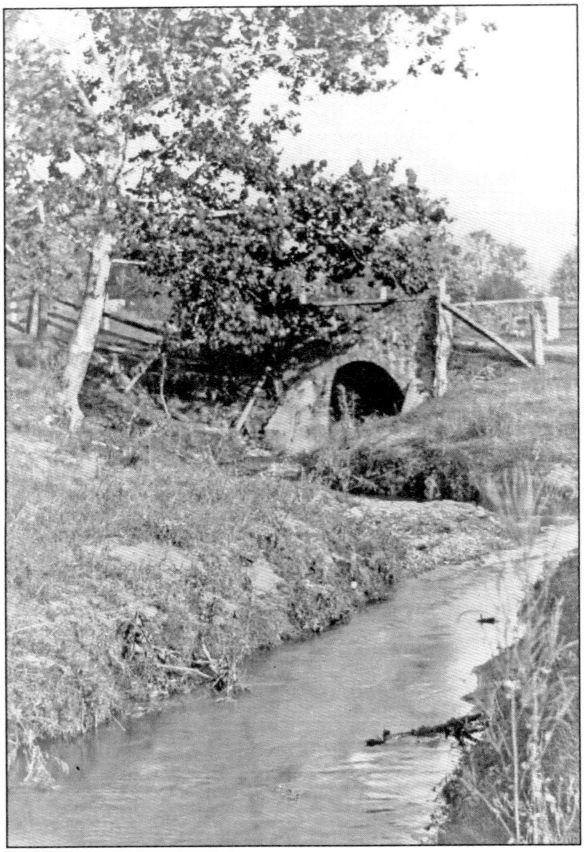

Marl Run Bridge. Perhaps because of its location on Marl Road, a little-traveled thoroughfare, the brick and stone arch span over Marl Run has survived as Old Harrison's oldest bridge. It has changed very little since this photograph was taken in the early 20th century; however, it is now surrounded and somewhat hidden by woodlands. Marl Run is a minor tributary of Oldmans Creek. (WPL.)

Harrisonville Gristmill. Established sometime prior to 1789, this mill was the village's pioneering business. After Thomas Cole replaced the original mill in 1810, the settlement became known as Coletown. In 1844, the town was renamed to honor the late president William Henry Harrison. Fire destroyed this building around 1875. It was replaced by the mill in this photograph. A tragic accident took place here in 1907, when John Keen was killed after his clothing became entangled in the machinery.

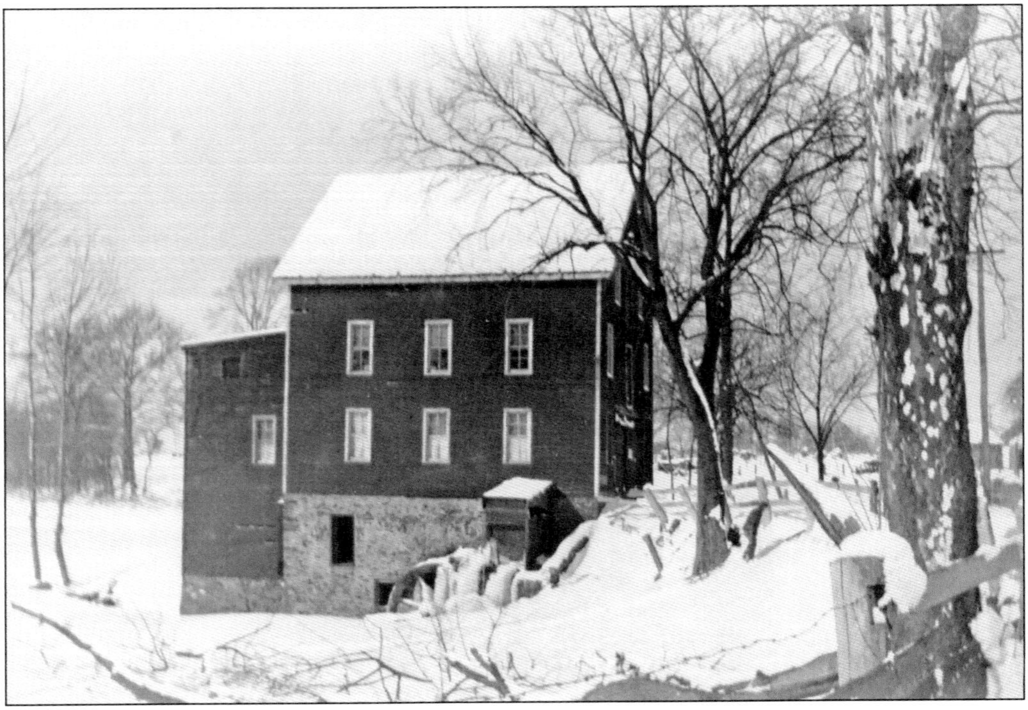

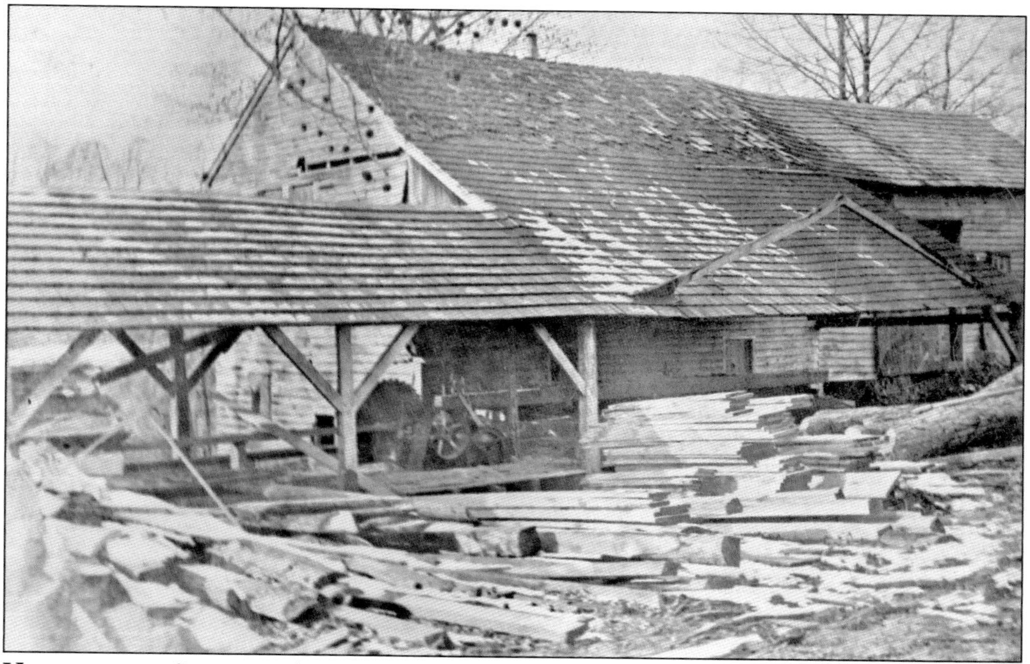

Harrisonville Sawmill. Like at Mullica Hill and Ewan, waterpower was sufficient at Harrisonville to operate more than one mill. The sawmill was constructed north of the gristmill along with an icehouse and slaughterhouse. Coletown slowly developed around this commercial complex, the largest on the upper reaches of Oldmans Creek. By 1835, the village consisted of nine houses.

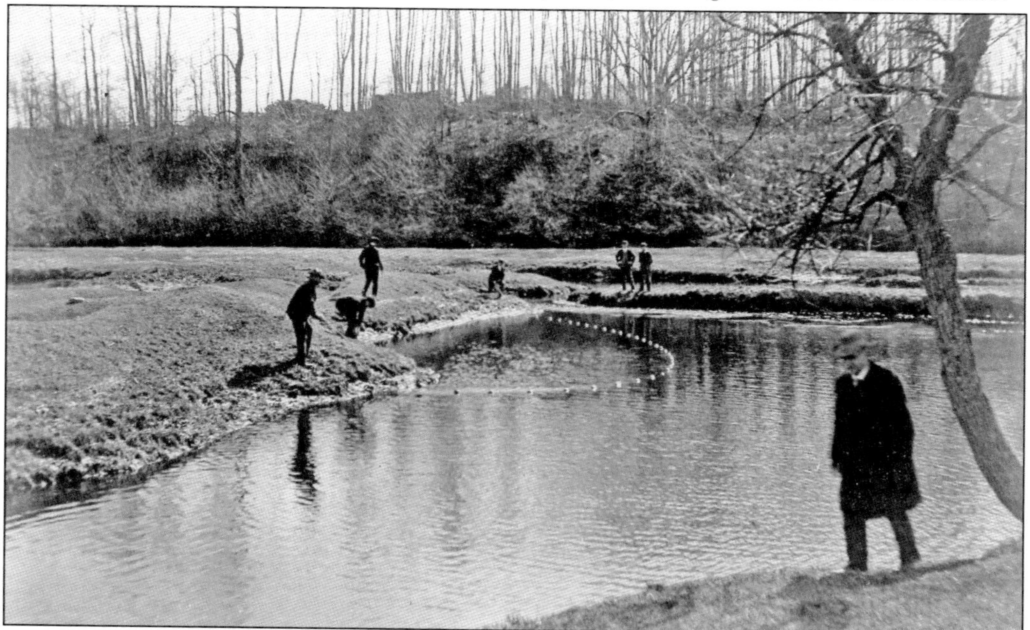

Seining on Harrisonville Lake. The New Jersey Division of Fish and Wildlife was established in 1892 with funding to establish a fish-breeding program to stock lakes throughout the state. Harrisonville Lake was a source for propagating stock for bass, here captured with nets around 1900. The division eventually purchased a 295-acre tract including the lake to establish the Harrisonville Lake Wildlife Management Area. (WPL.)

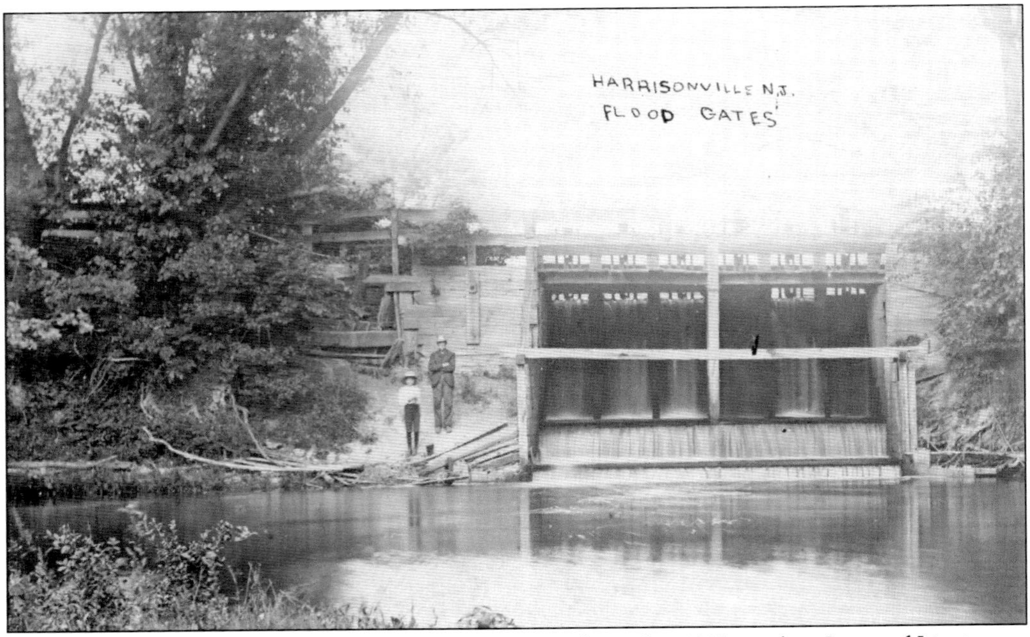

Harrisonville Lake Floodgates. After the bridge collapsed in 1917, resident Lamond Lippincott designed a new crossing and overflow. It was said that noise from the collapse could be heard all the way to the schoolhouse. The floodgates were configured so that the water level could be lowered during times of high water. Lippincott's bridge and dam did not fail during the September 1940 flood. (FSC.)

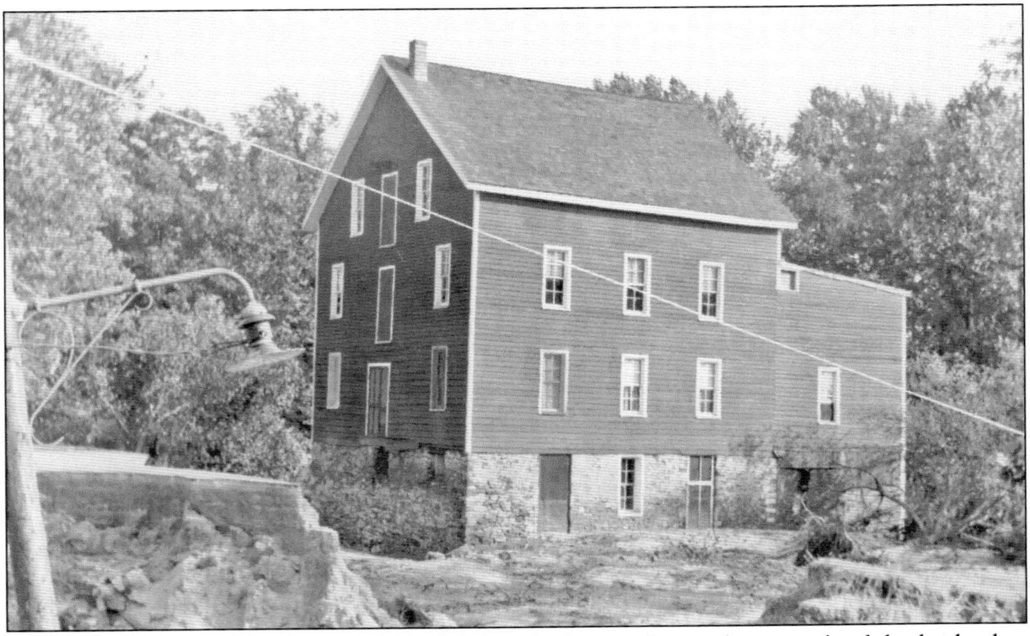

Flood at Harrisonville, 1940. The flood washed away the roadway north of the bridge but did not greatly damage the mill. While the building survived the deluge, milling operations ceased that year. After the state acquired the property, the mill was abandoned and became the target of vandalism. By the 1970s, the structure was ruinous and was razed in 1974. It was the last operating mill in the township.

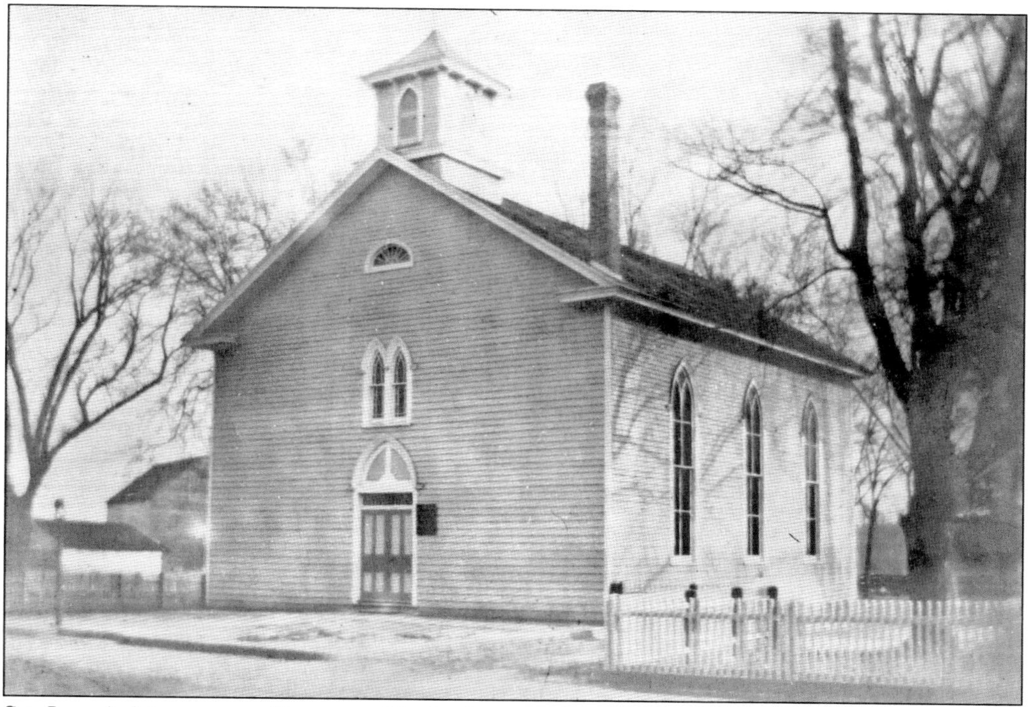

St. John's Methodist Church. Methodism in the neighborhood traces its origins across Oldmans Creek in Pilesgrove. There, a Methodist class meeting began around 1808, resulting in the construction of a meetinghouse called New Bethel in 1825. As Harrisonville's population grew, however, a movement arose to relocate into the village where the majority of members resided. St. John's Church was completed in December 1847, and New Bethel was sold three years later.

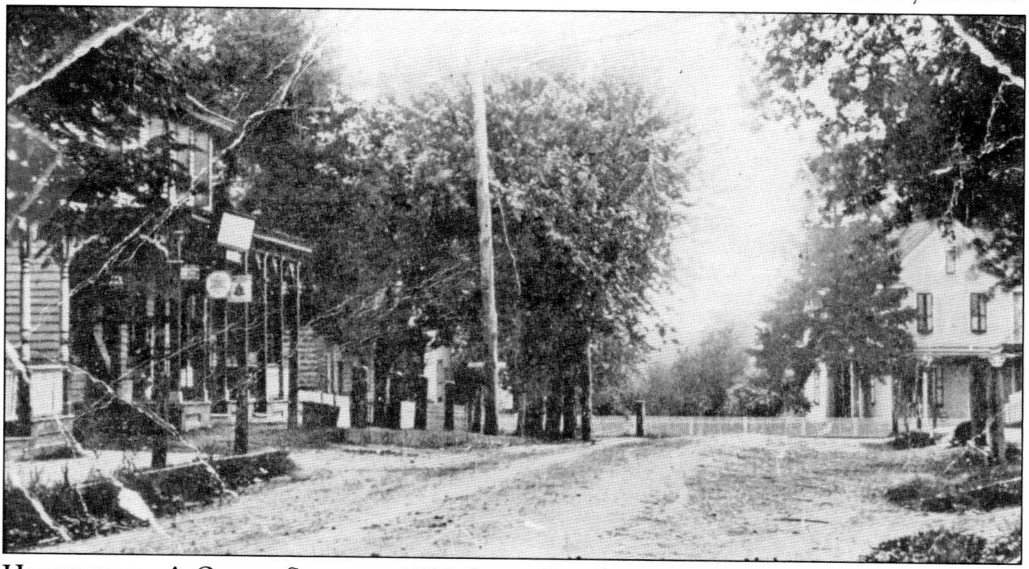

Harrisonville's Oldest Store, c. 1900. James Saunders opened the village's second general store on the south end of Main Street in 1848. A succession of owners continued the business for over a century. Franklin D. Bradway turned the store into living quarters in the mid-20th century after building a furniture store at the corner of Main and Jackson Streets. St. John's Parsonage, built in 1875, can be seen to the right. (FSC.)

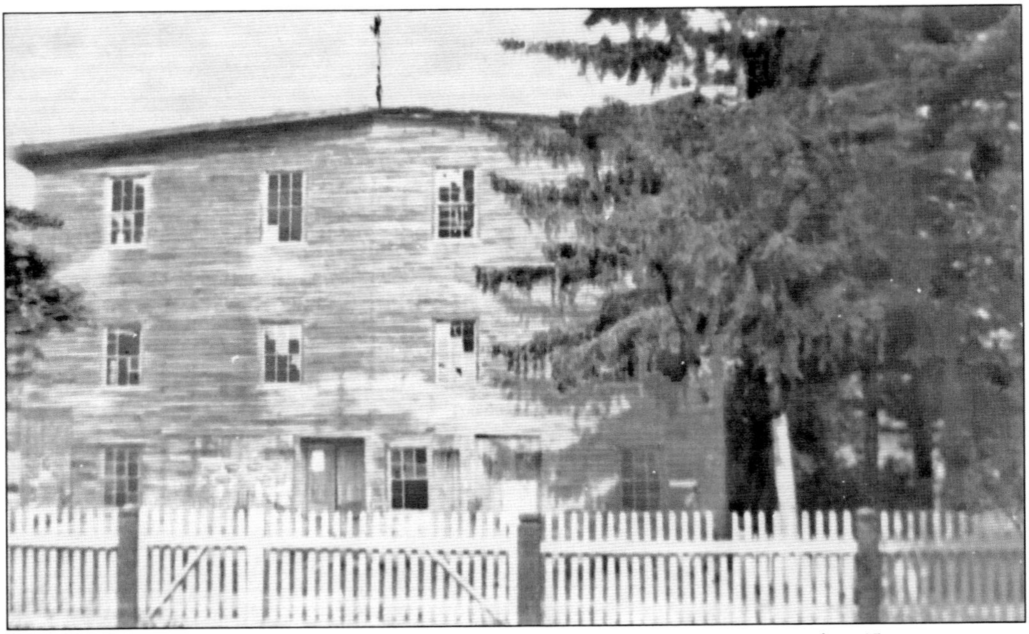

Harrisonville Hall. Iron Hall (as it was originally called) was built around 1865 near present-day Jackson Street. The first floor housed William Ladow's blacksmith and wheelwright shop; a paint shop for carriages and wagons occupied the second. The third-floor auditorium hosted entertainments, band concerts, and traveling shows. By 1900, however, the once grand building had deteriorated and was condemned and removed.

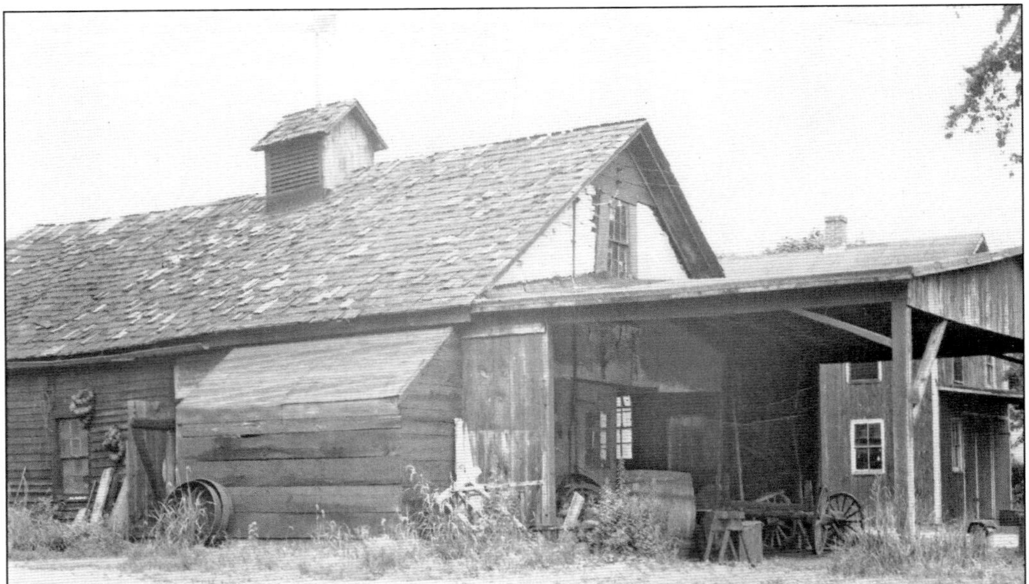

Pimm's Blacksmith Shop. Starting in 1820, four generations of the Pimm family operated a smithy on the west side of Main Street. The Pimms were noted as expert smiths and farriers. J. Lambert Pimm was the last member of his family to follow the family business, and his death in 1950 marked the end of blacksmithing in the village. Franklin D. Bradway removed the shop to build his new furniture store. (GCHS.)

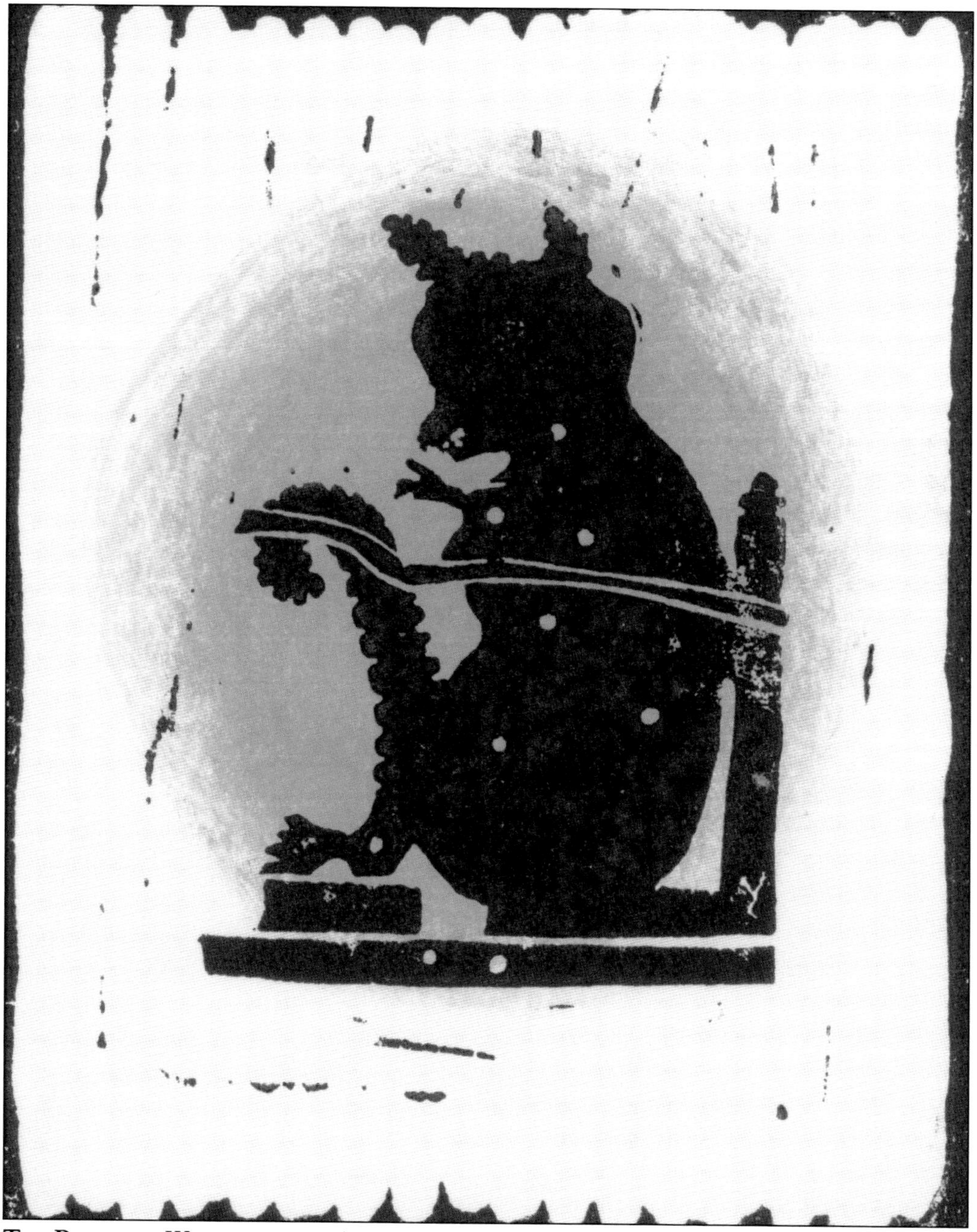

The Raccoon Weathervane. A curious relic of Whig politics of the 1840s, Harrisonville's Raccoon Weathervane was a familiar landmark in town for over a century. The Whig Party was instrumental in creating Old Harrison, whose name honored the memory of the party's president William Henry Harrison. The image of a raccoon thumbing its nose was adopted by the Henry Clay presidential campaign of 1844. This was Clay's third presidential race and Democrats pejoratively dubbed him "the same old coon." The Whigs decided to embrace the epithet and make Clay more appealing to the common man; however, he still failed to best Martin Van Buren. The weathervane was first mounted on a flagpole, and then installed atop Harrisonville Hall. When the hall was torn down, it was moved to Pimm's Blacksmith Shop until it, too, was demolished.

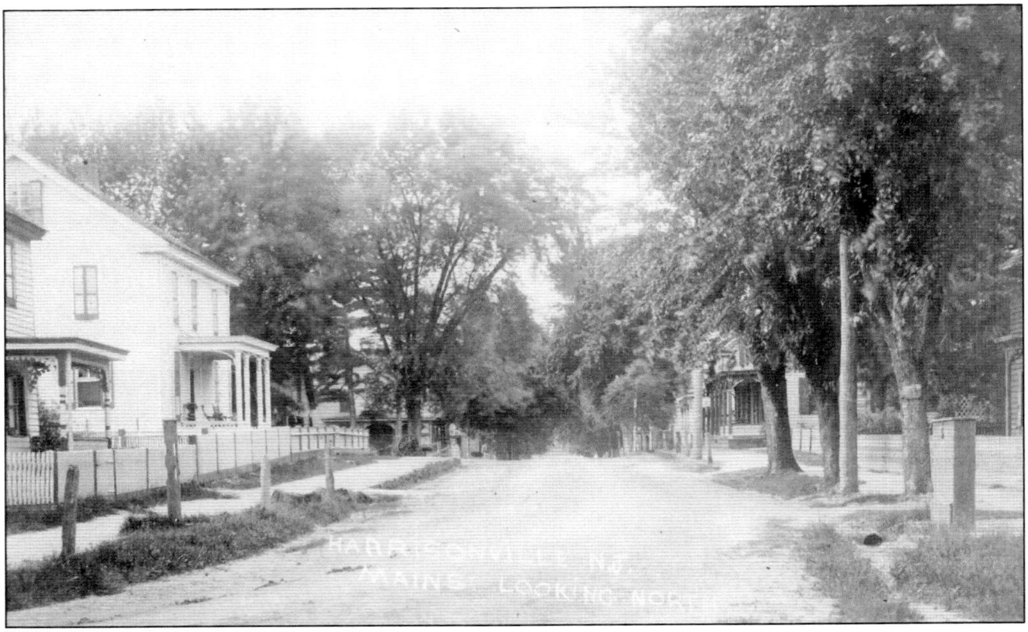

Main Street View Looking North. The Pimm Homestead, seen here on the left, is a familiar village landmark; the exterior has remained largely unchanged since it was built in 1868. The house replaced an earlier structure where Squire Samuel Pimm, the local justice of the peace for 25 years, resided. (FSC.)

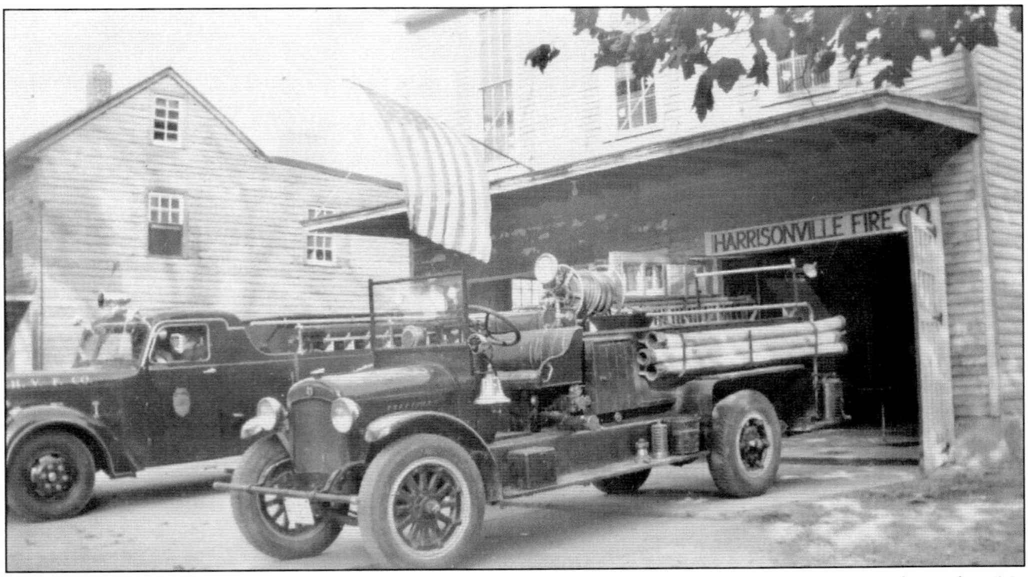

Harrisonville Fire Company. Although a fire company was not formally organized until 1938, a small building behind the Odd Fellows Hall long sheltered an antiquated, 18th-century hand pumper. A series of disastrous fires in the 1930s led citizens to acquire this 1924 Ruggles fire truck. The Odd Fellows Hall was converted into a firehouse and served the company until it was replaced by the modern station near the school. (HFC.)

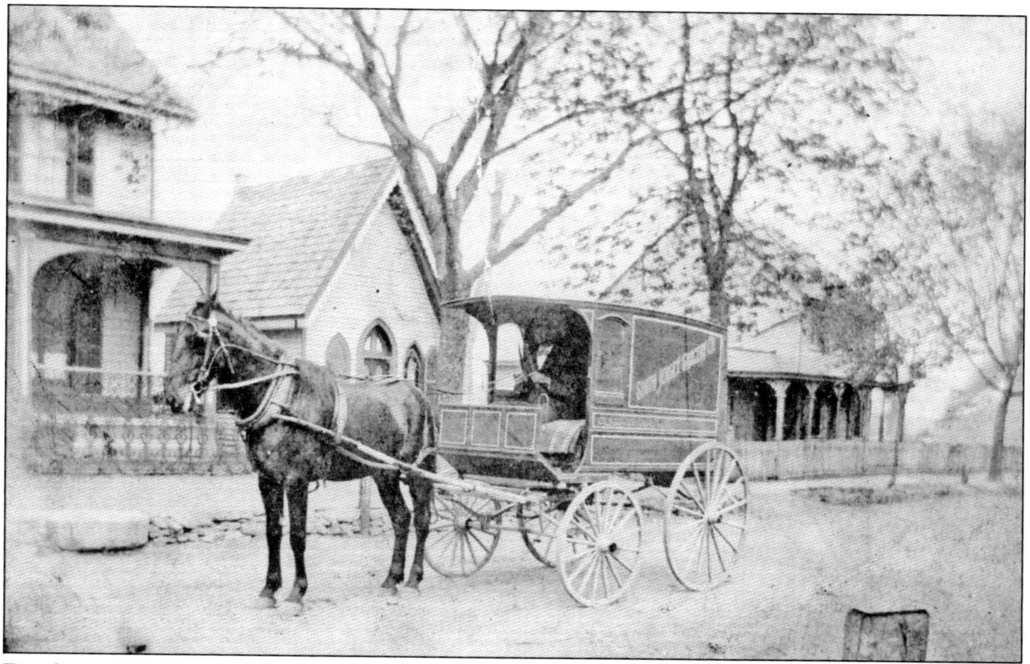

DR. SAMUEL STANGER'S HOUSE AND OFFICE. Dr. Samuel F. Stanger was Harrisonville's last resident physician (serving around 1877–1905). Stanger was well-regarded here and, in 1884, was elected township physician to provide care for the poor. His office was housed in the Gothic Revival building located in the center of the photograph and to the right of Stanger's residence. The building was later moved behind the house, where it remains today.

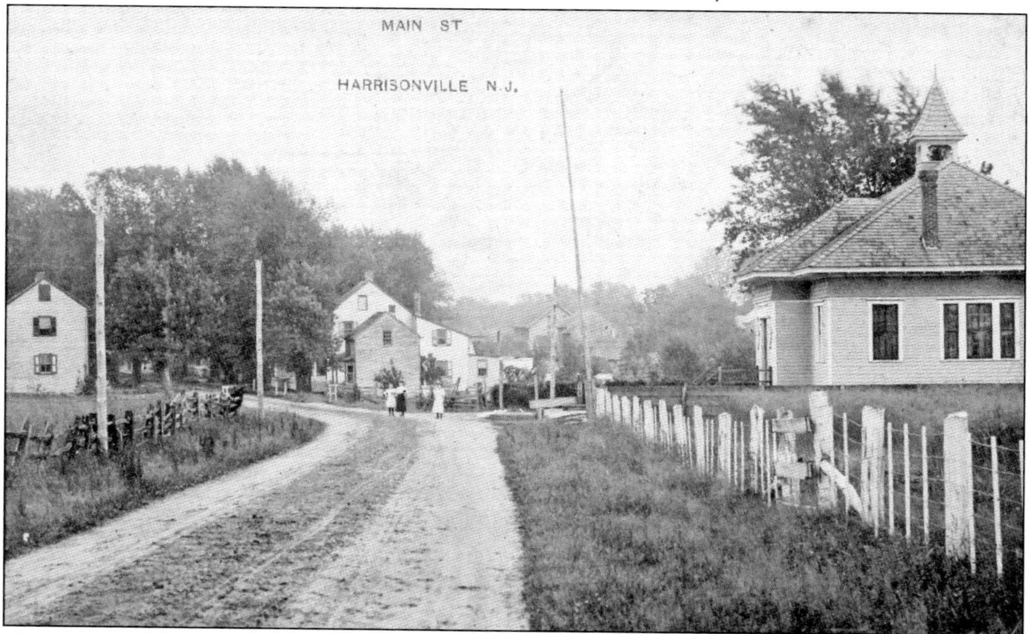

THE NORTH END OF HARRISONVILLE, C. 1900. Lewis Amme, Harrisonville's last shoemaker, conducted his business in the small building on the north end of the village, near the center of the photograph. It later housed Douglas McCauley's Harness Shop. The two-room schoolhouse replaced the "Red School," an earlier building at the same location. (KH.)

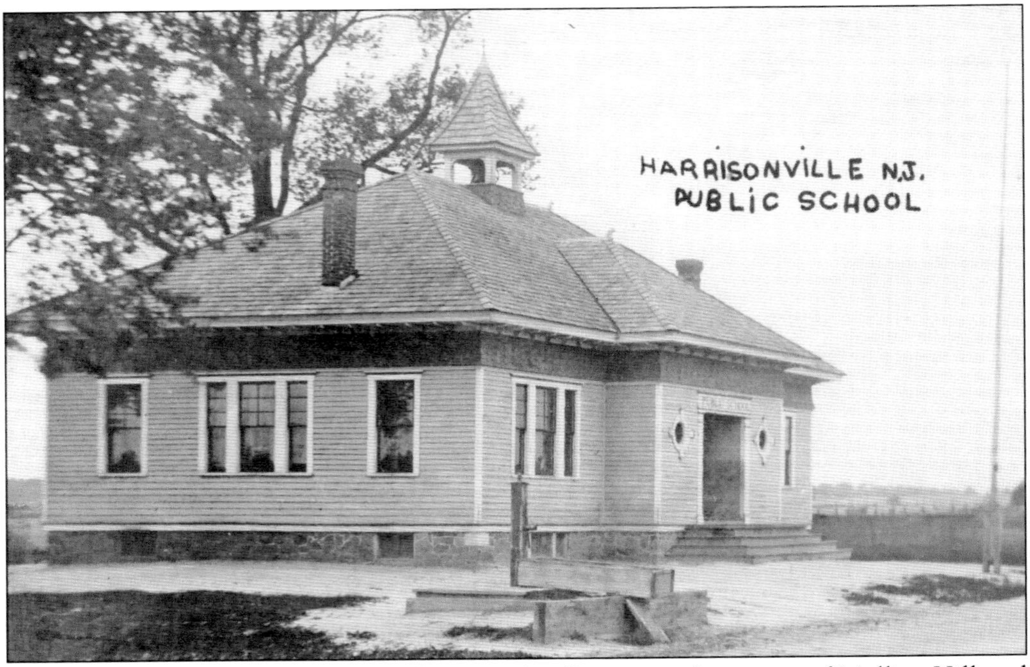

HARRISONVILLE SCHOOL. There has been a schoolhouse on the corner of Mullica Hill and Harrisonville Roads since the early 1800s. This school, the third in that location, was built in 1898 and enlarged in 1926 to accommodate all township students. Arson destroyed the building on July 26, 1947. (FSC.)

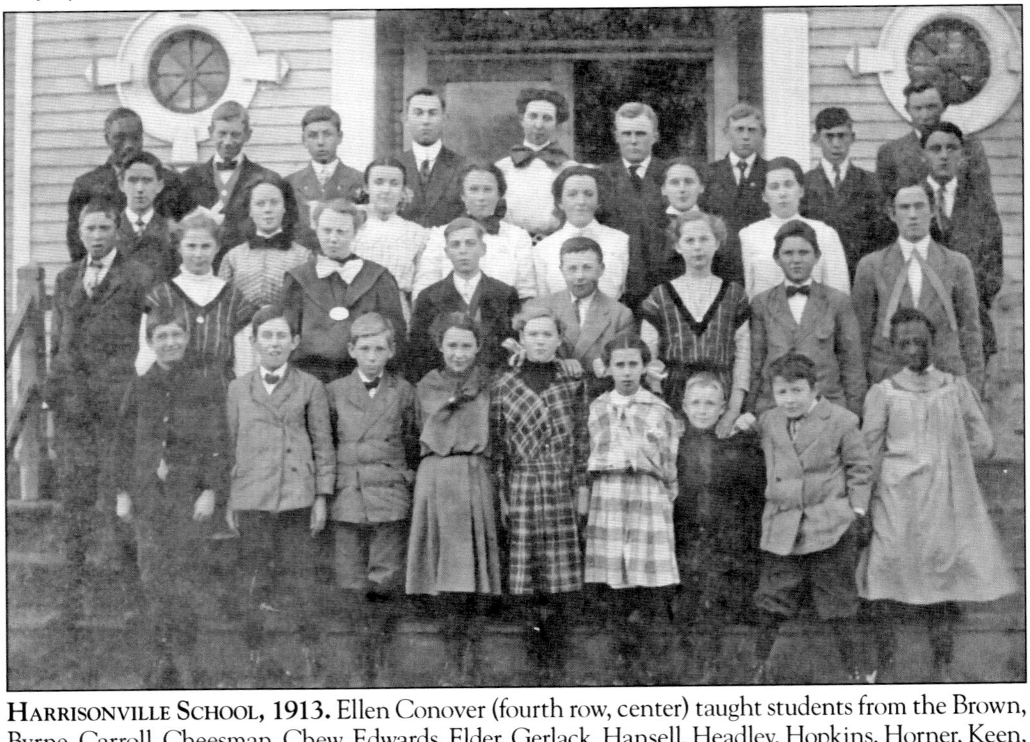

HARRISONVILLE SCHOOL, 1913. Ellen Conover (fourth row, center) taught students from the Brown, Byrne, Carroll, Cheesman, Chew, Edwards, Elder, Gerlack, Hansell, Headley, Hopkins, Horner, Keen, Kirby, Madara, Mattson, Moncrief, Pitman, Rainey, Randolph, Shaw, and Smith families.

SOUTH HARRISON TOWNSHIP SCHOOL. It took five years to build a new school after the fire. During the interim, students met in the Harrisonville Grange Hall, Harrisonville Fire Hall, and St. John's Church. Harrison Township permitted classes to be held in Jefferson School, which was no longer in service. When the school reopened, Raymond and Fannie Morgan resumed their duties as school custodians, positions they had held since 1926. (SHBOE.)

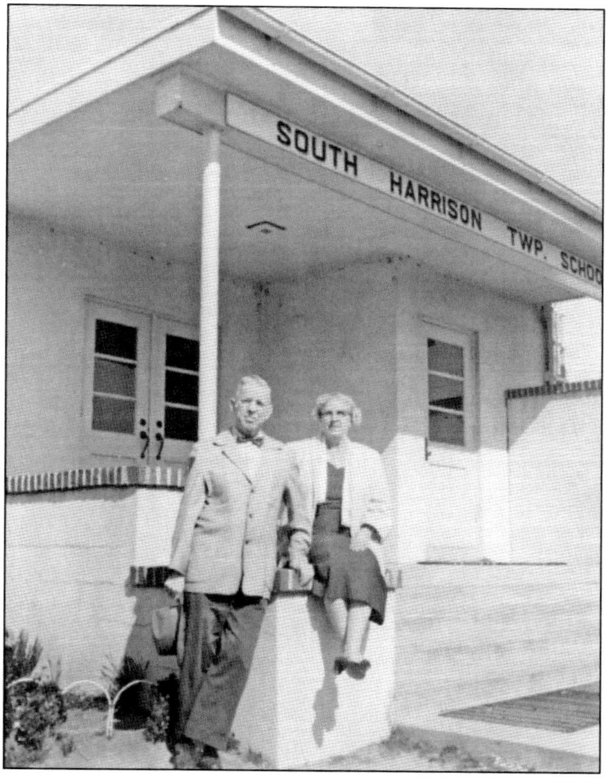

HARRISONVILLE SCHOOL, 1954. The first principal at the new school was Sara Lashley, seen here with students from the Atkinson, Banff, Clark, Crispin, Horner, Jackson, Leatherwood, Marino, Ridgway, String, and Tunnell families. The school has subsequently been enlarged and remodeled several times to accommodate the growing population. (KH.)

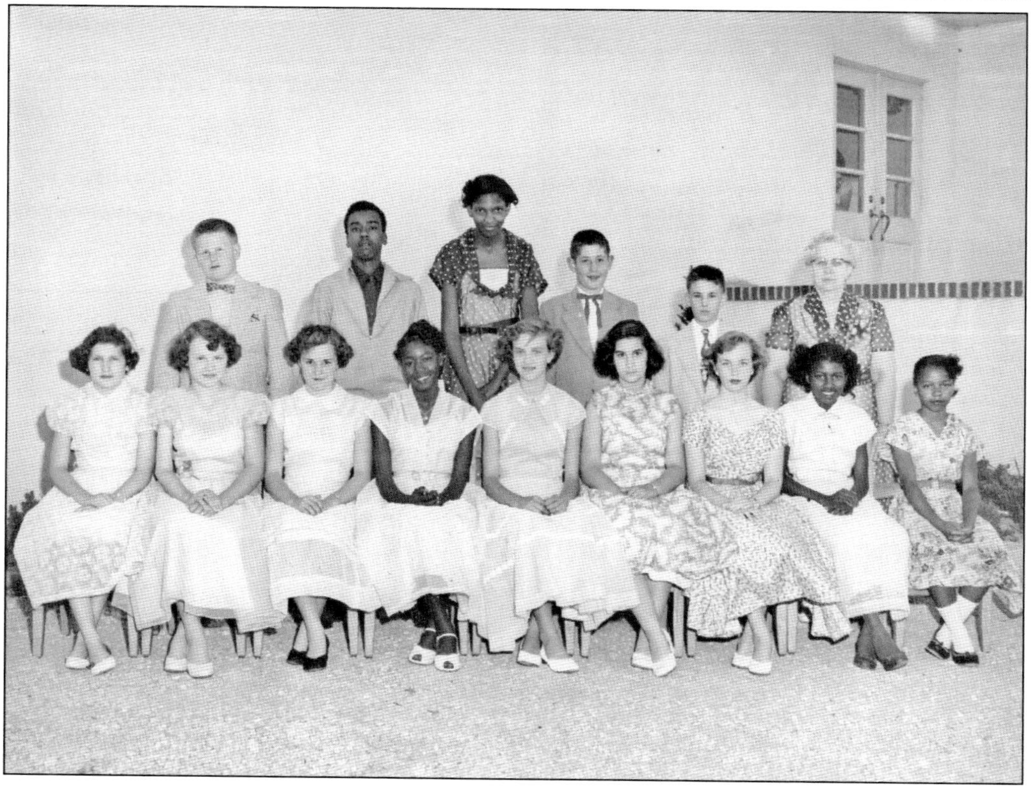

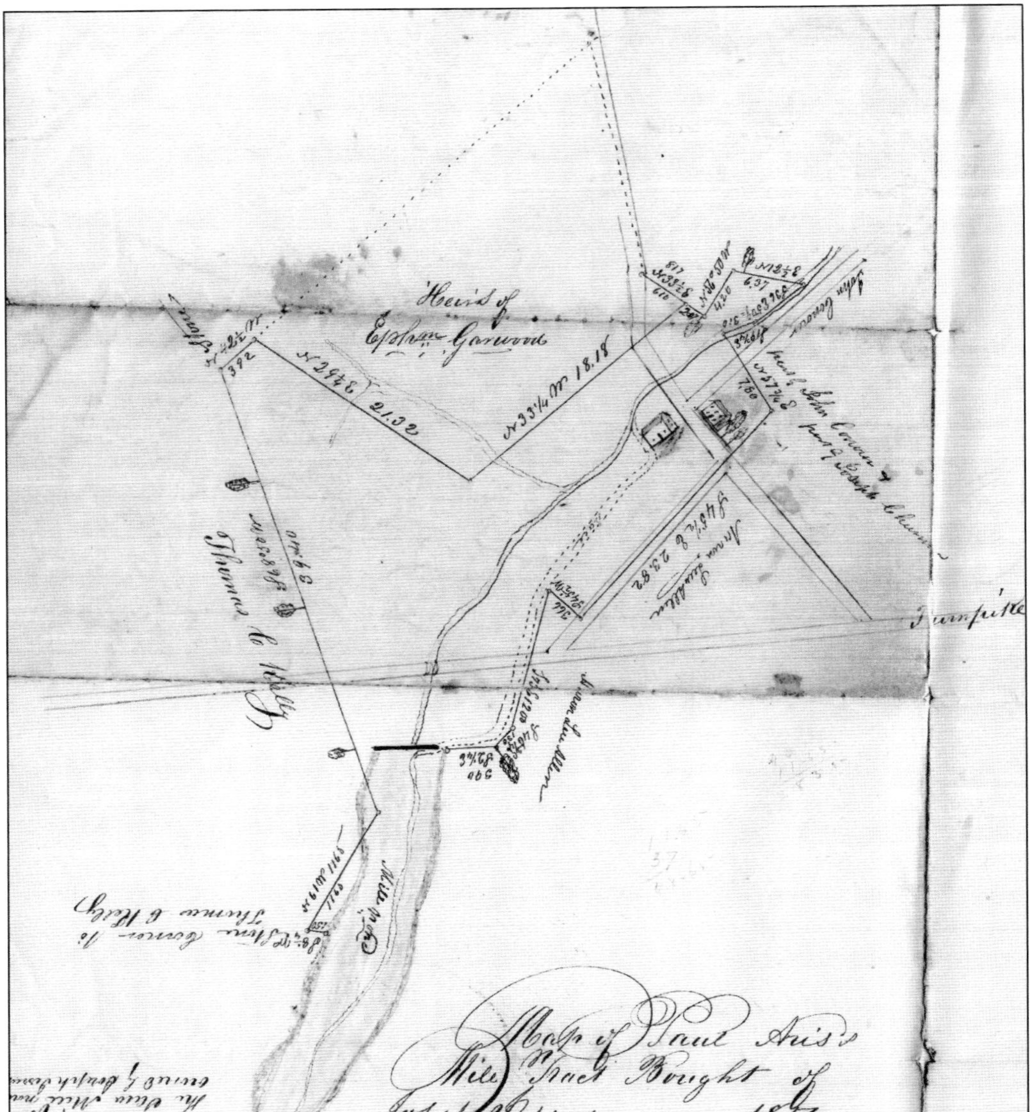

Survey Map, Paul Avis's Mill Tract, 1856. The upper reach of Oldmans Creek at Lincoln supported two mills, both shown on this map. Avis's millpond was located above Commissioners Pike, a considerable distance from the mill, which stood next to the creek at Lincoln Road. The lengthy raceway was necessary to increase the spillway's waterpower. A lane once ran along the raceway between the two roads. (RUASC.)

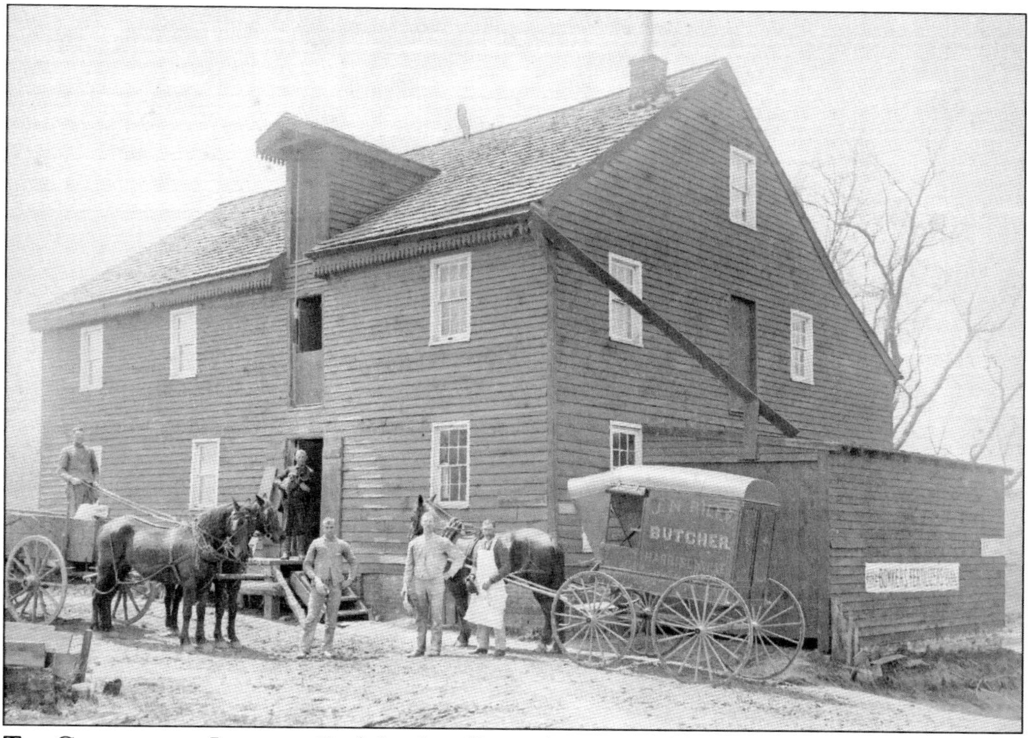

The Gristmill at Lincoln. Paul Avis's mill was the principal business in the village. Lincoln, originally called Stringtown after the String family, consisted of but a few houses, a blacksmith and wheelwright shop, and Oak Grove School. Although the mill is no longer extant, the miller's house still stands on the corner of Lincoln and Lincoln Mill Roads. (FSC.)

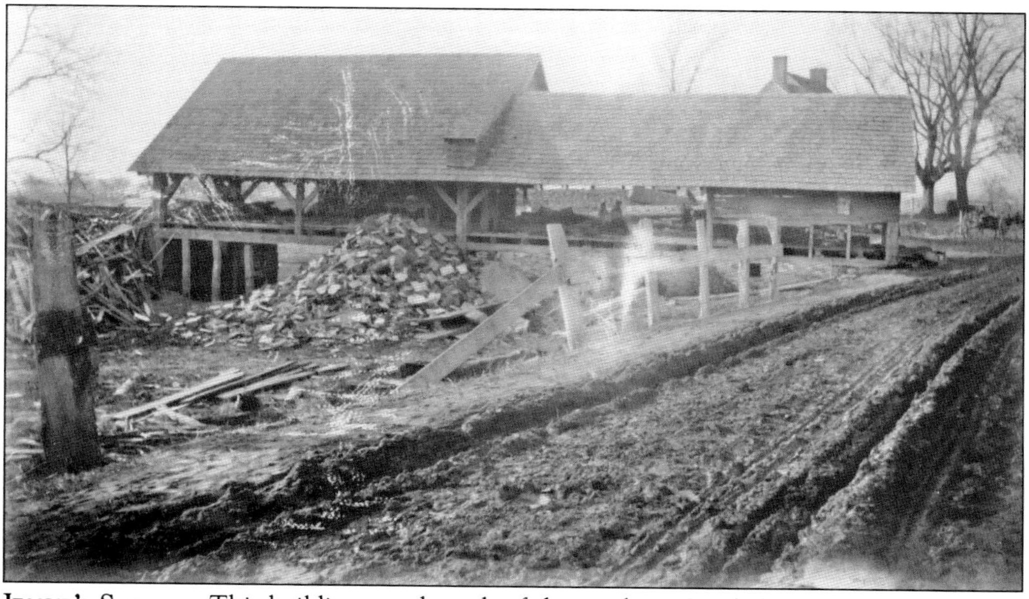

Jessup's Sawmill. This building stood north of the creek on Swedesboro-Monroeville Road. Operations at this location included both saw- and woolen mills. The sawmill continued in business into the 20th century; however, today, little evidence remains of either the pond or building save some stone foundations and the sawyer's house, which is visible in the background. (SCHS.)

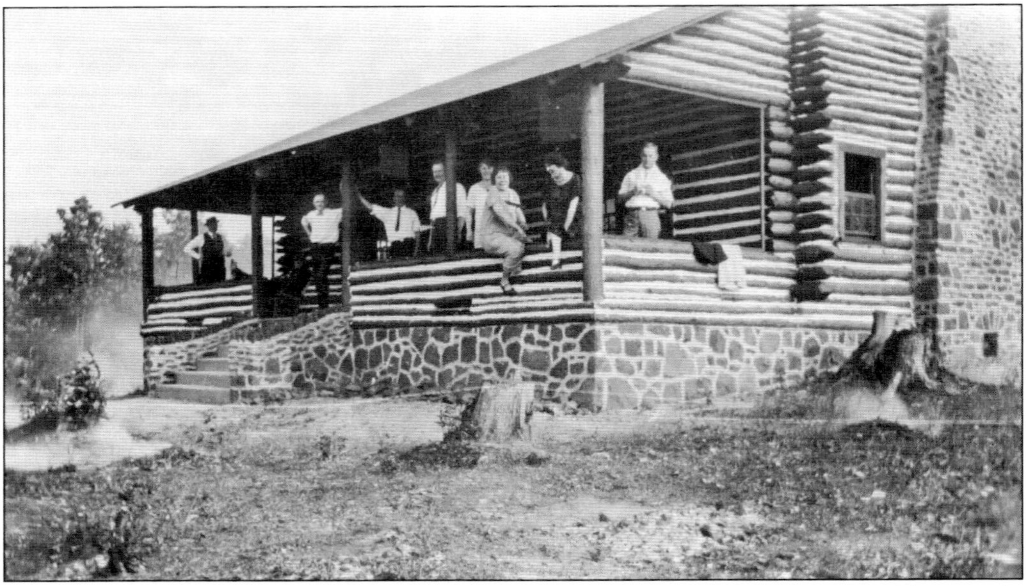

ALGONKIN CLUB, 1925. A group of Camden County businessmen purchased the site of the Lincoln Mill pond on Commissioners Pike and surrounding land in 1920 to establish a sportsmen's club. The group first rebuilt the dam and then constructed the clubhouse, which was completed around 1925. The club featured swimming, boating, hunting, and trapshooting and became a popular place that organizations and businesses could rent for outings and company picnics. (JHB.)

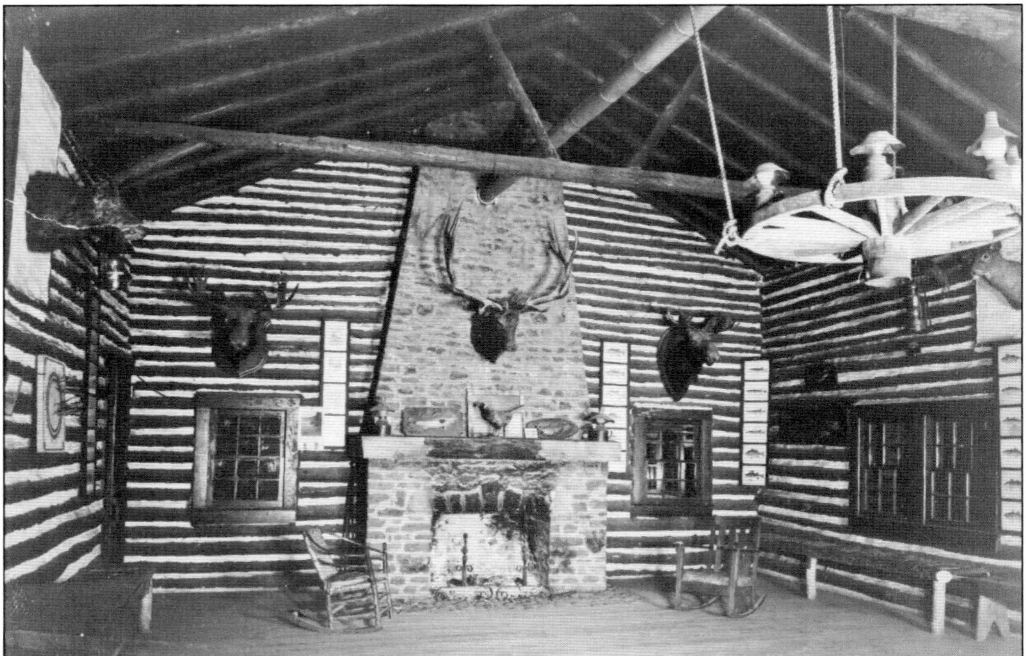

ALGONKIN CLUBHOUSE. The clubhouse was the principal structure on the property and was built in classic hunting-lodge style. There was a small sleeping loft, and the fireplace provided the only heat. By 1970, with membership dwindling, the property was sold to Bancroft School, which established there an innovative residential program for adults with intellectual and developmental disabilities. The clubhouse, however, had deteriorated and was torn down. (JHB.)

Four

Trails and Crossroads

Ancient Indian trails and a network of 18th- and 19th-century roads are still the principal roadways of Old Harrison Township. The Cohawkin Road, later known as the Cumberland Road, is the oldest and is today's Bridgeton Pike. It provided access to Philadelphia's markets and brought commerce that led to the establishment of a number of inns and taverns to cater to the needs of travelers. Roads to Glassboro, Swedesboro, and Franklinville also facilitated movement and opened the township to settlement.

In the early 19th century, clusters of houses sprang up at prominent crossroads and became small villages. A schoolhouse was often the first public building, followed by a church and a general store. Blacksmith shops and carriage works were established in the days of horse-drawn vehicles and gave way to garages and gas stations with the rise of the automobile. Richwood became the largest of these crossroads towns, followed in size by Jefferson, Ferrell and Cedar Grove.

For Richwood, the roads that brought prosperity are today bringing dramatic change as farmland and older homes give way to residential and commercial development. Jefferson has some commercial activity but its well-known old businesses are gone, and since the church closed, there is nothing left to identify it by name. Ferrell can still be identified by its firehouse and church and sits at a busy intersection with access to Route 55. Cedar Grove is located at a busy five-point intersection, but no public building or sign names the place.

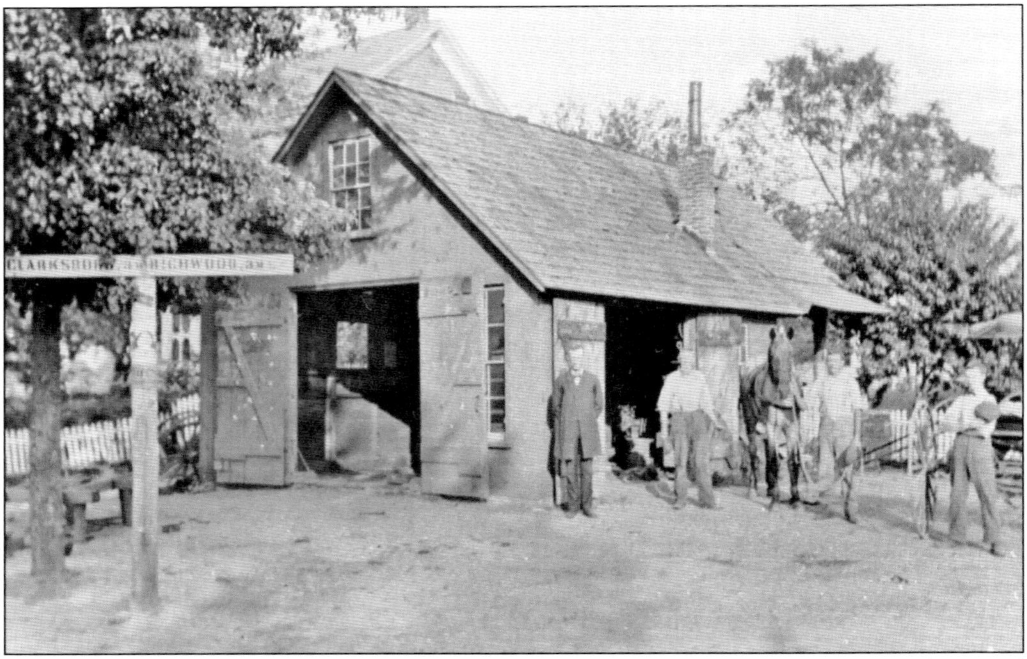

Jenkins Blacksmith Shop, c. 1900. Running east from the Delaware River, Cohawkin Road made a right turn at what is now Jefferson and headed south through Mullica Hill toward Salem and Cumberland Counties. Jenkins's shop stood at the northeast corner of that turn. The village was first called Cox's Hill, then Allenboro and Lawrenceville or Lazy Lawrence, pejoratively suggesting the inhabitants lacked ambition. It was finally renamed Jefferson in 1872.

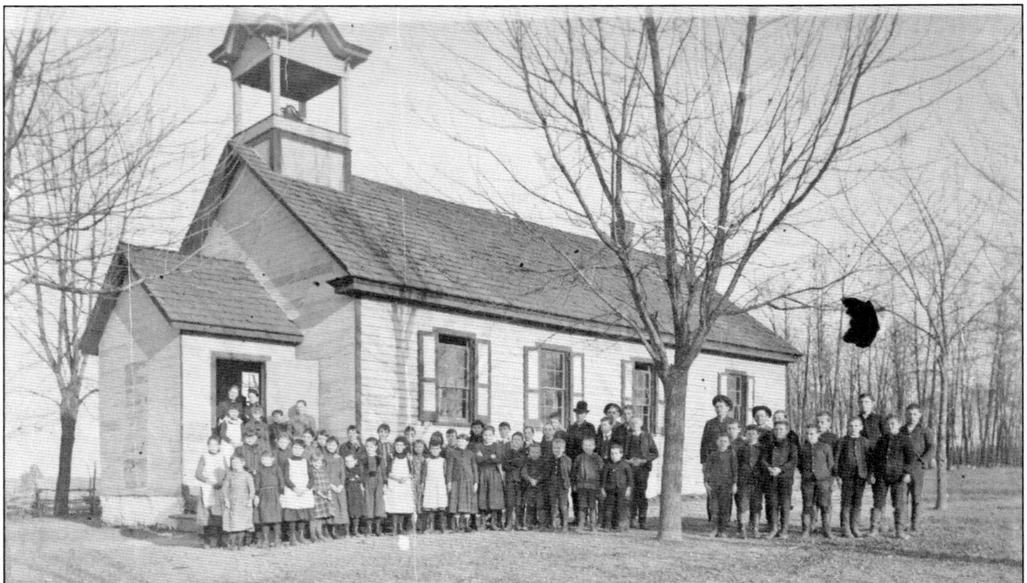

Jefferson School. The original one-room school in Jefferson was built in 1859 on land donated by the Gooden family and was divided into two rooms in 1895. In 1905, when a new two-room school was planned for the site, the one-room schoolhouse was sold and moved a short distance, where it was used as a blacksmith shop. The Jefferson School closed in 1944, but was brought back into service when Harrisonville School burned down.

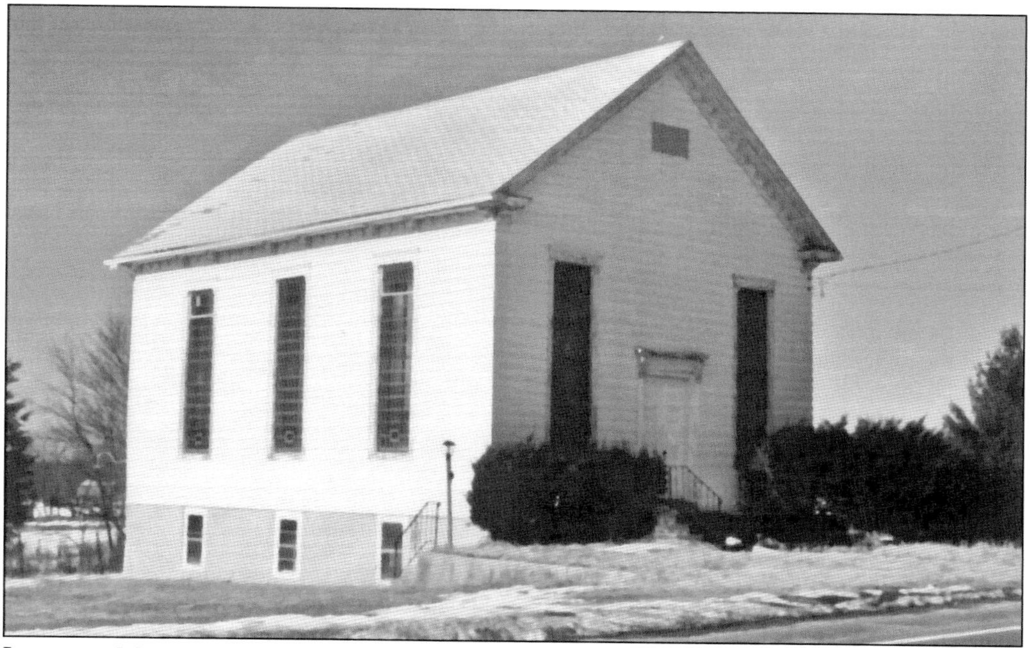

Jefferson Methodist Church, 1987. Methodist classes began in Jefferson in the 1830s, and by 1845, they were being led by David A. Shute. Construction of a church began in 1867 on land donated by John Sitley and his wife, Rebecca, and was completed in 1868.

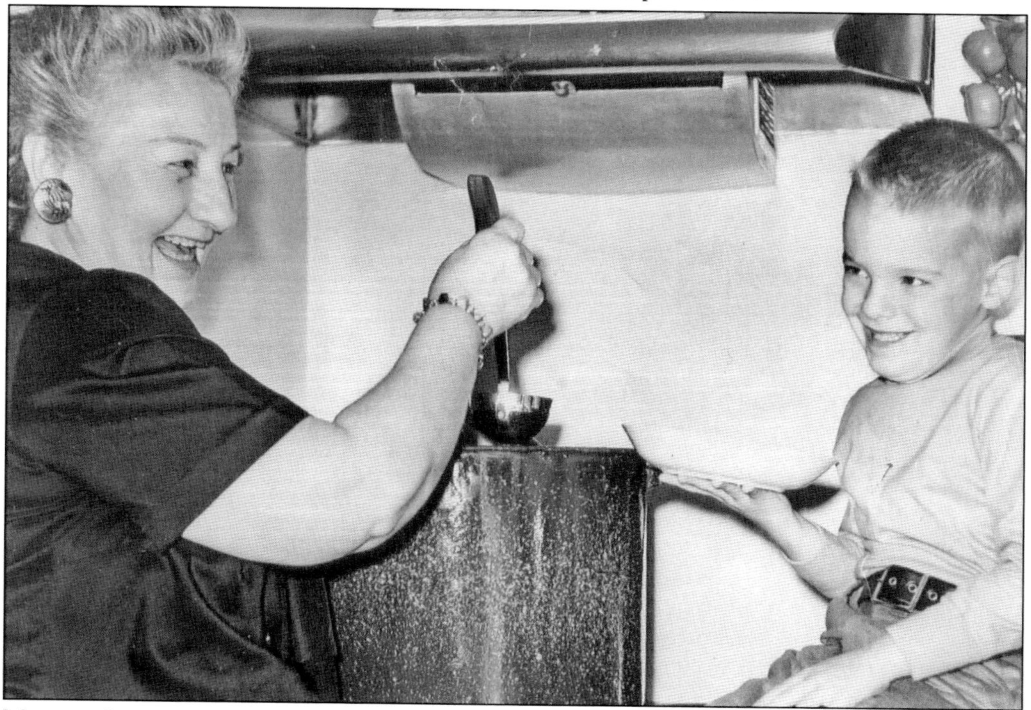

Making Soup for the Church Bazaar, 1969. Chris Gwin watches while Estel Steffen serves up a pot of soup for a Jefferson Methodist Church bazaar. Eight years later, the church closed and the congregation merged with Trinity United Methodist Church in Mullica Hill. The building still stands and is a commercial establishment.

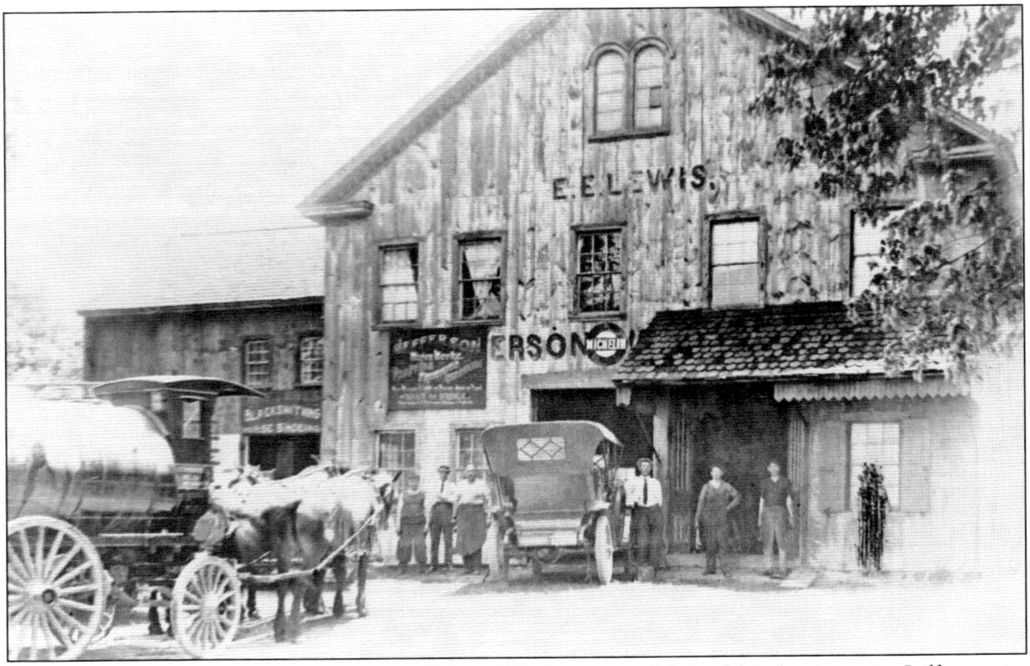

E. E. Lewis Carriage Works, 1912. Edward E. Lewis established his business in Jefferson in 1874. He manufactured a wide variety of carriages, wagons, and sleighs and employed expert mechanics, blacksmiths, and farriers. As transportation evolved in the early 20th century and automobiles became popular, he offered auto repair services as well.

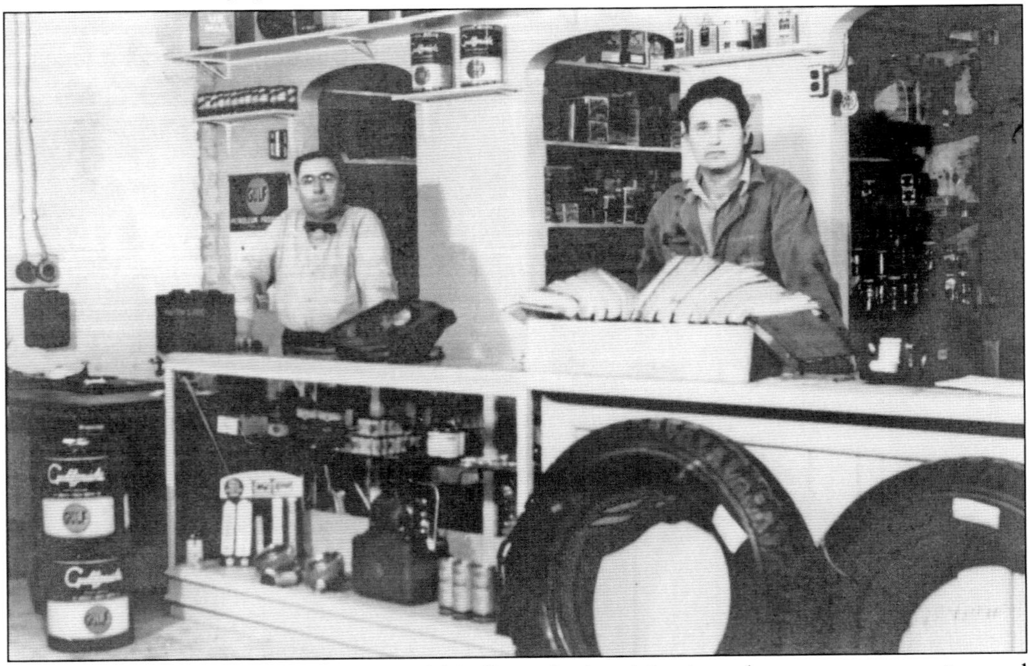

Oscar Jenkins Service Garage, c. 1940. Oscar Jenkins's business began as a gas station and service garage in Jefferson in the 1920s. By 1950, it had expanded to include a sporting goods store that sold fishing and camping equipment. The store was so well known that local residents referred to its location as "Oscar Jenkins Corner." Pictured are Jenkins (left) and Joe Bailey.

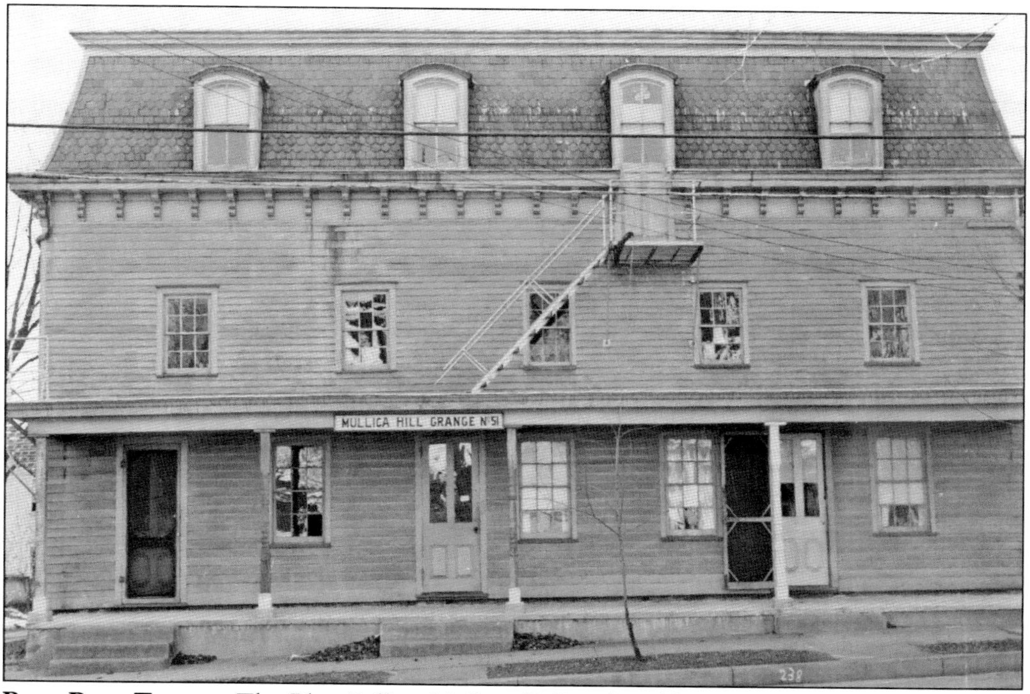

Blue Ball Tavern. The Blue Ball in Mullica Hill is the oldest tavern site in the township. Robert Gerrard petitioned for the first license in 1724, and in 1838, James Tomlin became the most prominent of its innkeepers. First called Blue Bell, it took its more familiar name from a later sign in the shape of a blue ball. The building served as home to the Mullica Hill Grange until it was razed in the 1950s and replaced with a new hall.

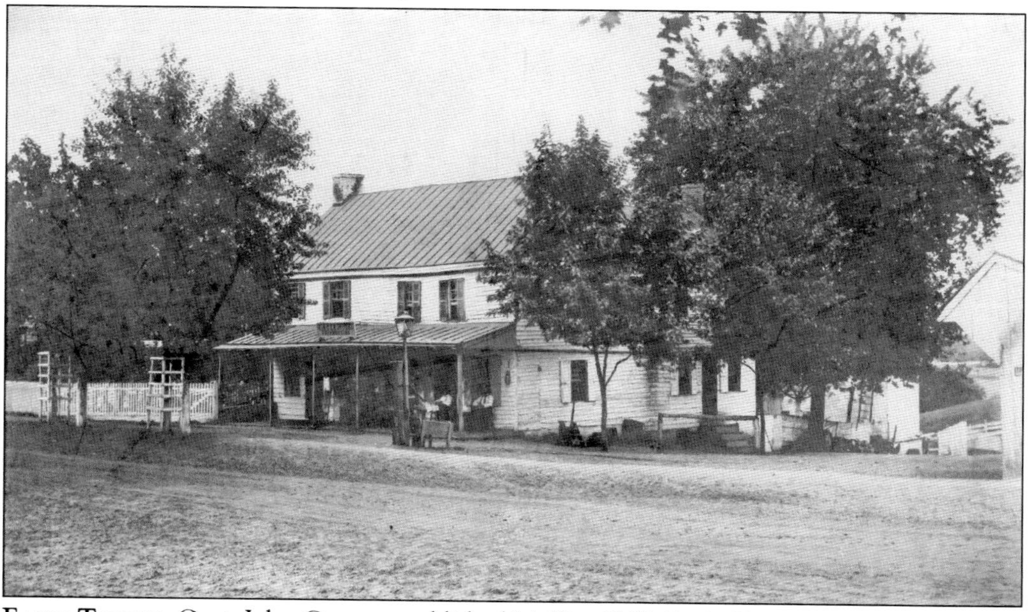

Eagle Tavern. Capt. John Cozens established Mullica Hill's Eagle Tavern in 1772. Sixty years later, local citizens met here to petition the state to establish Harrison Township, and township committee meetings were held here until Old Town Hall was built in 1871. Enlarged in the 1890s, the building operated as a hotel into the 20th century and contains apartments today.

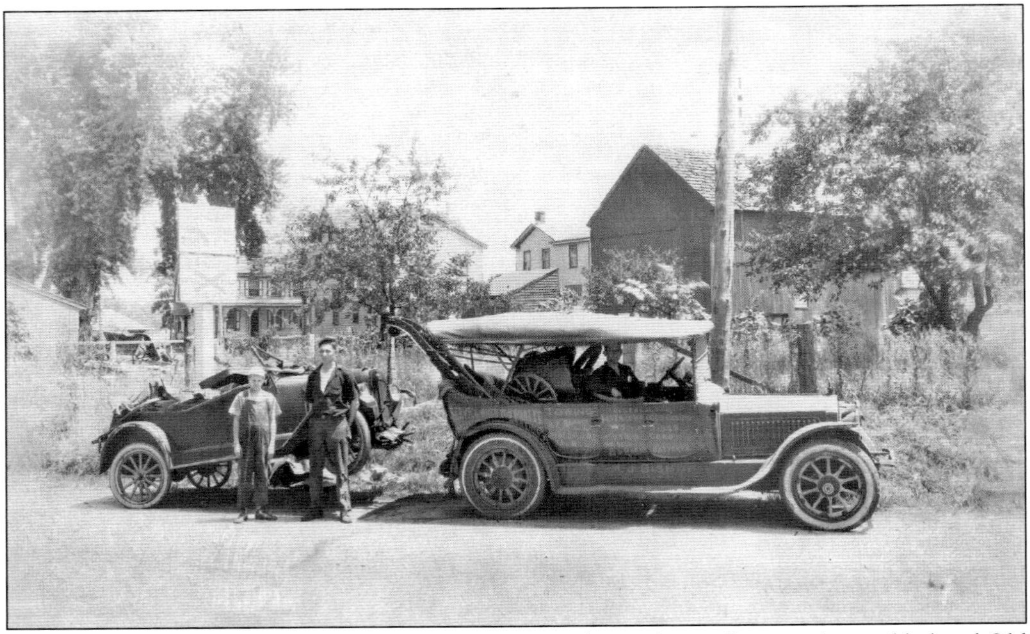

M. J. Bishop's Towing. Bishop's Towing first operated out of a small garage located behind Old Town Hall in Mullica Hill. The business began as a blacksmith shop, and as automobiles became popular, Bishop added a gas pump and operated it as a service garage. The towing rig advertised "Service When You Want It," listed the services offered, and provided a phone number.

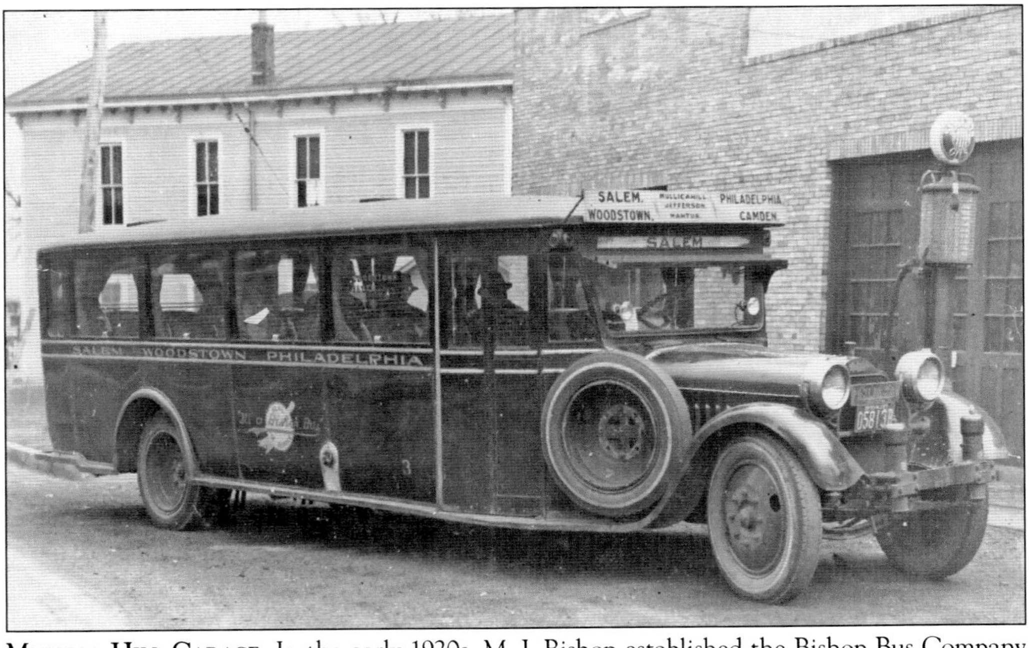

Mullica Hill Garage. In the early 1920s, M. J. Bishop established the Bishop Bus Company and built the Mullica Hill Garage to replace his smaller original building. The garage served as the headquarters for the bus company, sold gas, and offered automotive services. The company operated two bus lines: one from Philadelphia to Bridgeton and the other from Philadelphia to Salem. The building later housed a corn-chip factory and was briefly a lumberyard before becoming an antique mall.

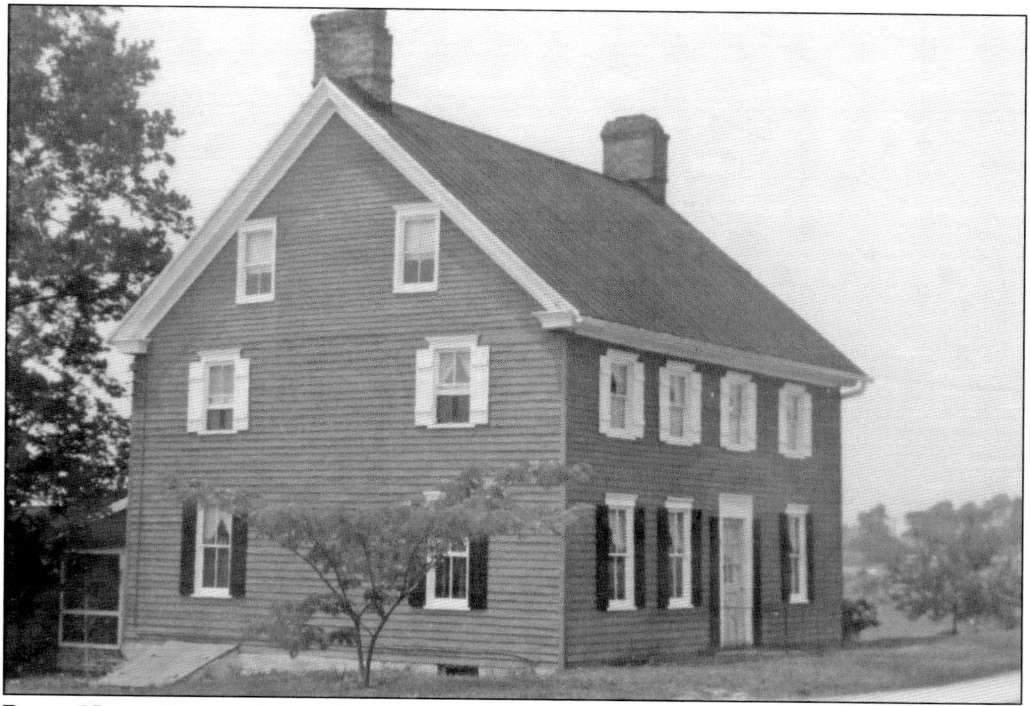

Black Horse Tavern. Located south of Mullica Hill on the Bridgeton Pike at Ewan Road, the Black Horse was established by William Gosling shortly after 1800. The original tavern burned in 1822. It was immediately rebuilt and, in the 1830s and 1840s, was a popular destination for sleighing parties. It is now a private residence.

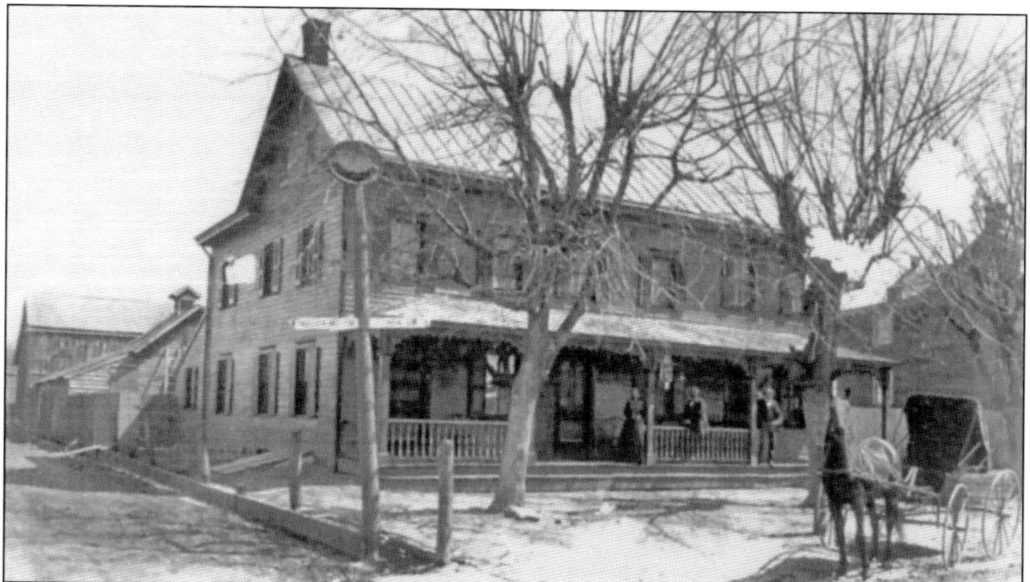

Meister's Hotel. John Meister of Ewan established the last tavern in the township in the late 1800s. He was succeeded in the early 1900s by John Rachor, who held horse and mule auctions in the livery behind the building. The hotel holds the distinction of briefly operating as a speakeasy during Prohibition. It is now a private residence and has been extensively remodeled and reduced in size.

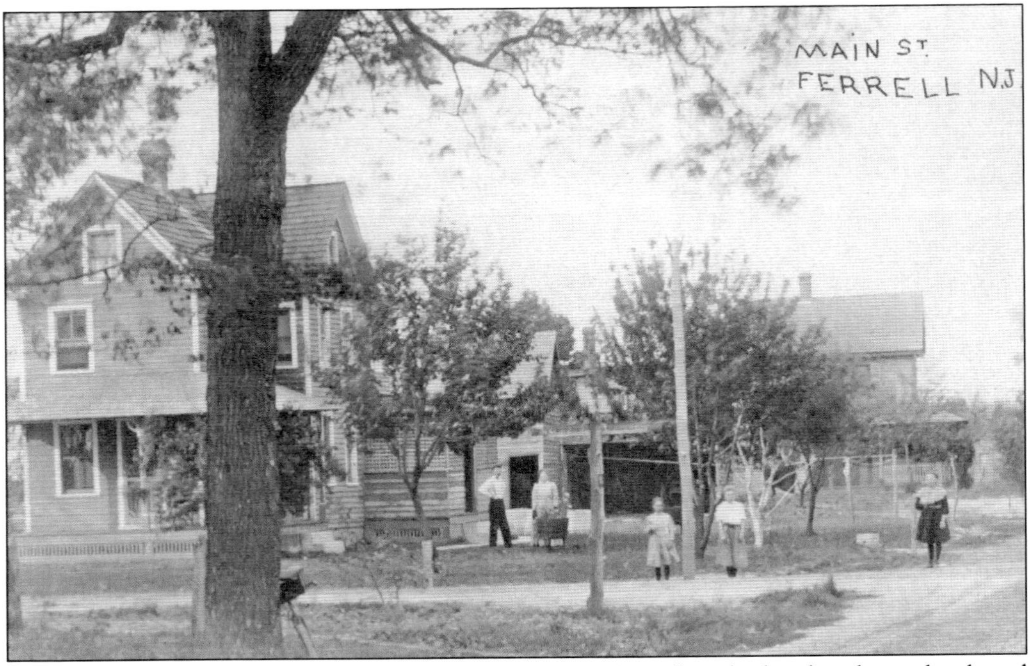

MAIN STREET, FERRELL. Originally known as Fairview, the village had a church, a school, and a handful of houses in the 1880s. It was mainly an agricultural settlement but there was also a small basketmaking industry. In 1891, residents renamed the village after Congressman Thomas M. Ferrell, a politician from Glassboro. (FSC.)

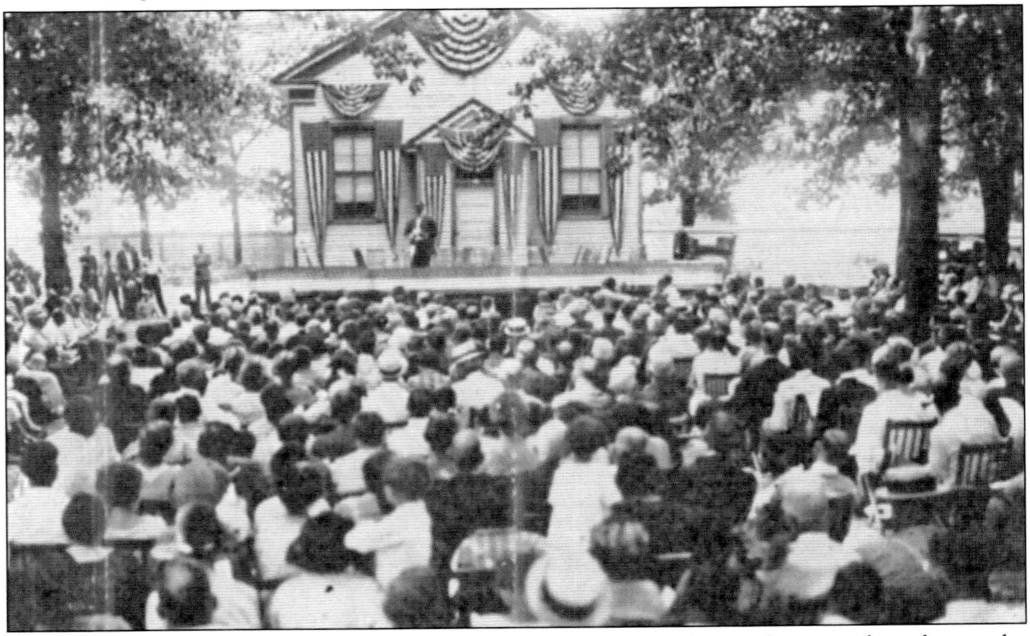

FERRELL SCHOOL. In 1925, when the Starking Red Delicious apple was discovered on the nearby farm of Lewis Mood, a celebration was held at the schoolhouse in Ferrell. Built in 1875 to replace the earlier log cabin school, it remained in use until 1944, when students were sent to Aura School. In 1945, the Ferrell Fire Company bought the property and built a firehouse onto the school building. The school was later torn down.

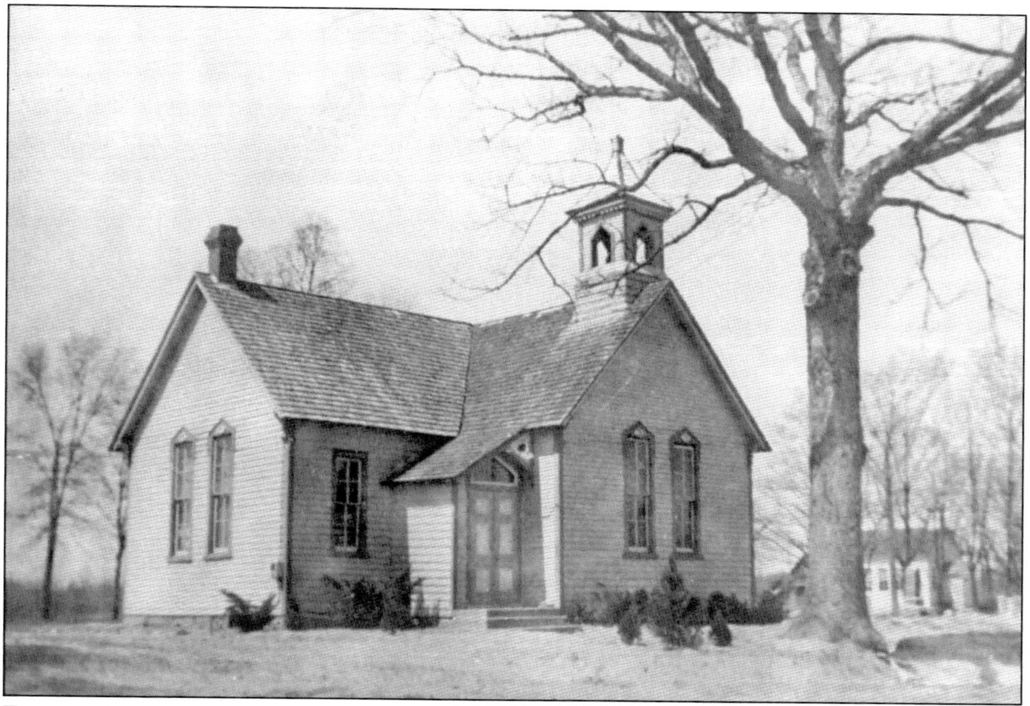

FERRELL METHODIST CHURCH. The community's Methodists first met for services in the old Fairview School, and in 1876, a church building was proposed. Construction began in 1883 on land purchased from James Lafferty, and the Fairview Methodist Church was dedicated in January 1884. It retained that name until 1960, when it became Ferrell Methodist Church. (FUMC.)

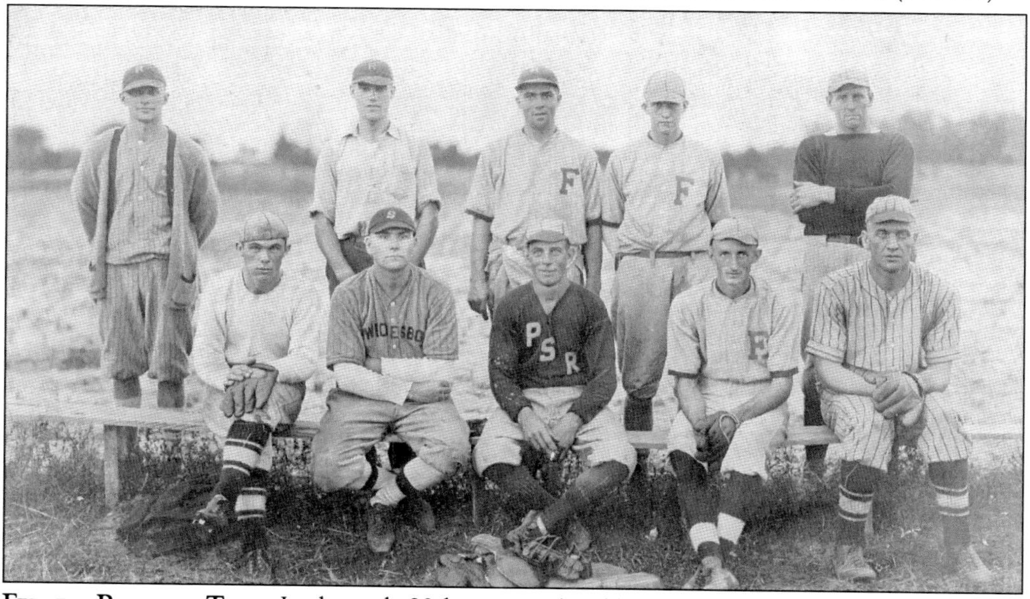

FERRELL BASEBALL TEAM. In the early 20th century, local baseball teams often welcomed players from other towns. The Ferrell team, which played games on the field across from the Methodist church, was no exception. From left to right are (first row) E. McGonigle, Charles Holtzhauser, E. Ernest, Ben Cassidy, and S. Carver; (second row) Charles Roth, Fletcher Souders, Howard Boyd, Harry Eastlack, and Maurice Bates.

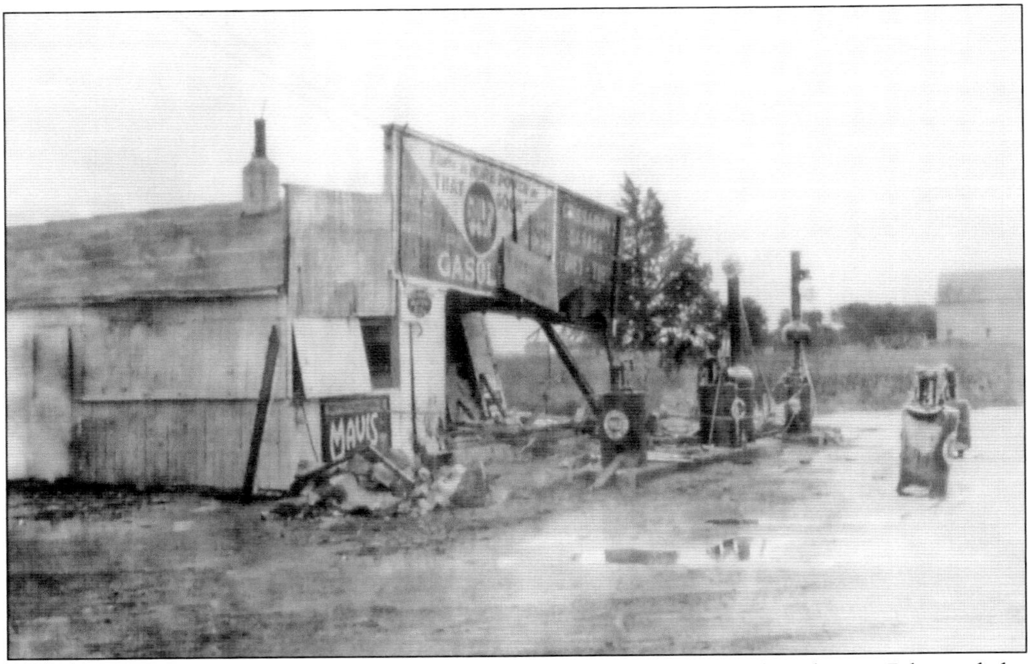

CASSADAY'S GARAGE, 1929. Cassaday's Garage stood at the corner of Bridgeton Pike and the Swedesboro-Franklinville Road near Ferrell. In 1929, a bus crashed into the front of the building and severely damaged it. It was later replaced with a gambrel-roofed store and garage built by H. R. Hubschmitt. (GCHS.)

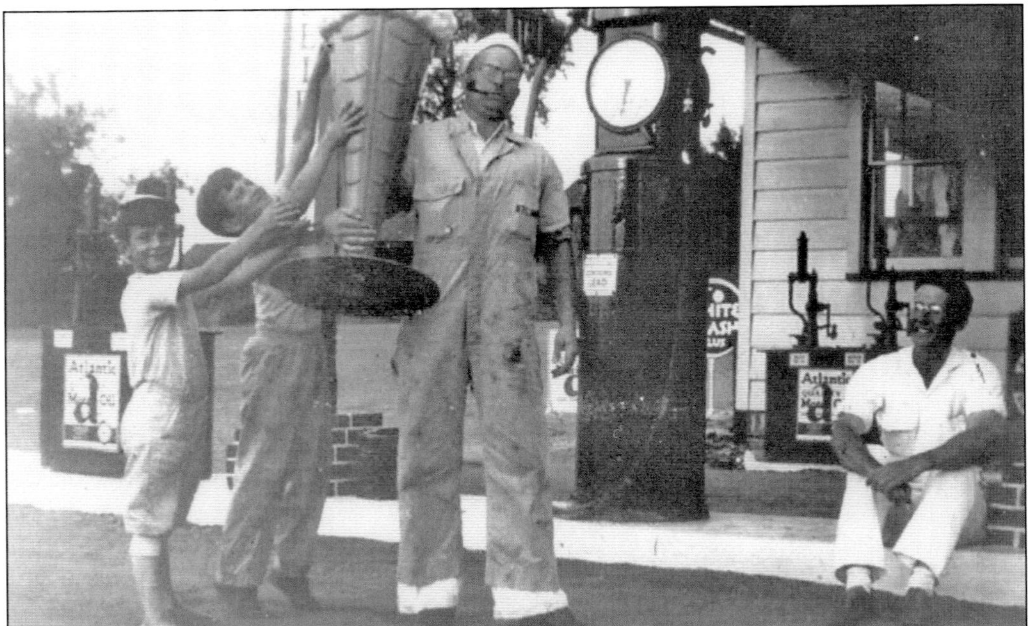

HUBSCHMITT'S STORE AND GARAGE. The giant ice-cream cone that stood outside Hubschmitt's Store and Garage was a local landmark, and travelers would stop to have their pictures taken with it. The building later fell into disrepair and stood empty for years before recently being demolished. (GCHS.)

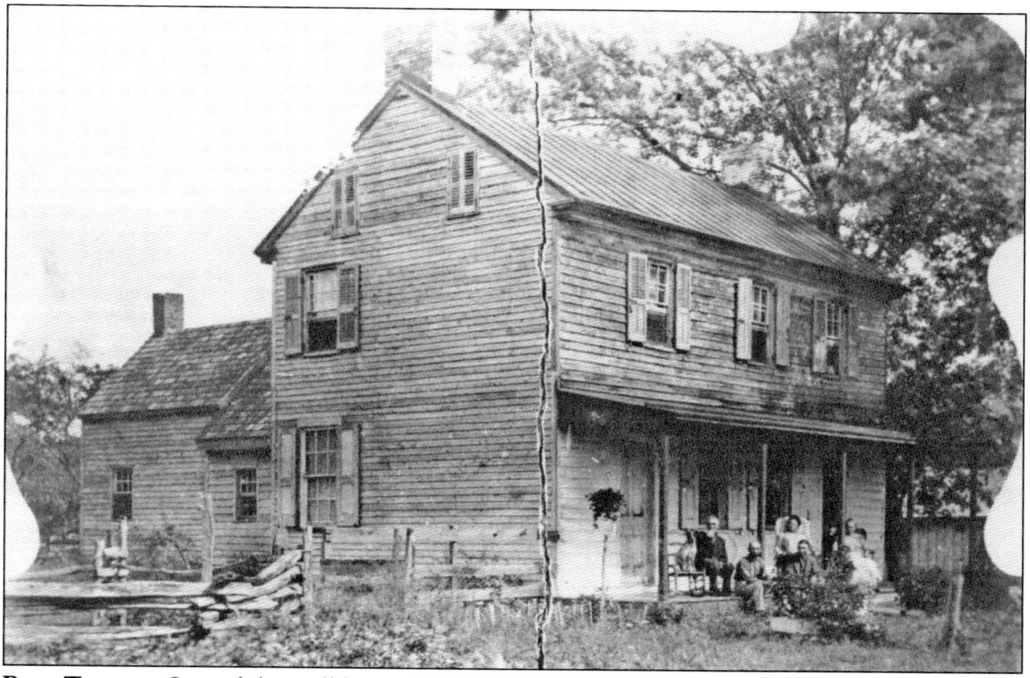

Pine Tavern. One of the well-known coaching inns along the Cumberland Road, the tavern stood just north of Oldmans Creek. William Lindsey held the first license in 1752, but by the 1840s, the inn was badly kept and in disrepair, and no further licenses were granted. In 1849, the locality was known as Pineville, and the former tavern was a store and post office. It later became a private residence and was demolished in 1994. (GCHS.)

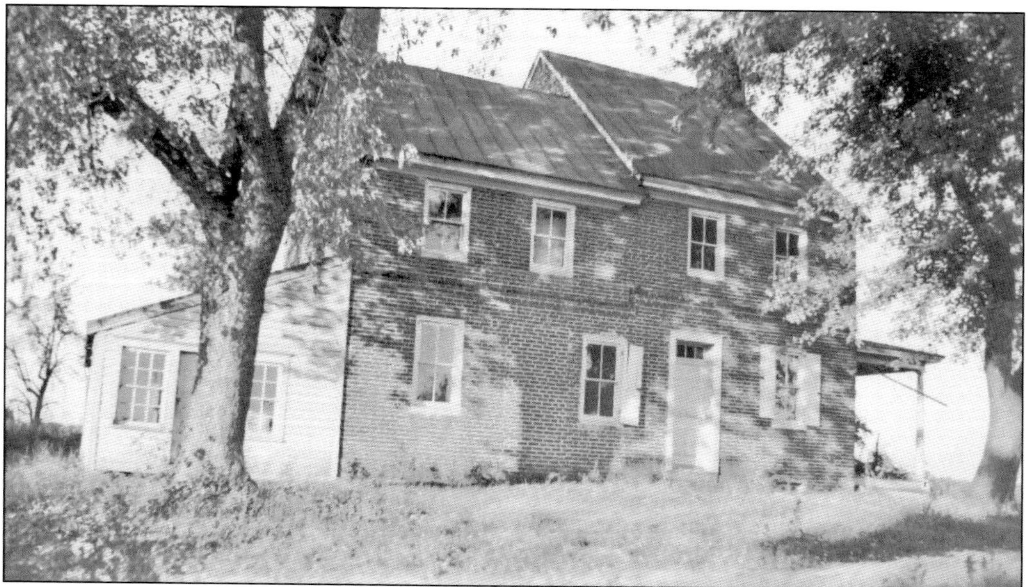

Jerusalem the Golden, 1939. Thomas Iredell Folwell, a descendent of Quaker settlers, made three trips to California between 1849 and 1851. With the gold he found, he bought a house near Cedar Grove built by a member of the French family. He named it Jerusalem the Golden after a hymn and in honor of his success in the Gold Rush. He died in 1871 when, in the midst of a nightmare, he jumped from his bedroom window. (GCHS.)

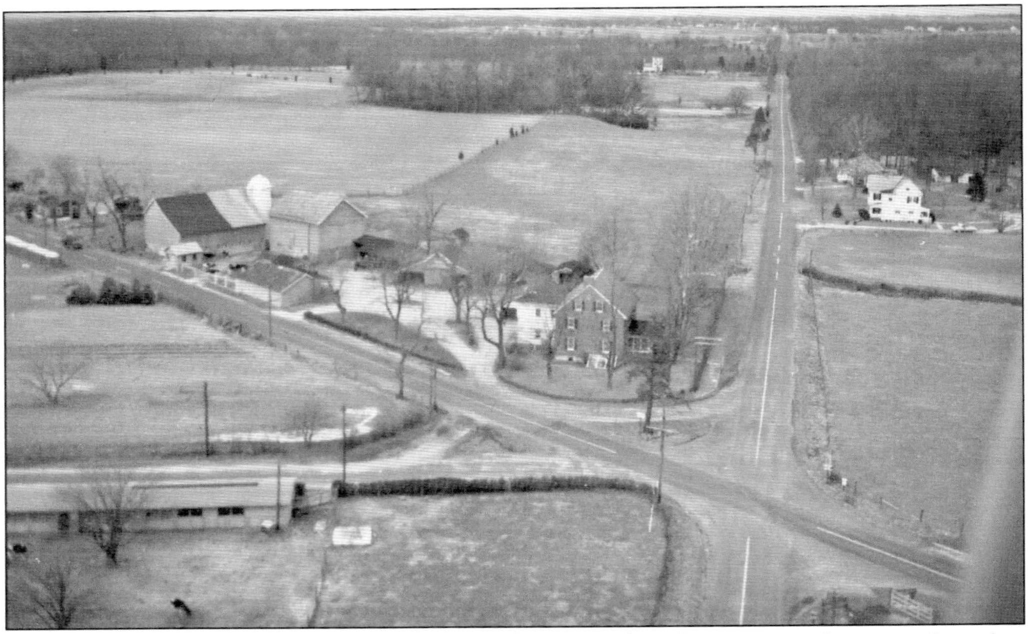

CEDAR GROVE. Signs still direct drivers to Cedar Grove, but there is no indication when that destination has been reached. Nestled at the convergence of Swedesboro-Franklinville Road, Commissioners Pike, and Harrisonville-Richwood Road, the area was settled by Quaker families in the 1700s. Although there has been residential development in recent years, it remains a largely rural area. (GCHS.)

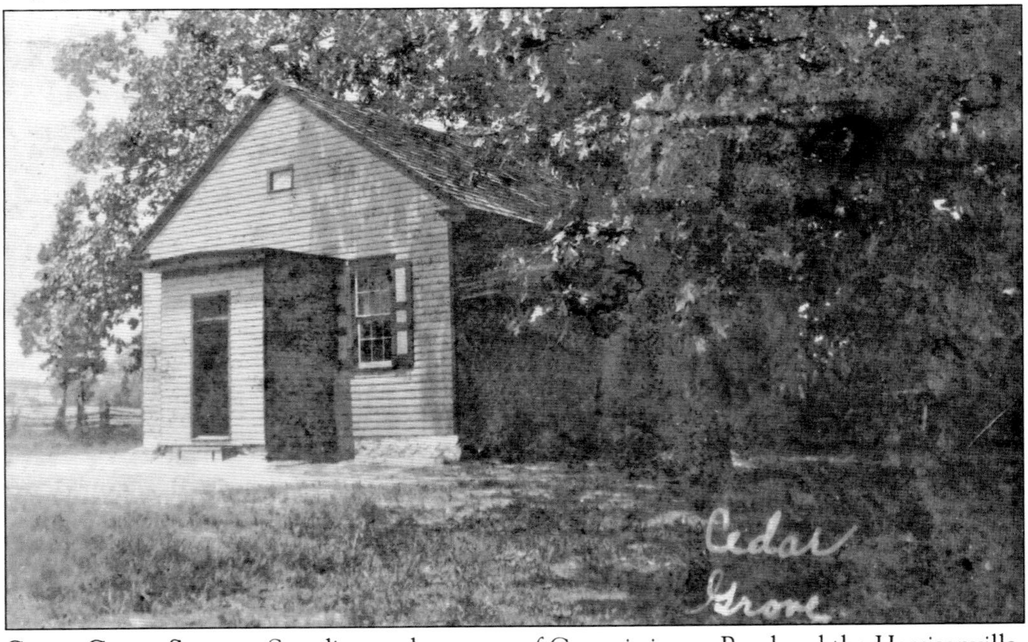

CEDAR GROVE SCHOOL. Standing at the corner of Commissioners Road and the Harrisonville-Richwood Road, the school was built around 1852 and was the only public building in the little settlement. The school closed in the early 1920s, and the children of Cedar Grove were sent to Harrisonville School. After retiring from farming in 1929, local resident Asa Moore bought the building and made it into a private home, which it remains today. (SHBOE.)

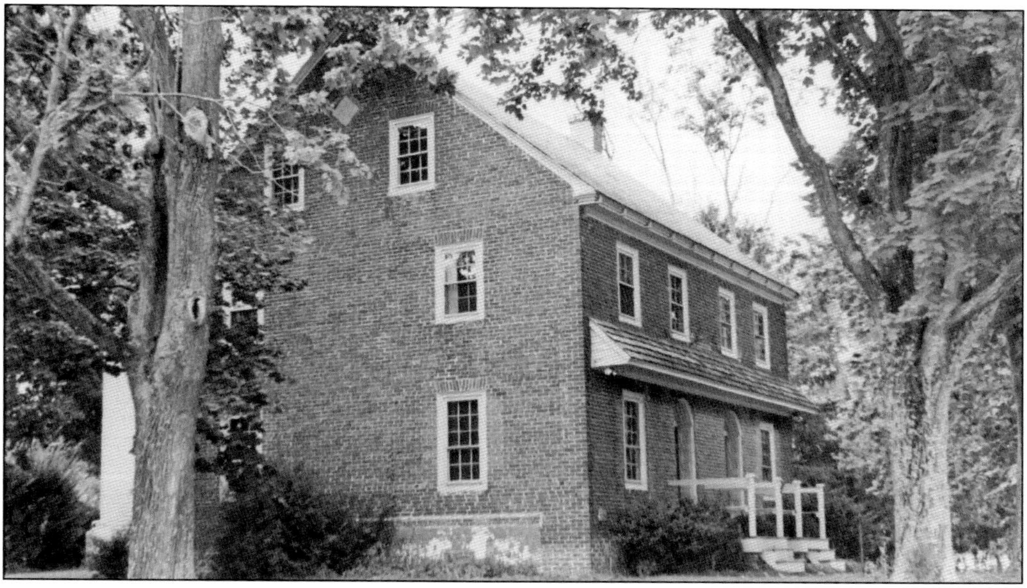

MOORE-GARDINER HOUSE, 1997. Benjamin Moore, a Quaker from Burlington County, purchased land in Cedar Grove from John Gosling in the 1700s. This elegant house, built by a descendant in 1818, is not typical of the local Quaker style. The property remained in the Moore family until Willard Gardiner purchased it in 1930.

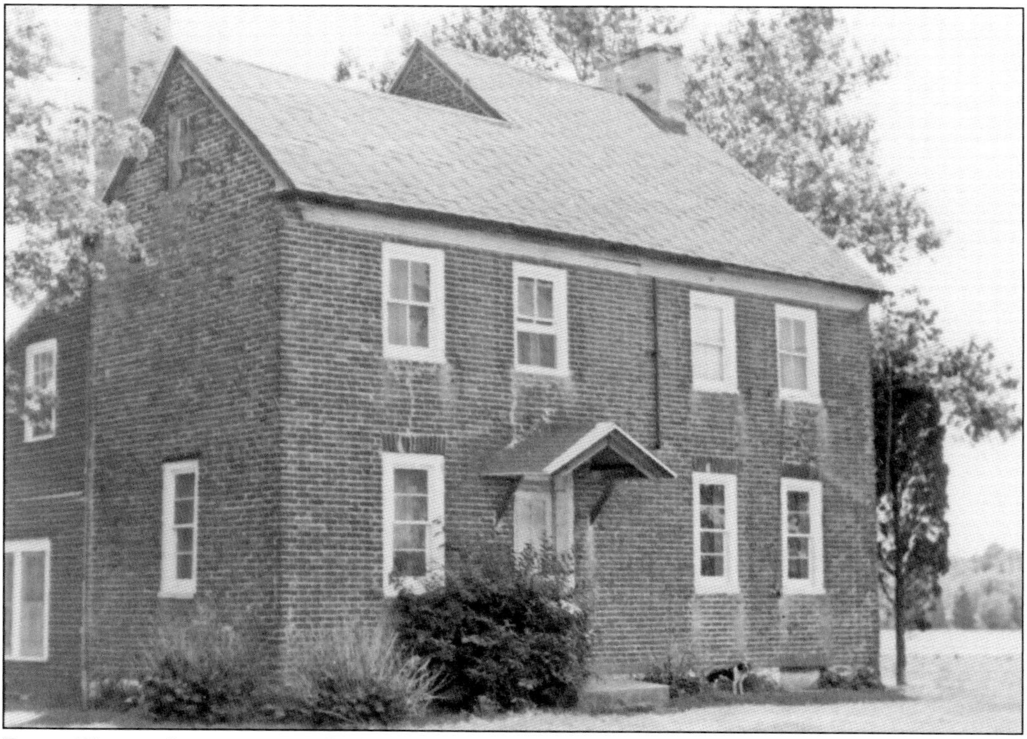

ENGLE HOUSE. In contrast to the Moore-Gardiner House, the Engle House provides an example of a more typical Quaker dwelling. It was built in 1818 in the drop-wing style, with one end of the house taller than the other. It stood empty and dilapidated for several years before finally being demolished.

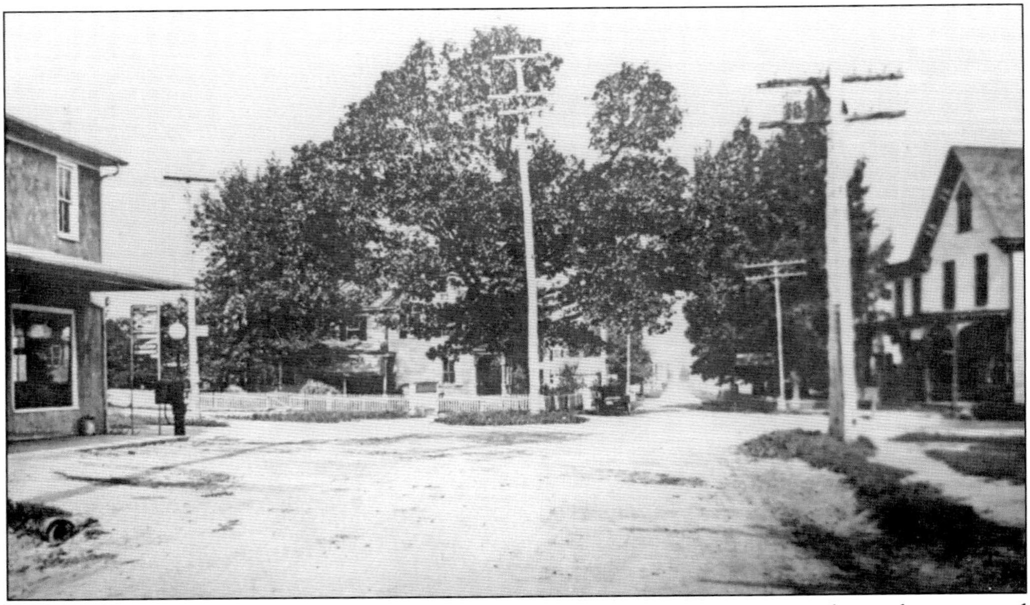

Center of Richwood, c. 1915. The village of Richwood grew up around two five-pointed intersections with the Mullica Hill-Glassboro Road. Its earliest name was White Horse after a notorious tavern that also earned it the nickname "Hell Town." It was successively known as Campbell's Crossroads, Mount Pleasant, and Five Points before finally becoming Richwood in 1888.

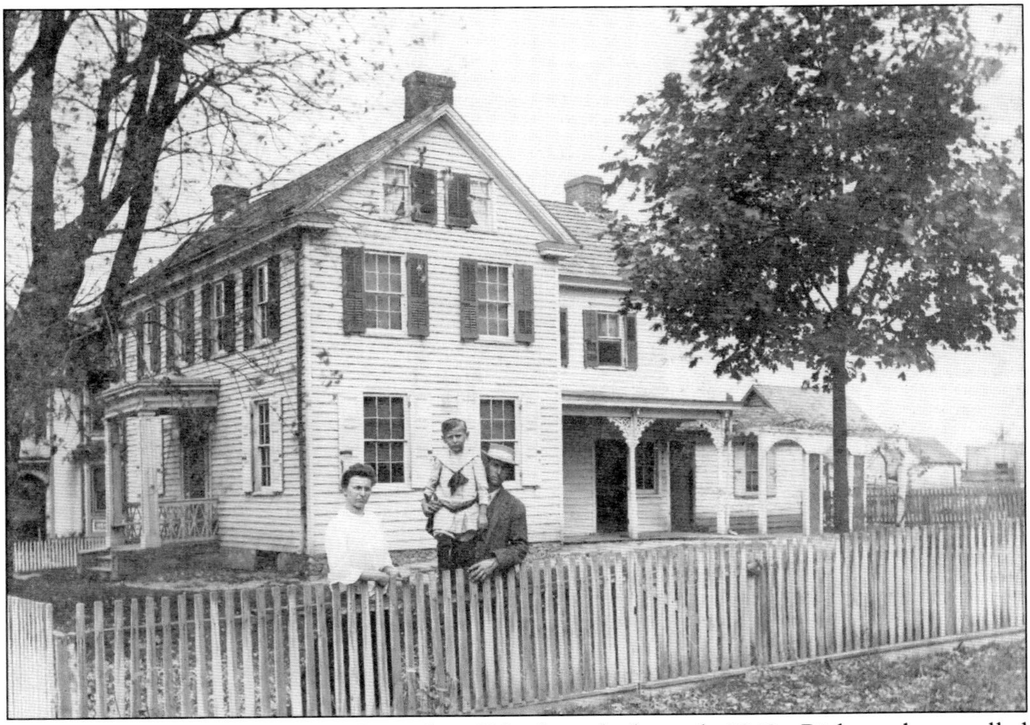

F. A. Campbell House, 1908. From the 1830s through the early 1840s, Richwood was called Campbell's Crossroads after pioneer settler Francis A. Campbell, who built his house at the corner of Barnsboro Road and Mullica Hill-Glassboro Road. In 1908, it was occupied by W. Wade and Clara Heritage and their son W. Howard.

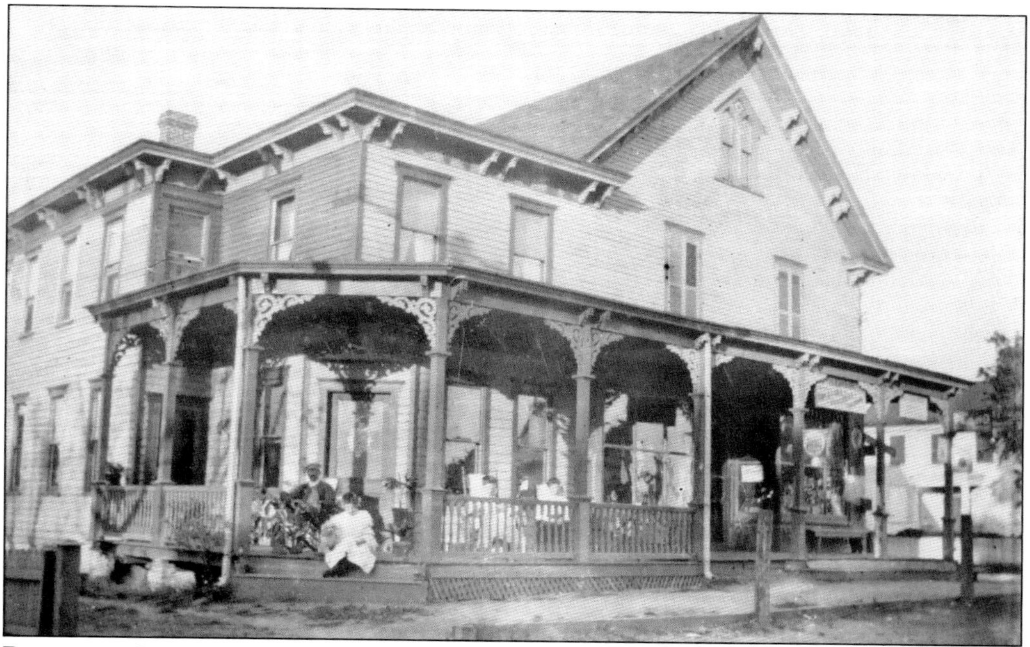

Richwood General Store, c. 1905. Francis A. Campbell built the first store in Richwood in 1846, and when the post office was established in 1862 it, too, was housed there. Abraham Tomlinson bought the store in 1900 and added a residence on the western end of the building. The store ceased operation in 1966, and the post office moved to its present location in the late 1990s. The building is still in commercial use.

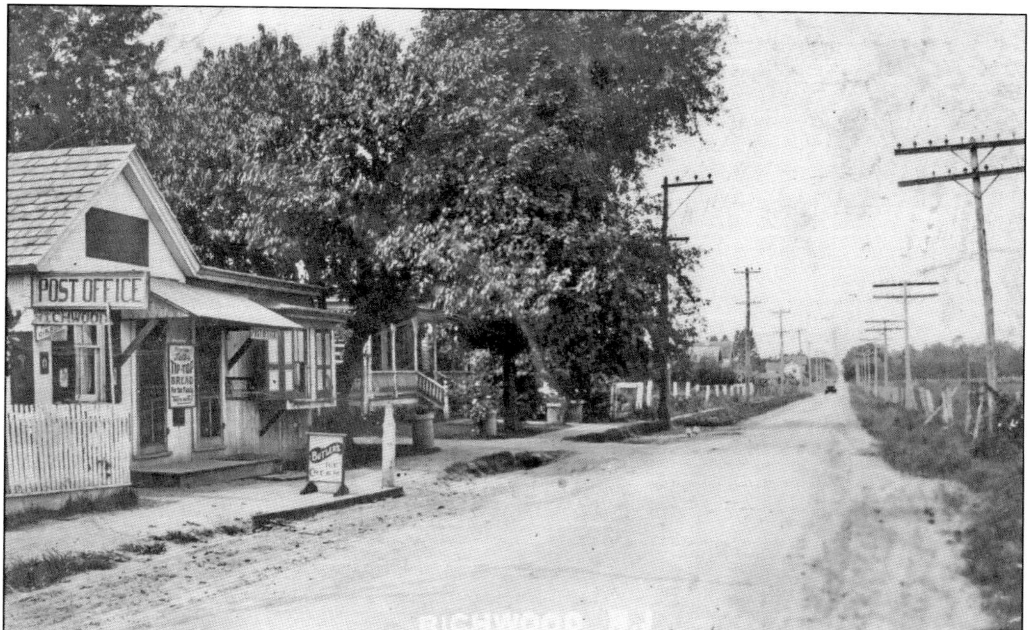

Richwood Post Office. For most of its existence, the Richwood Post Office was located in the general store, but from 1907 through 1928, it occupied a small building on Mullica Hill-Glassboro Road constructed by John J. Rulon. He served as postmaster and also sold groceries. In 1929, the post office returned to the general store. (FSC.)

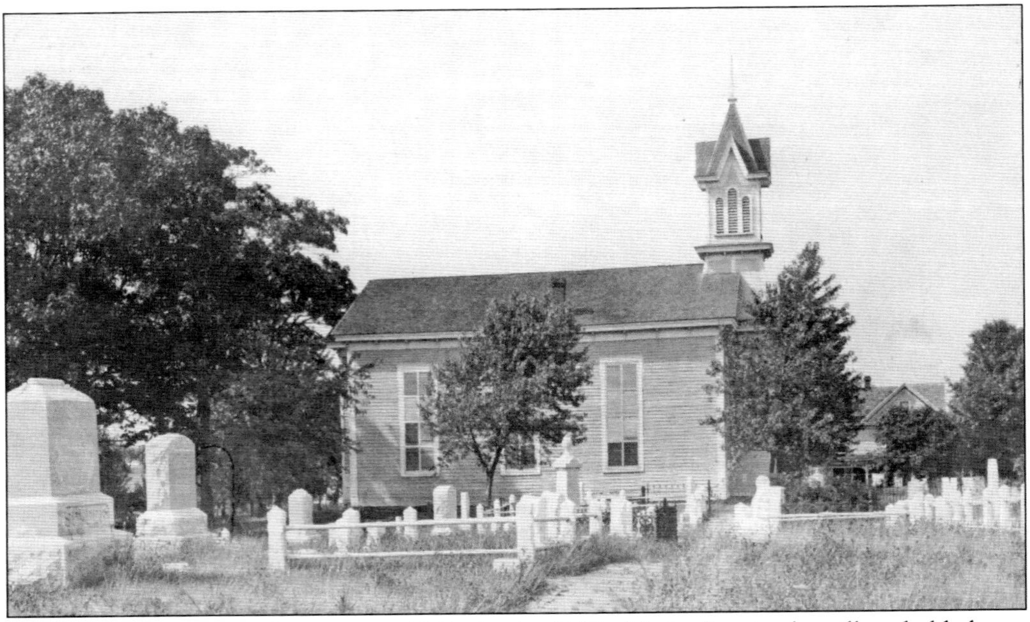

Richwood Methodist Church, c. 1908. In the 1840s, Methodists in the village held classes in the home of Francis A. Campbell and then at Clems Run School. In 1860, they purchased land and built the church across the road from the site of the infamous White Horse Tavern. The building has been expanded over the years and was added to the National Register of Historic Places in 1979.

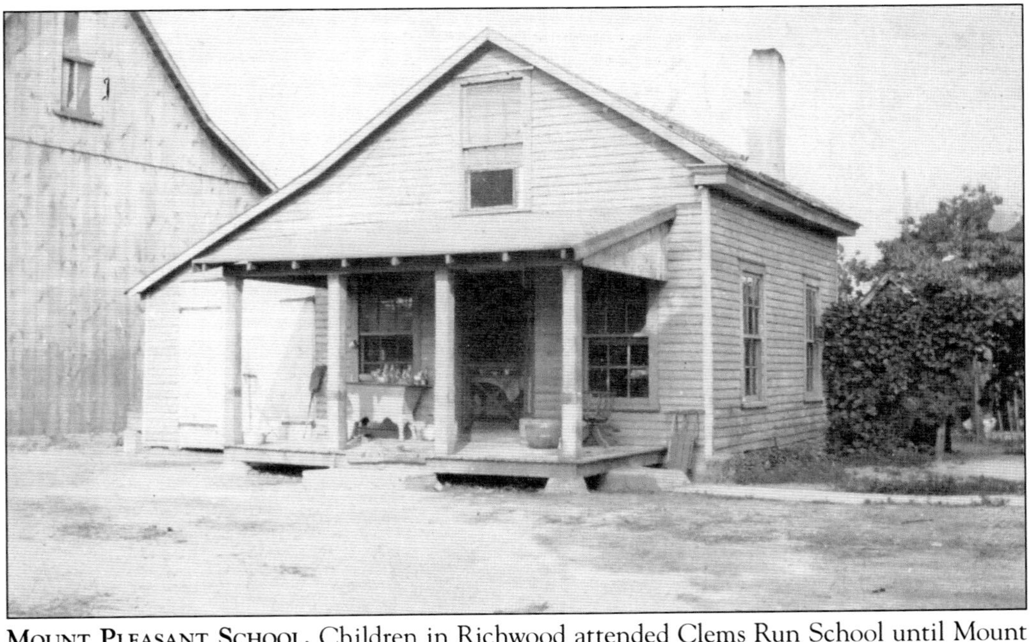

Mount Pleasant School. Children in Richwood attended Clems Run School until Mount Pleasant School was built in 1855 at the corner of Mullica Hill-Glassboro Road and Lambs Road. It served until 1870, when Richwood Academy was built. Elisha C. Heritage bought the old school and moved it to his property west of the general store. It was destroyed by fire in 1934.

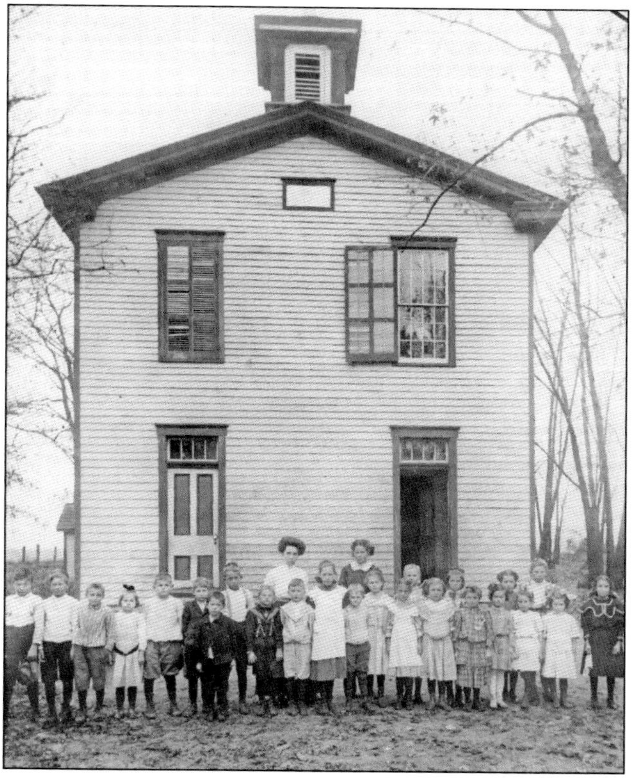

Richwood Academy, 1908. The Richwood Academy stands on the site of the old Mount Pleasant School. It closed in 1950, when Harrison Township School opened in Mullica Hill. Students in 1908 came from the following families: Cattell, Datz, Dougherty, Evans, Johnson, Kier, Morgan, Nicholson, Oldt, Reuter, Roth, Schleicher, Shute, Skinner, Souder, Turner, and Vanlier. The teacher was Margaret B. Nutt.

Old Home Day, 1954. In 1951, the Richwood Academy Association was formed and bought the old schoolhouse to use as a community meeting place. The first Old Home Day baked ham supper was held here in 1953 as a fundraiser and was an annual event into the 1990s. The academy now houses the French Lodge No. 89 of the IOOF.

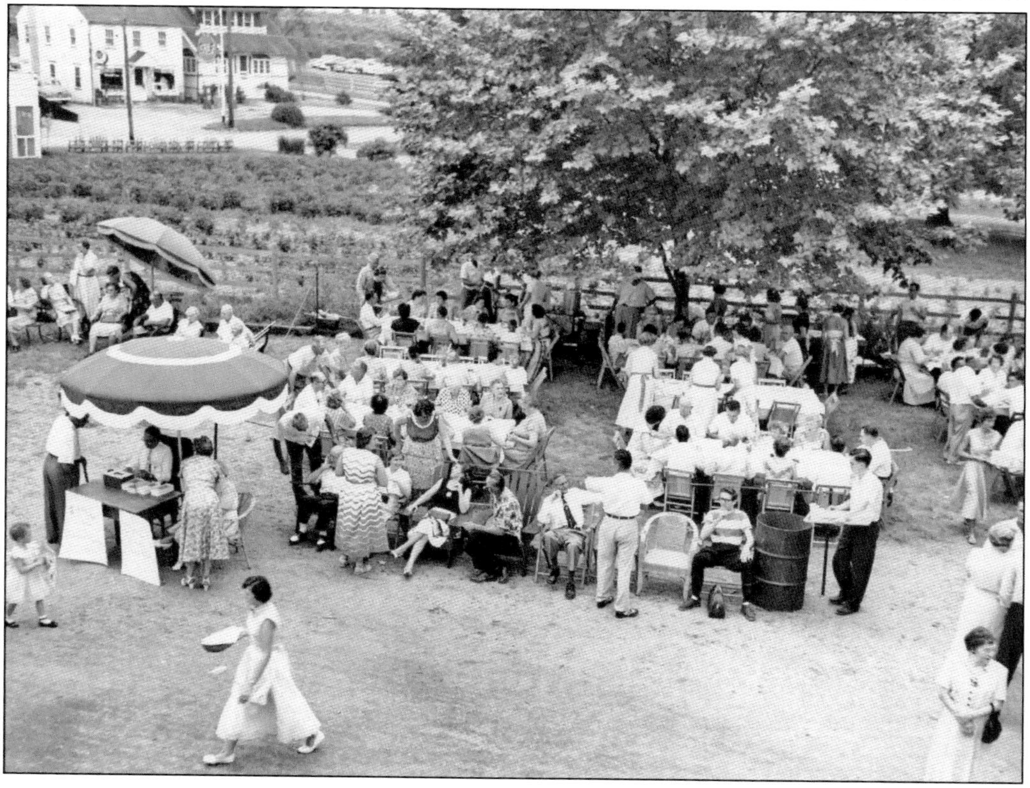

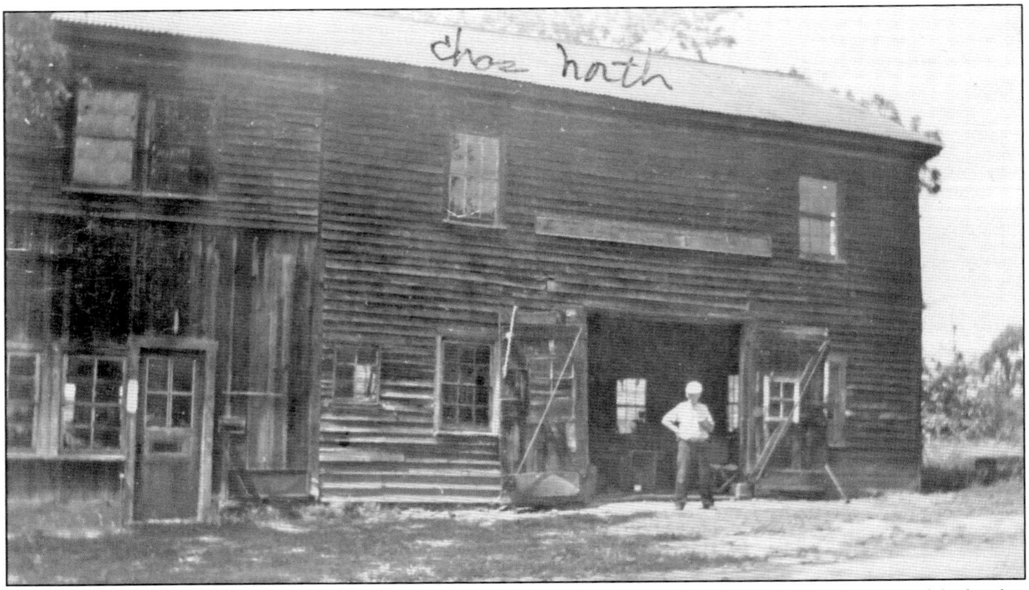

North's Blacksmith and Wheelwright Shop. In 1874, Robert McKeighan established a blacksmith shop in Richwood that was subsequently bought by Charles W. North. Upon North's death in 1947, J. Evans Elkins purchased the building and used it as a workshop. In the 1960s, it served as a warehouse until it was demolished in the late 1980s to make way for a convenience store.

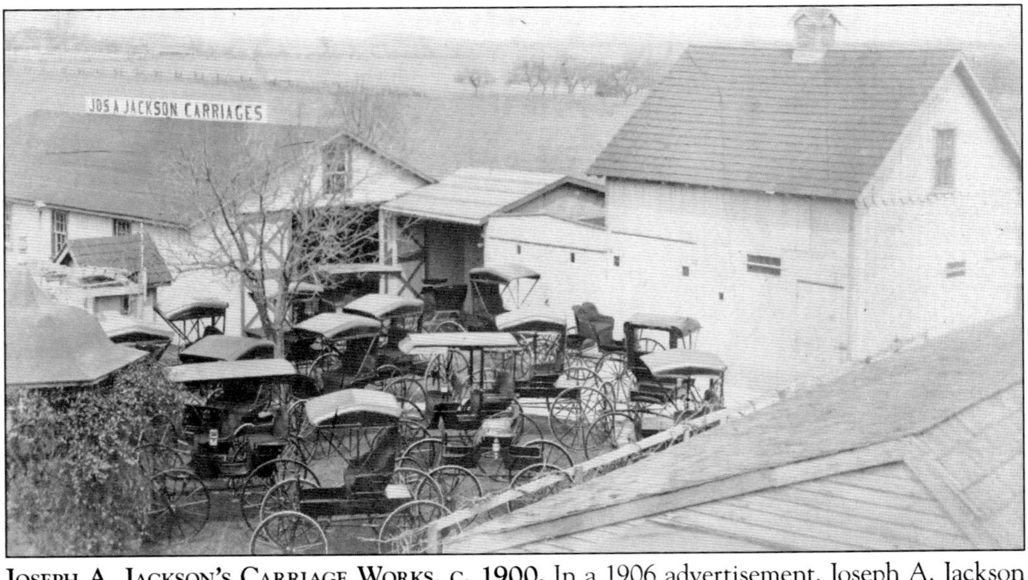

Joseph A. Jackson's Carriage Works, c. 1900. In a 1906 advertisement, Joseph A. Jackson promised his customers "High-grade, made-to-order vehicles at lowest prices possible." By then, he had been in business next to the general store for 18 years. Known as "Fancy Joe," he was influential enough to convince fellow residents to change the name of their village from Five Points to Richwood after his young nephew G. Richwood Marshall.

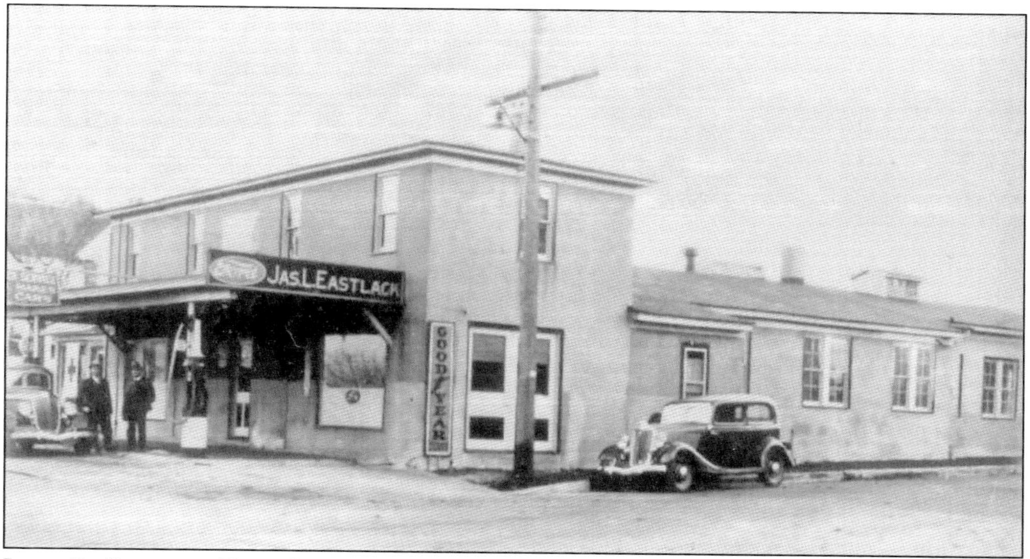

JAMES L. EASTLACK FORD AGENCY. James L. Eastlack started in business as a bicycle dealer and, in 1910, began selling Hupmobiles at his shop in Richwood. By 1914, he had added Fords and Buicks and, in the 1920s, expanded the business to sell Ford tractors. Automotive sales later relocated to Woodbury and the Richwood agency continued to sell tractors through the 1980s. In the 1990s, tractor sales moved to Peach Country Ford and Eastlack's closed. It was razed in the fall of 2009.

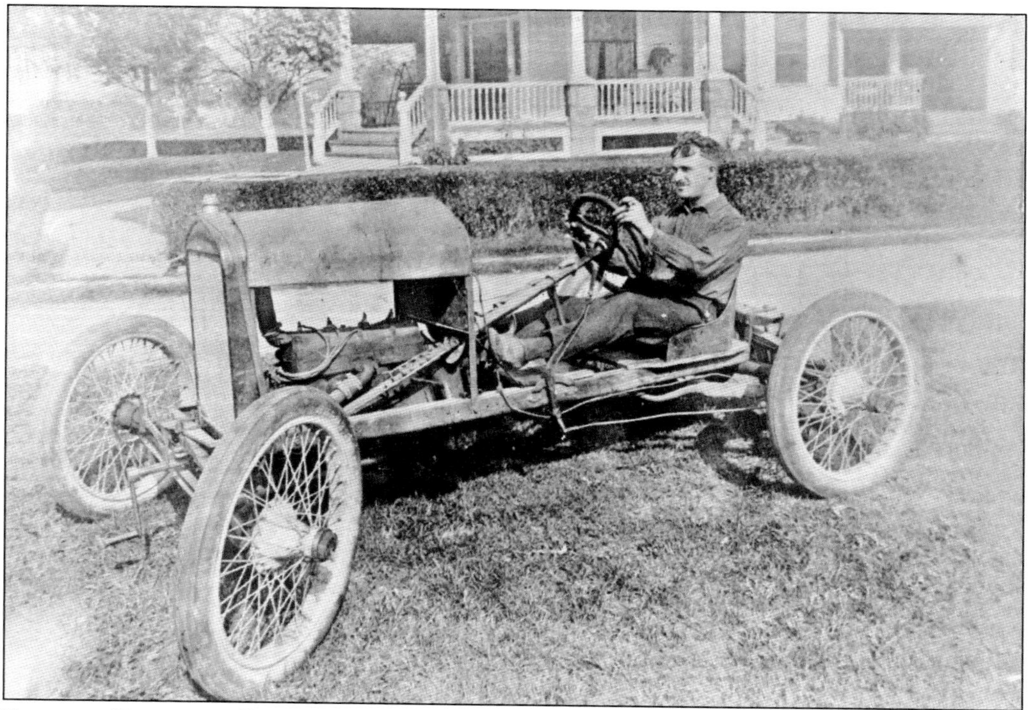

EASTLACK PORCH AND RACING CAR. When automobiles became popular in the early 20th century, so did automobile racing. Local enthusiasts like Harold Stratton of Mullica Hill and Eastlack Porch of Richwood often raced at Alcyon track in nearby Pitman. Porch lived on the family farm on Barnsboro Road and enjoyed showing off his Model T Speedster.

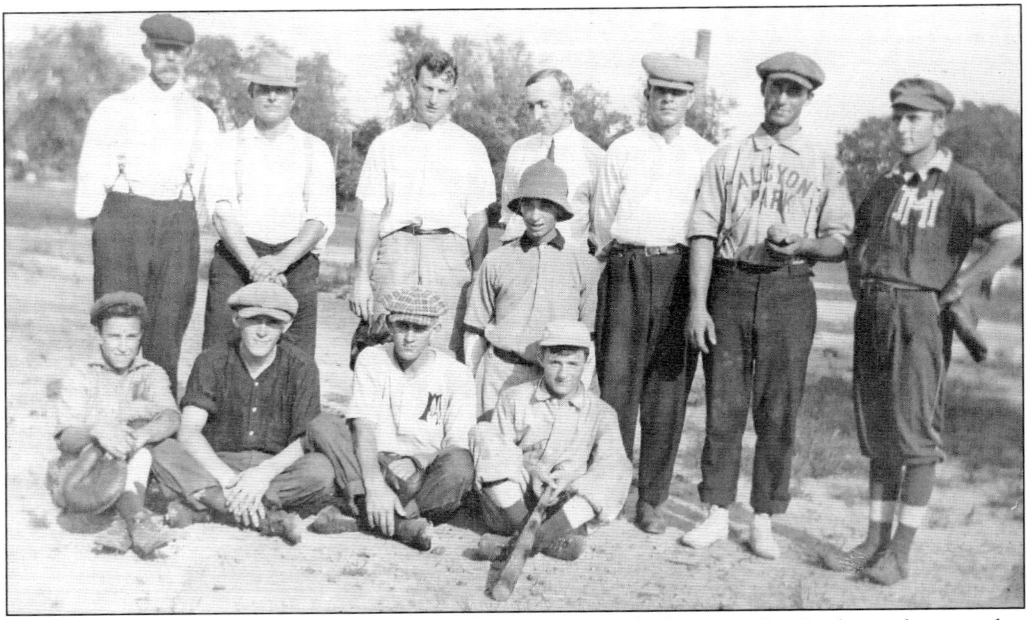

RICHWOOD BASEBALL TEAM, 1912. Like the Ferrell baseball team, the Richwood team also welcomed players from other local communities. From left to right are (front row) Harry Oldt, Andy Johnson, Daniel Oldt, Tremont Murphy, and John Clendining; (second row) Thomas Costello, Charles Roth Sr., Frank Ramsey, J. Evans Elkins, William Kier, Walton Elkins, and George White. (RAA.)

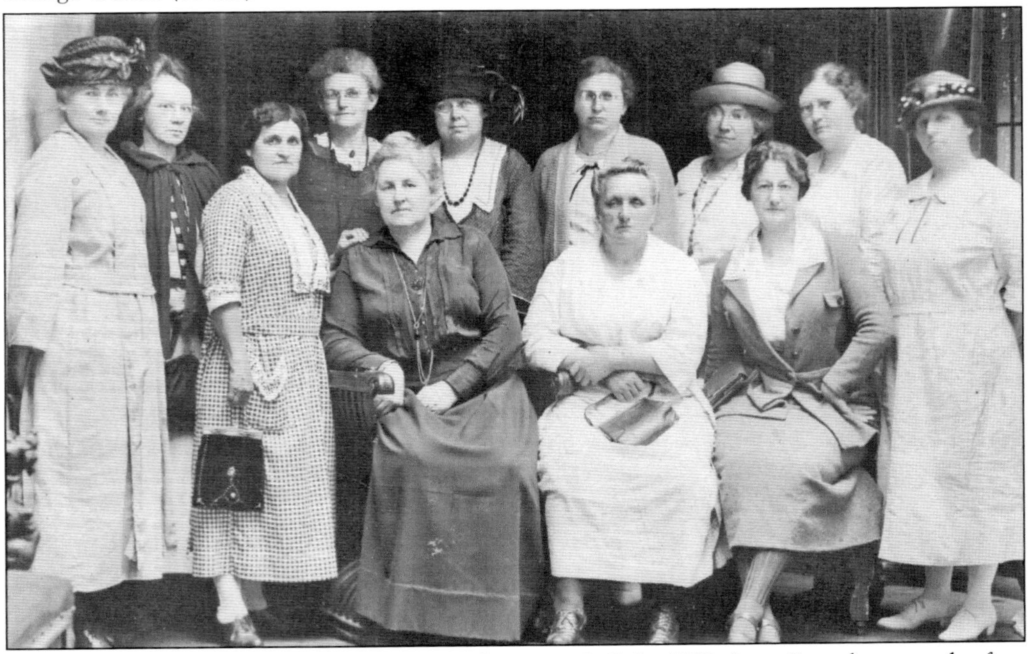

LUCY LACY WITH THE RICHWOOD SEWING CIRCLE, 1915. In 1933, Lucy Lacy became the first woman to serve on the Gloucester County Board of Chosen Freeholders. She took over the seat of her husband, William Lacy, after he died in an automobile accident. She was active in several civic and community organizations, including the sewing circle. She is pictured standing in the back, second from the left.

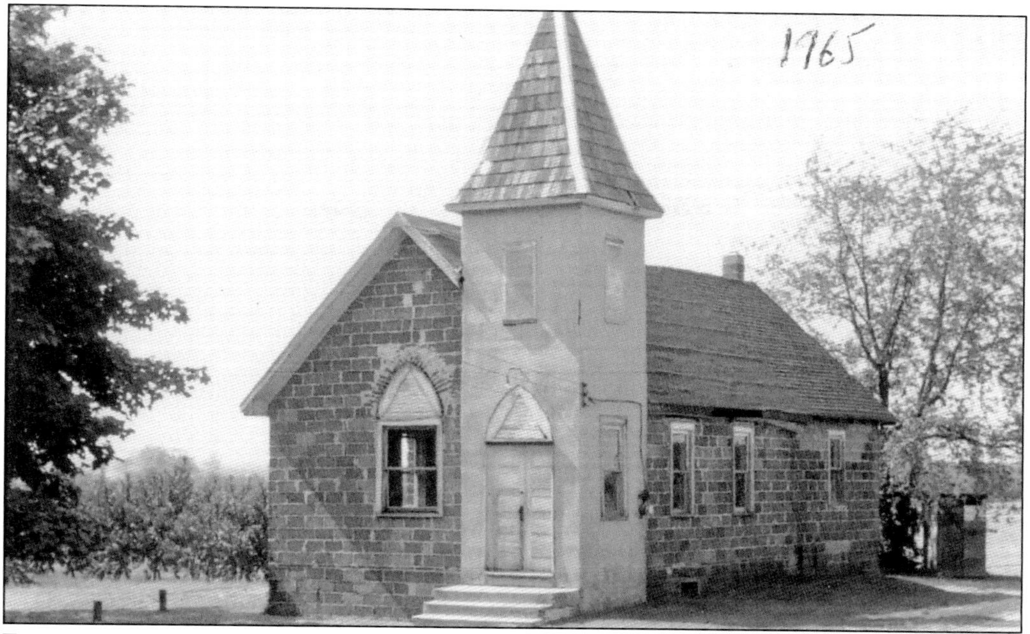

First Baptist Church of Richwood, 1965. African American Baptists in the Richwood area, many of whom worked on local farms, built their first church on Harrisonville Road in the 1930s. By 1970, the building was in disrepair and the congregation built a new church near Harrisonville. The Richwood church was used by various other congregations until it was destroyed by arson in 2003.

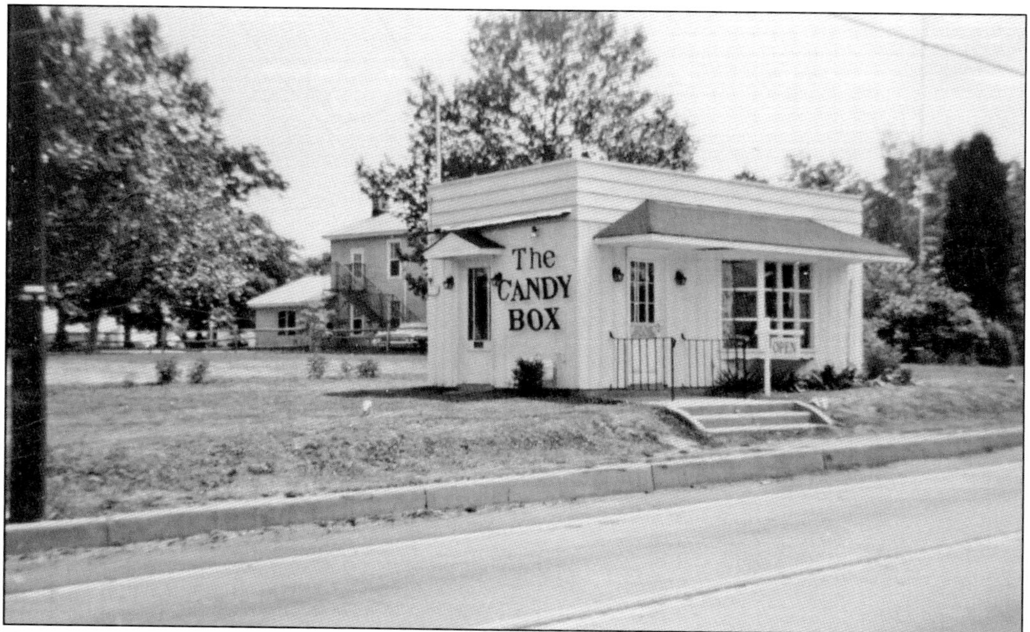

The Candy Box. In the early 1950s, Mildred Price opened a little shop on Mullica Hill-Glassboro Road to sell handmade Bayard's Chocolates. The Reiner family bought the shop in the early 1960s and, sometime before 1970, attached the small building to the back of their house next door. In 1981, Eleanor and William Madara moved the business to their home on Lambs Road, where it continues to offer Bayard's Chocolates.

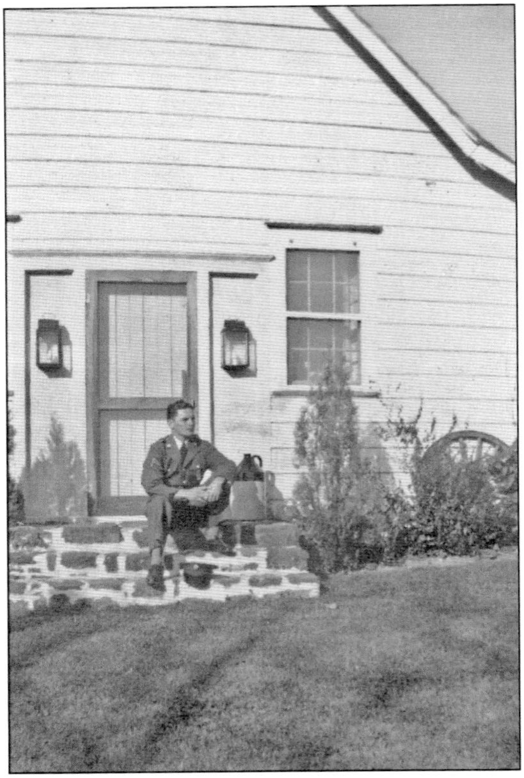

Maj. Louis Reuter Jr. (1913–1998). Louis Reuter Jr. was born into a farming family in Richwood and served in the US Army during World War II. He saw action in the Pacific, where he was shot in the head and gravely wounded. He required years of therapy to regain his speech and motor abilities. Reuter became a noted civic leader, and his home at Mount Pleasant Orchards was a local showplace.

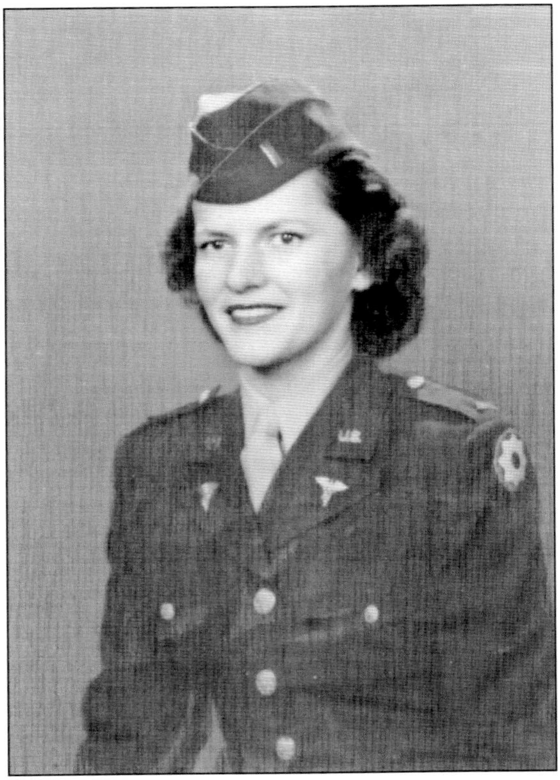

Carolyn Marie Reuter (1921–1996). Carolyn was sister to Louis Reuter Jr. She too served in World War II, as a second lieutenant in the US Army Nurse Corps. After her brother Louis was wounded, she was permitted to work as part of his Army medical team, which initiated his rehabilitation.

Five

THE FARMLANDS

Agriculture has dominated the local economy for most of the township's history. The diversity of soil types in the area allowed a wide variety of crops to be grown on even small tracts of land, and the discovery of marl, a natural soil conditioner, enhanced the productivity and prosperity of the surrounding fields and orchards.

In an 1866 letter to the editor of the *Constitution*, a visitor to the township notes "fine looking farms, houses, barns, etc., with cultivated fields all around." Two decades later, local farming spurred the construction of a rail connection to Philadelphia and made Mullica Hill one of the largest shipping points of fresh produce in America. Vegetables and grain were staples on early farms, and cows, pigs, and chickens were often kept. Fruit began to dominate local agriculture at the beginning of the 20th century, and Richwood became one of the country's largest centers of peach production. The discovery of the Starking Red Delicious apple in Ferrell helped popularize that well-known variety.

Although the number of acres in production has declined, agriculture remains deeply rooted in the community. Fruit and vegetables are still grown on a smaller scale, supplying thriving farm markets, while wineries and horse farms are growing, replacing orchards and dairies. Five Century Farms, each having remained in the same family for 100 years, dot the township, and participation in the Farmland Preservation program ensures that agriculture will continue to play an important role for years to come.

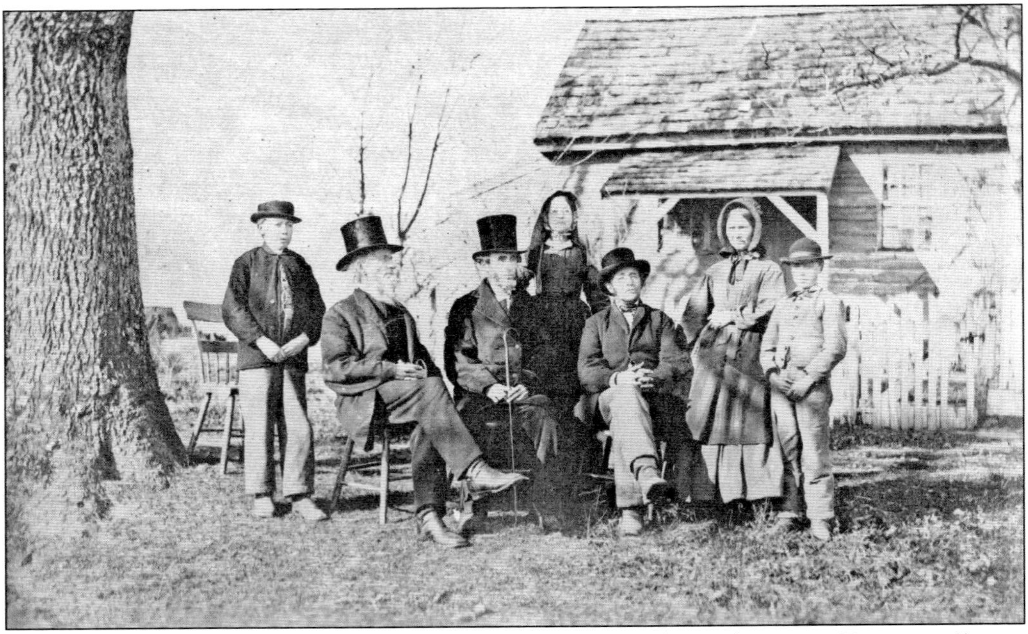

Ridgway Farm. Established in 1797, the Jacob and Keziah Ridgway farm near Harrisonville was typical of the diversity of crops grown in the township. The Ridgways raised corn, wheat, rye, flax, white and sweet potatoes, turnips, asparagus, and potatoes. Sheep, dairy cows, hogs, and poultry were also kept. Keziah Ridgway is said to have dyed wool in a cauldron by the house, earning the farm name Dye Pot Hill. The farm remained in the family until 1989. (RBR.)

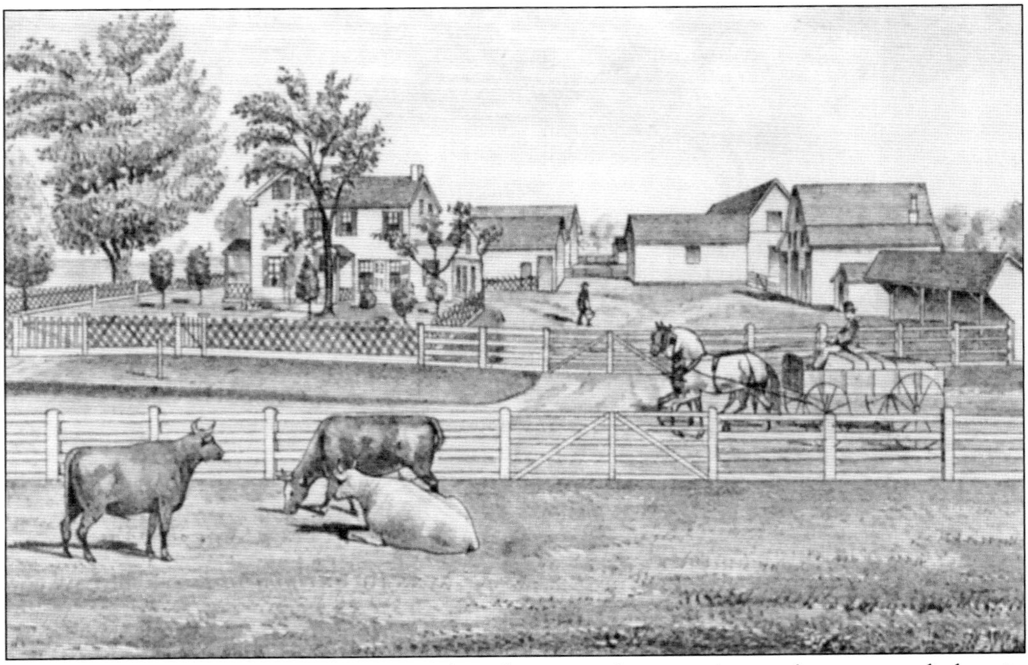

Dunn Farm, 1876. The most common farm layout in the township is the courtyard plan, in which the house and outbuildings are arranged in the shape of a horseshoe. A fine example was the Dunn farm in Jefferson, later known as Cherry Grove. Although the farmstead as pictured no longer stands, it still exists and is owned and operated by the Grasso family.

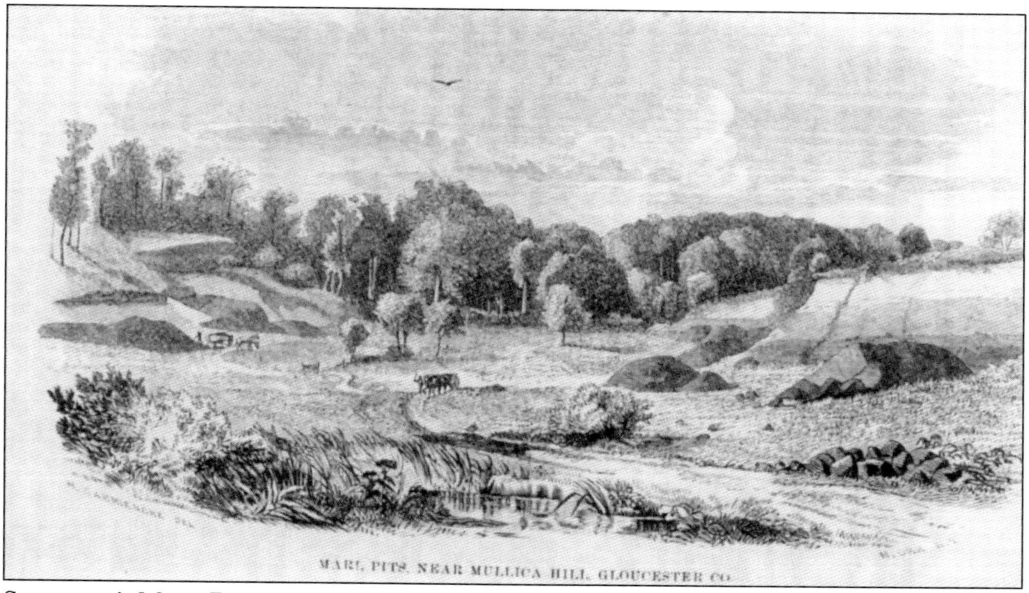

STRATTON'S MARL PITS, MULLICA HILL. Greensand, locally known as marl, is a highly effective soil conditioner, and by the 1850s, there were quarries near Mullica Hill, Ewan, and Harrisonville. It is composed of glauconite, a mineral that helps soil store nutrients and hold water. This enhancement contributed greatly to the prosperity of farming in the area.

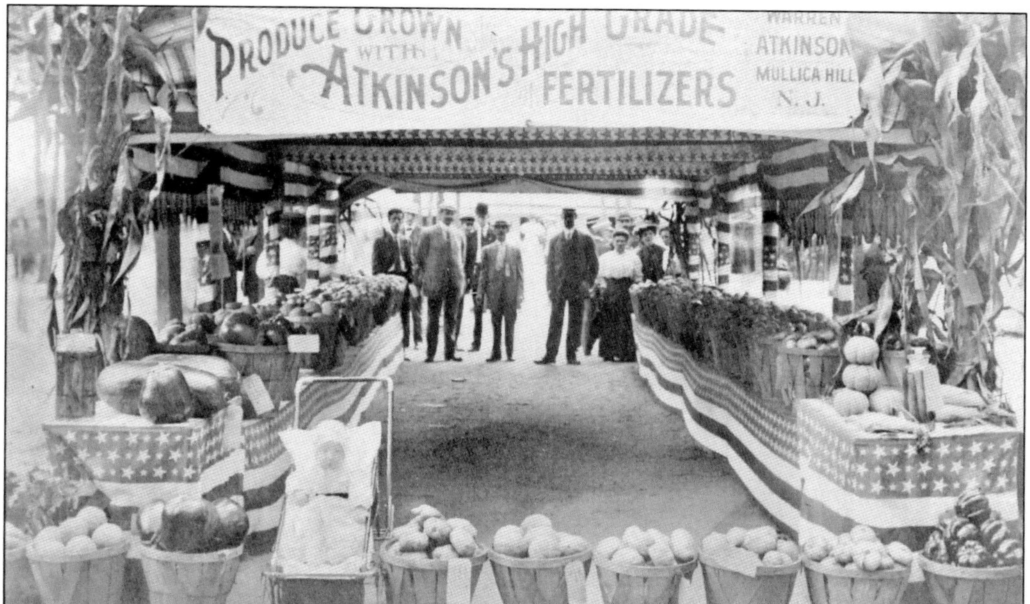

ATKINSON FERTILIZERS. Warren Atkinson was a farmer in Mullica Hill and also a pioneer in fertilizer production. His display at a Granger's Picnic at Alcyon Park in Pitman provides a snapshot of the diversity of the township's vegetable farming in the early decades of the 20th century.

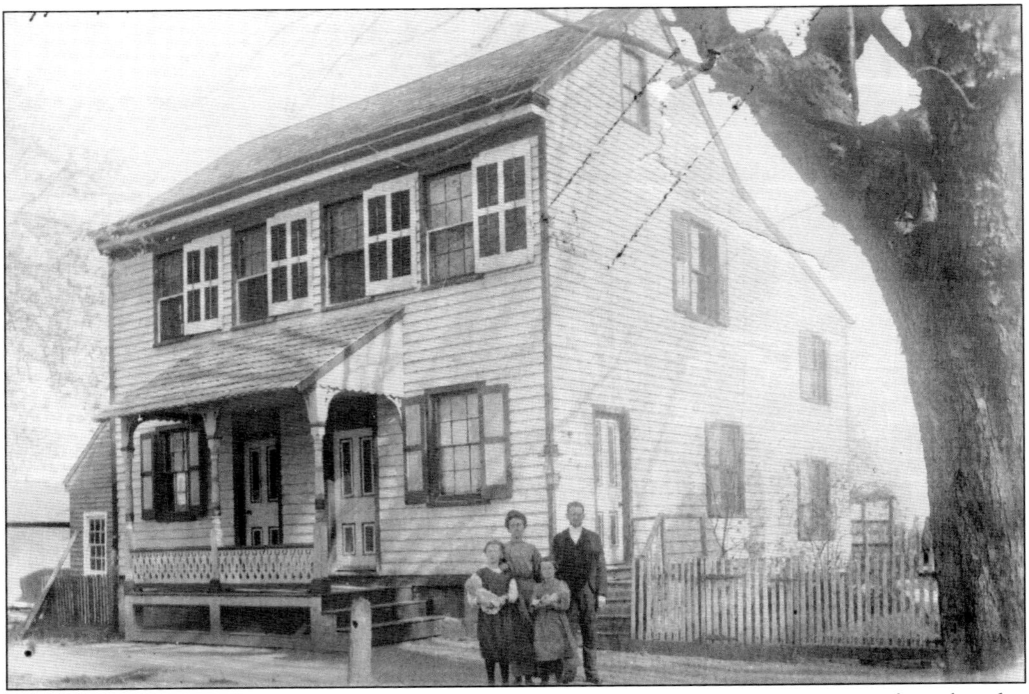

Harrisonville Grange Hall. The National Grange of the Order of Patrons of Husbandry was founded in 1867 to advocate for farmers and their families on both the national and local levels. Commonly referred to as the Grange, it lobbied for issues important to farmers and rural residents. The Harrisonville Grange organized in 1873 and still exists although it no longer owns the building. (GCHS.)

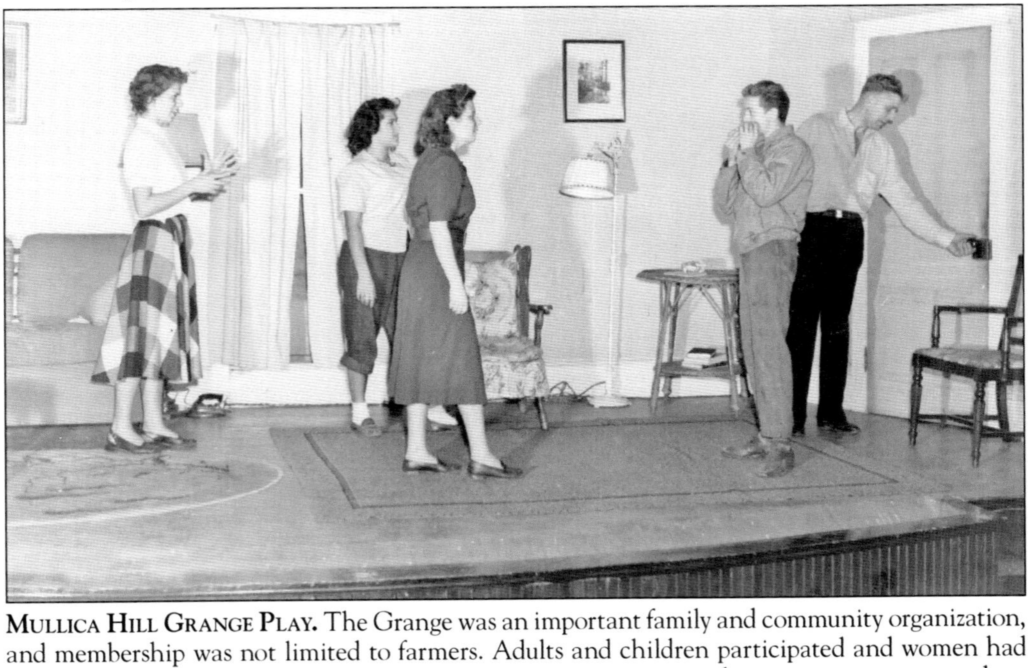

Mullica Hill Grange Play. The Grange was an important family and community organization, and membership was not limited to farmers. Adults and children participated and women had equal status from the beginning. Grangers were active in civic and community events, such as the play *Jumpin' Jupiter* staged at Old Town Hall.

Farmers National Bank. Local farmers were instrumental in organizing the bank, built in 1903 on North Main Street in Mullica Hill. It moved to its present location farther north in 1963 and opened a branch in Richwood 10 years later. An example of modern bank consolidation, it was bought by Equity Bank, which was in turn bought by Susquehanna. Susquehanna was acquired in 2015 by current owner BB&T.

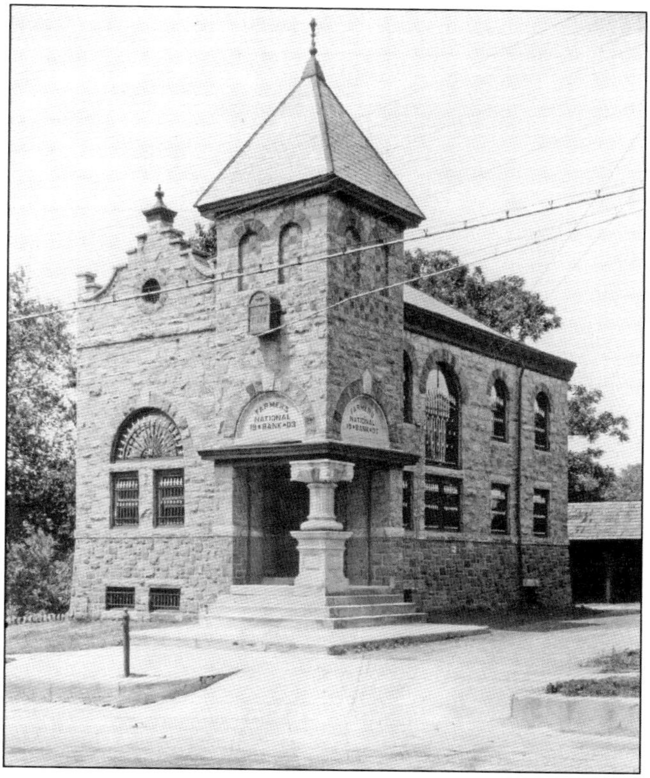

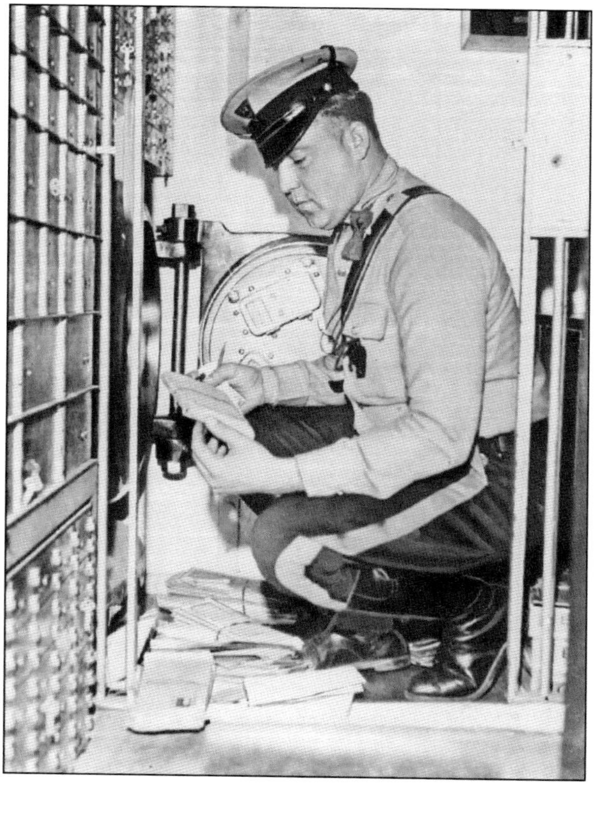

Farmers National Bank Robbery, 1932. On October 11, 1932, four young men bound two bank employees and two customers, made them lie facedown on the floor, and escaped by car with $8,370. The owner of a garage across the street and another man pursued the bandits but were unable to catch them.

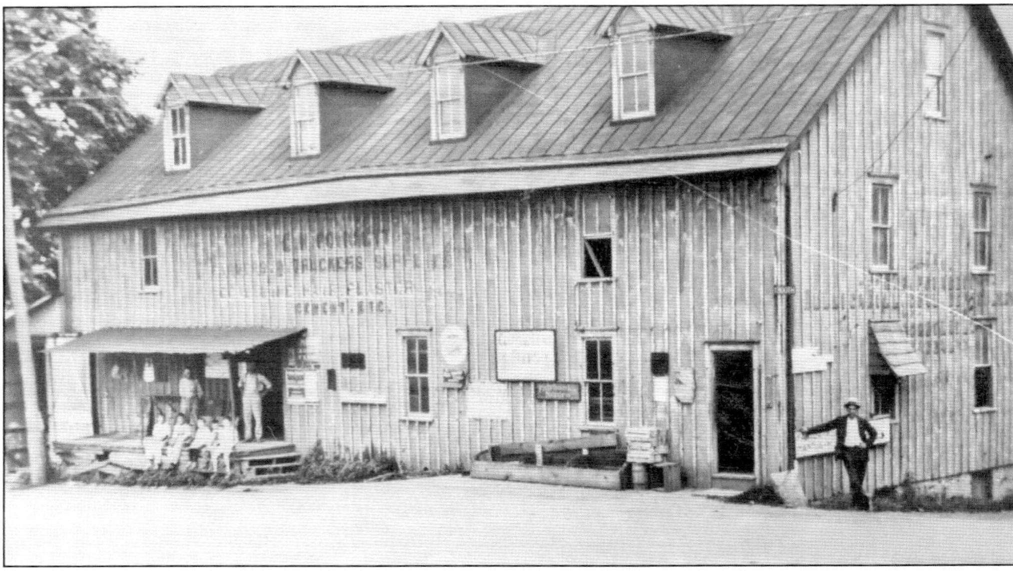

Poinsett's Feed Store, c. 1920. Located at the corner of Main Street and Mullica Hill Road in Mullica Hill, Poinsett's was a feed mill that also carried other supplies needed by farmers, such as coal, lime, and plaster. It was built in the 1880s, at the same time the railroad spur was under construction. It was later owned by W. A. Jones and now houses several businesses including an antique mall.

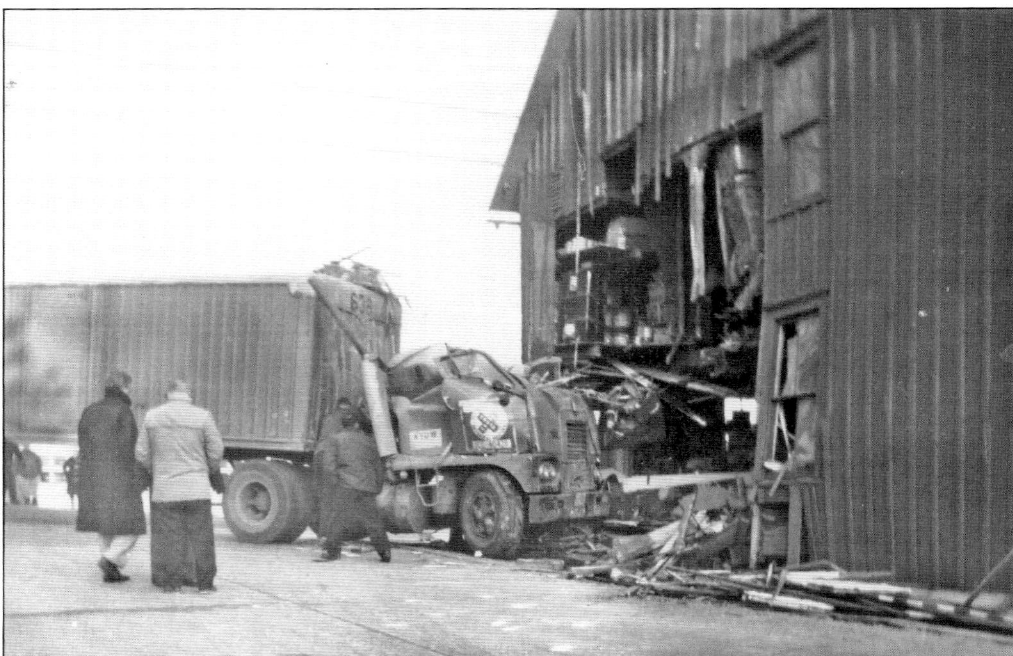

W. A. Jones & Sons Hardware and Feed Store, 1964. On the morning of March 19, 1964, a tractor-trailer crashed through the southwest side of the building, causing extensive damage. All the diesel fuel in the truck leaked into the basement, and local farmers brought loads of dirt to absorb it. The hardware section was closed for over six months, but the feed section remained open. It was not the first accident to the building, nor was it the last.

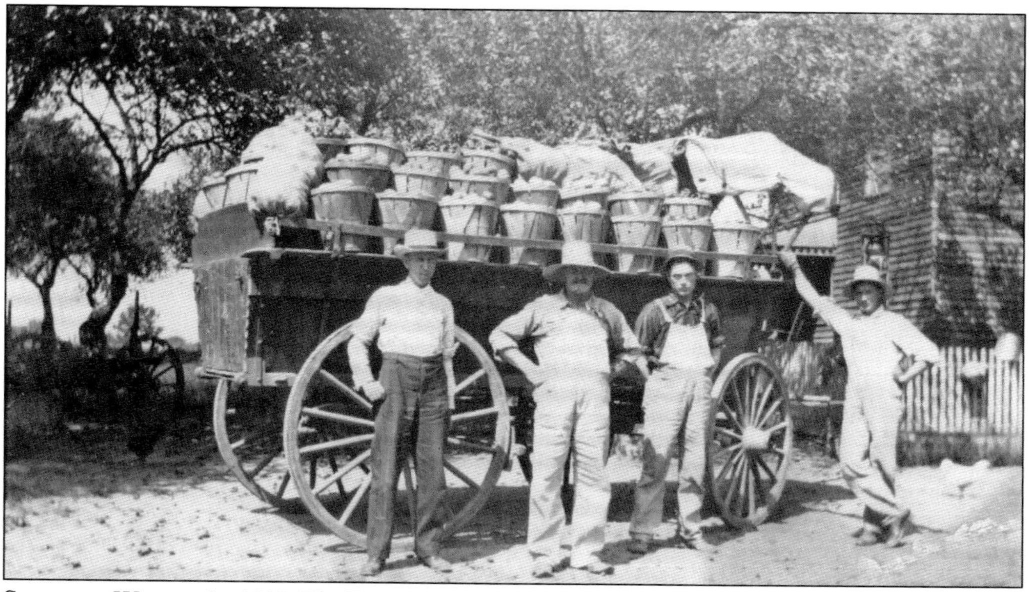

Shelving Wagon. In 1913, *The Farm Journal Directory of Gloucester County* acclaimed it as "the County that feeds Philadelphia." Transporting produce to market was a primary concern for farmers, and the horse-drawn shelving wagon was an early vehicle used for this purpose. This wagon at the Kier farm in Ewan is loaded with the diverse selections of produce typical of the area's farms.

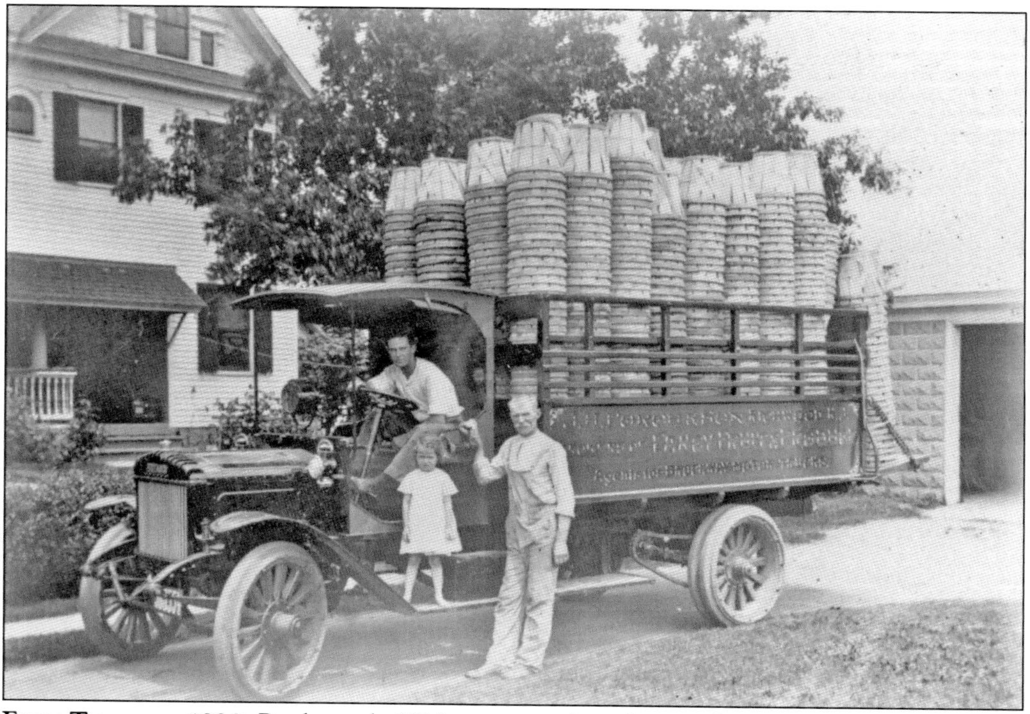

Farm Truck, c. 1920. By the early 1920s, motorized trucks were being used to transport farm products to market and would eventually supplant the horse-drawn wagons. J. Howard Porch was an early dealer in Brockway trucks at his farm in Richwood. One of the first farmers in the area to plant a large orchard, he planted 8,000 peach trees in 1910.

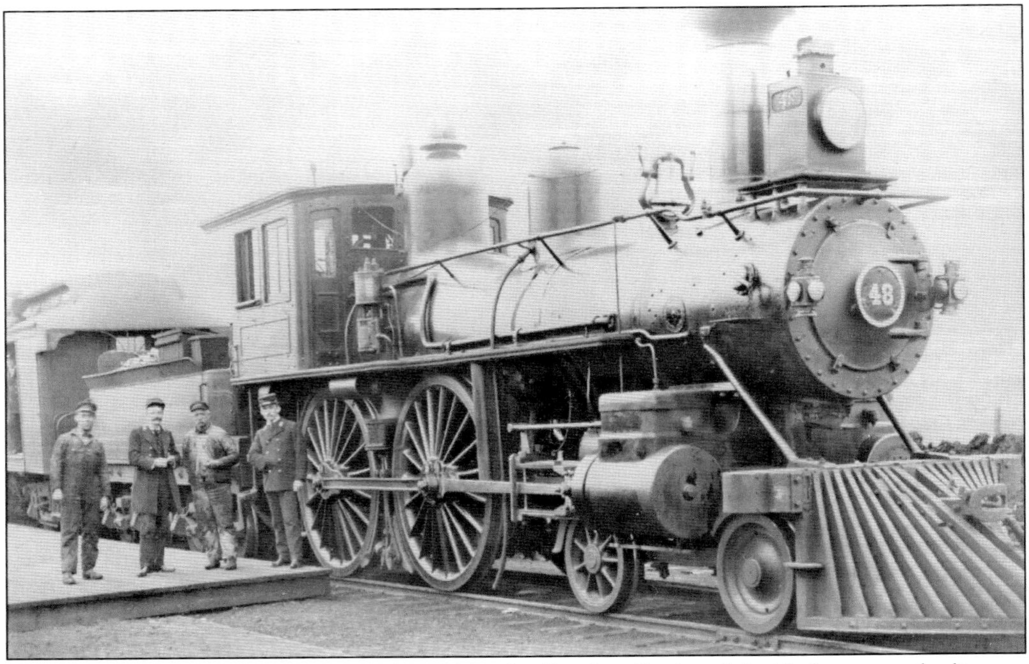

First Train to Mullica Hill. In the 1880s, the Reading Railroad decided to extend a line on its Williamstown Branch from Glassboro to Mullica Hill. Work began in 1887 and continued into 1889. "The coming of the railroad has wakened the town with new life," according to the February 13 issue of the *Constitution*. (GCHS.)

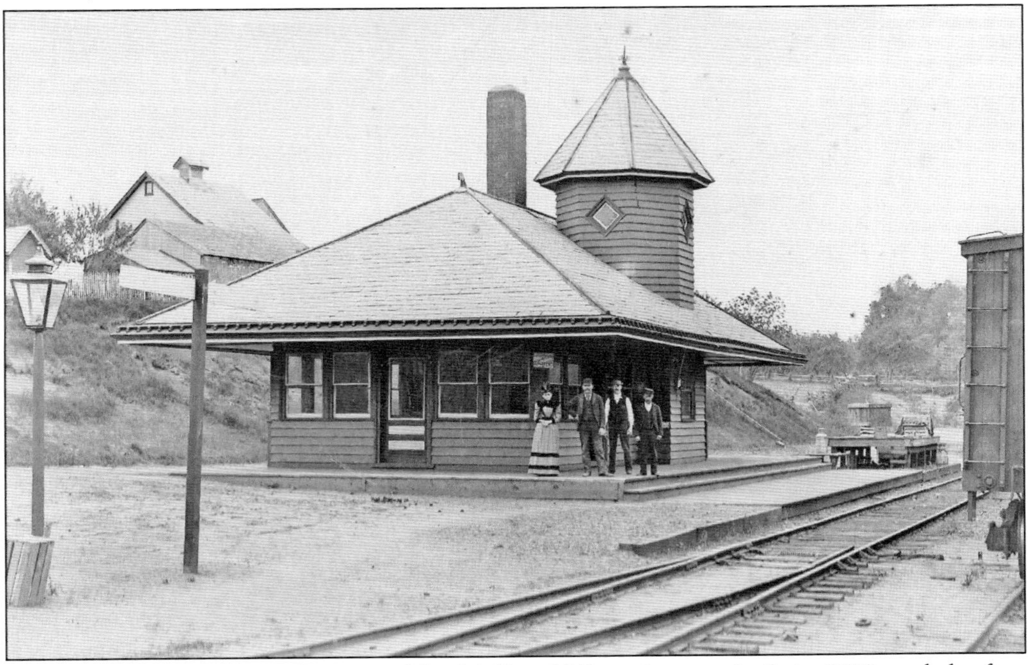

Mullica Hill Railroad Station. The Mullica Hill station was built in 1889, and the first passenger train arrived in May of that year. Mullica Hill was the end of the line, and trains had to back along the tracks into a wye to turn around for the return trip to Glassboro. The site of the station is part of the property of Harmony Fire Company.

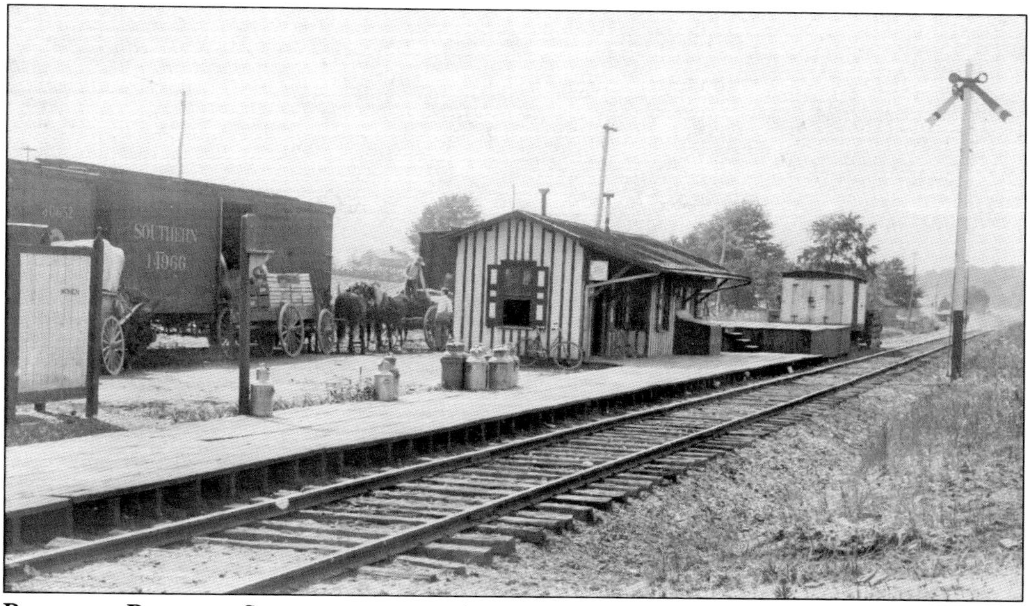

Richwood Railroad Station, c. 1910. Although there was passenger service, the railroad line was built primarily to facilitate shipment of produce to markets in Philadelphia and beyond. Farmers increased production and farming became an even more profitable industry in the township. The Richwood station was located on what is now the Lt. James Stratton Bypass.

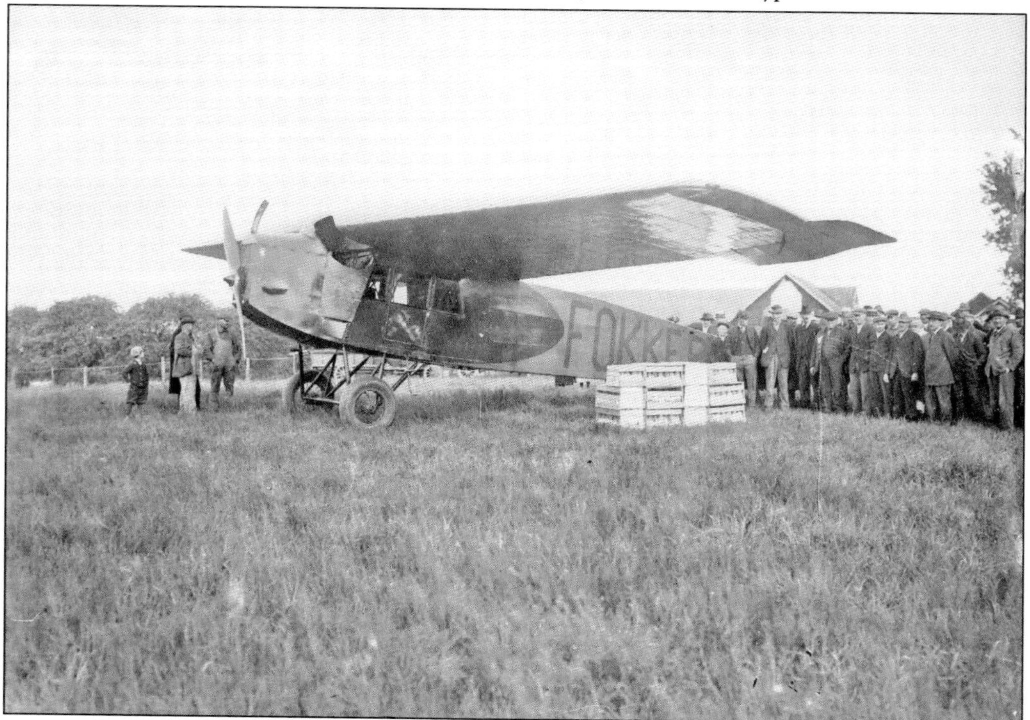

Air Shipment of Produce, 1922. The first air shipment in the United States of fresh produce occurred on May 17, 1922. That morning, a Fokker monoplane loaded with 1,000 pounds of locally grown asparagus took off from the farm field of W. D. Iredell in Mullica Hill and landed in Boston five hours later. (SCUARUL.)

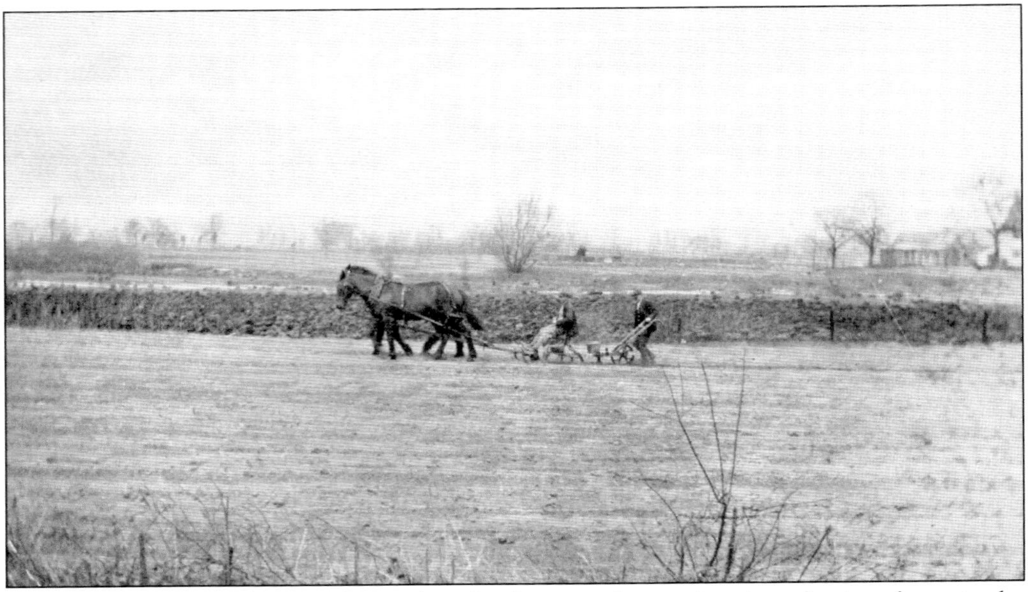

SPRING PLANTING. Before peaches and apples dominated agricultural production, farms in the township were intensively cultivated, producing multiple crops in a single growing season. A variety of vegetables and grains were grown, and poultry and dairy cows kept. Planting began in the spring and in the days before tractors horse drawn cultivators were used. (TSH.)

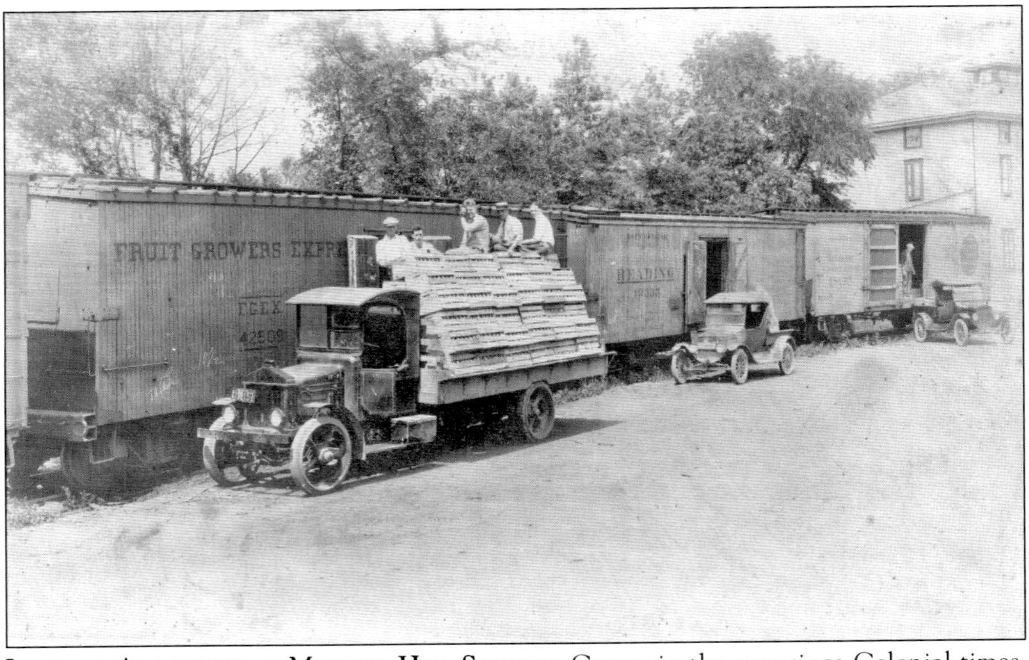

LOADING ASPARAGUS AT MULLICA HILL STATION. Grown in the area since Colonial times, asparagus heralds the arrival of spring. It became a major crop here in the early 20th century, and by the 1920s, Gloucester County was the largest producer of asparagus in the country. As a consequence, Mullica Hill Station became one of the busiest shipping points for this crop and other produce.

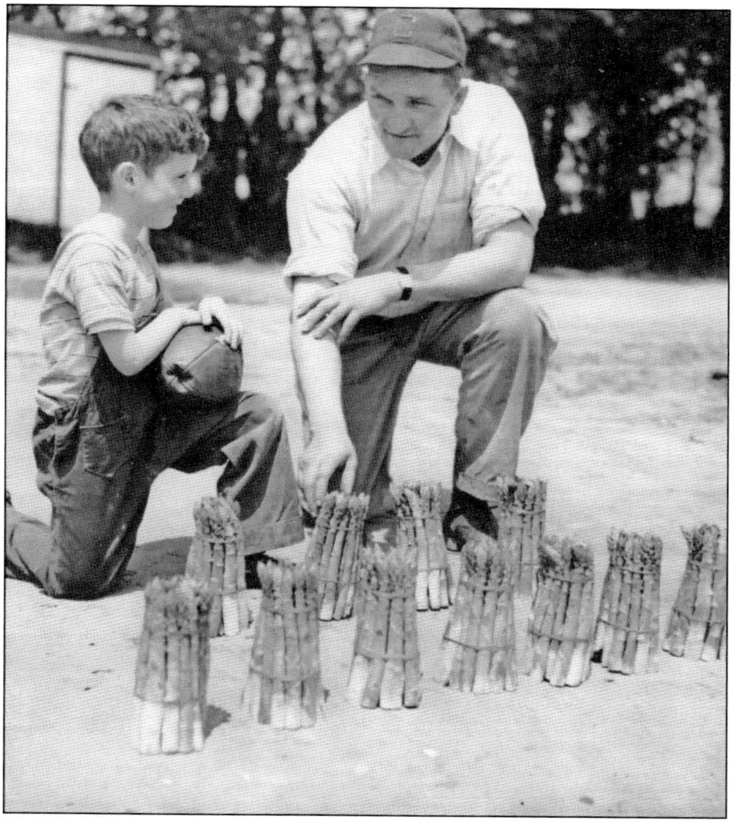

JAMES LEONARD SR. (1910–1993). Jim Leonard Sr. was a professional athlete and a coach of both professional and college football teams. When he retired, he returned home to his Mullica Hill farm. He kept coaching on the local level, however, working with Interstate League team the Swedesboro Devils in the 1950s. Family members recall that he used anything at hand to lay out football plays, including bunches of asparagus.

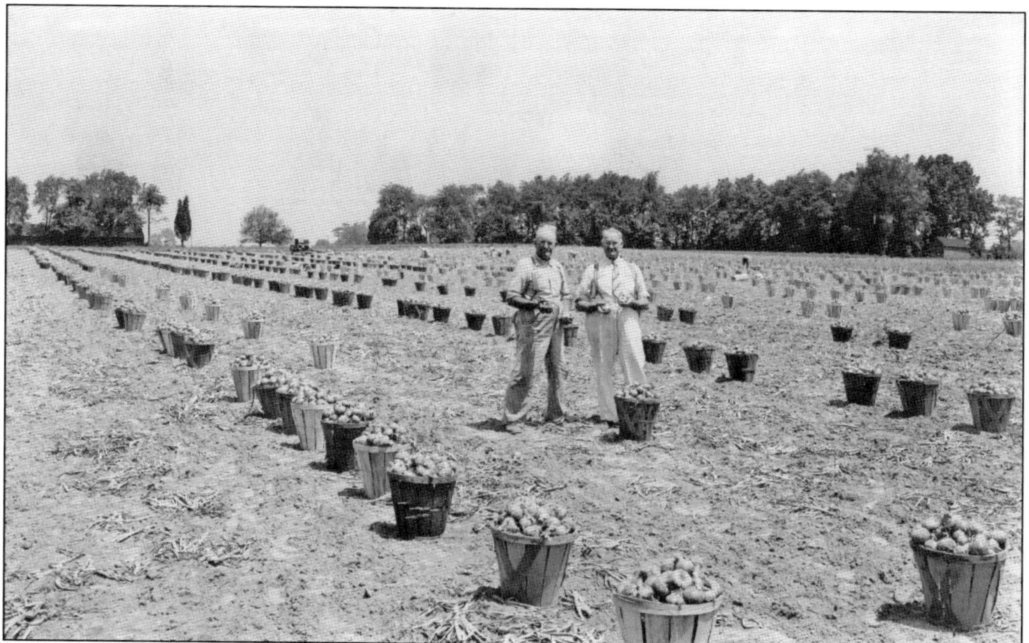

ONION HARVEST. Onions were widely grown in the township in the late 19th and early 20th centuries. They were a versatile crop that could be harvested as scallions in the spring or allowed to mature into late summer, like these on the Chalkley Kirby farm in Mullica Hill.

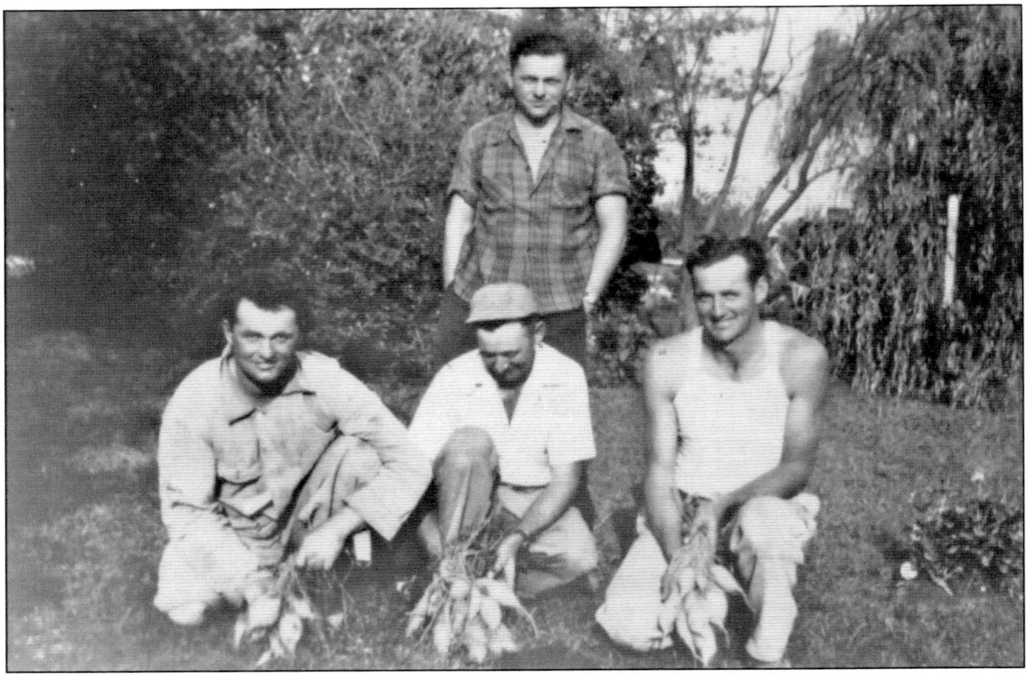

Sweet Potato Harvest, c. 1940. Sweet potatoes were an important crop in Gloucester County throughout most of the 20th century. After they were cured, sweet potatoes kept well and could be marketed through the fall and winter. The harvest on Mount Pleasant Farm in Richwood is shown off by (first row) from left to right, Jake Reuter, David Turk, and Walter Turk; (second row) Milton Reuter.

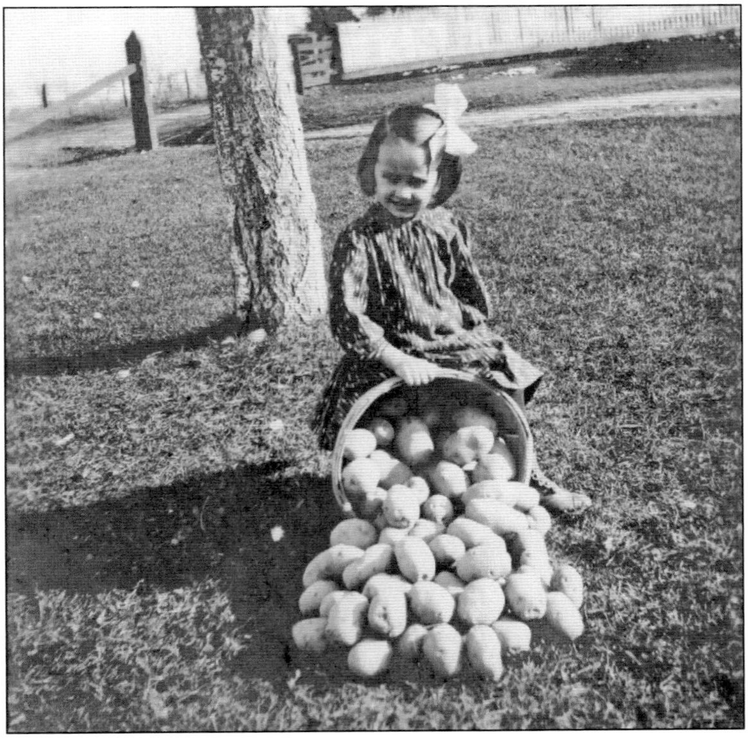

White Potato Harvest, c. 1905. *The Farm Journal Directory of Gloucester County* of 1913 declares that "the great crop of Gloucester County is potatoes." White potato production was second only to sweet potatoes and yams, with the combined harvest that year totaling almost three million bushels, much of it shipped from Mullica Hill Station. Here, Ella Evans showed off a bushel of prize potatoes at Cherry Grove on Wolfert Station Road.

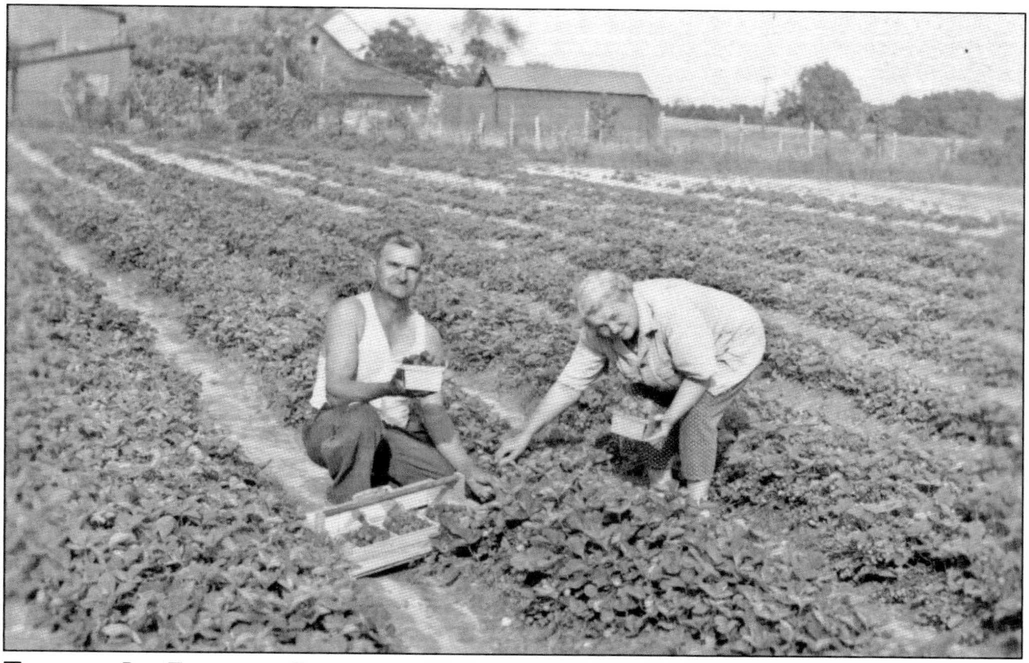

Theo and Ida Eggert in Strawberry Patch, 1948. Strawberries, like asparagus, were a good springtime cash crop. Highly perishable, they had to be shipped quickly to nearby markets. The Eggert farm was only a few acres, which was not locally unusual. The Eggerts lived in Ewan in the Israel Ewan house across from the firehouse, which was torn down in the late 20th century.

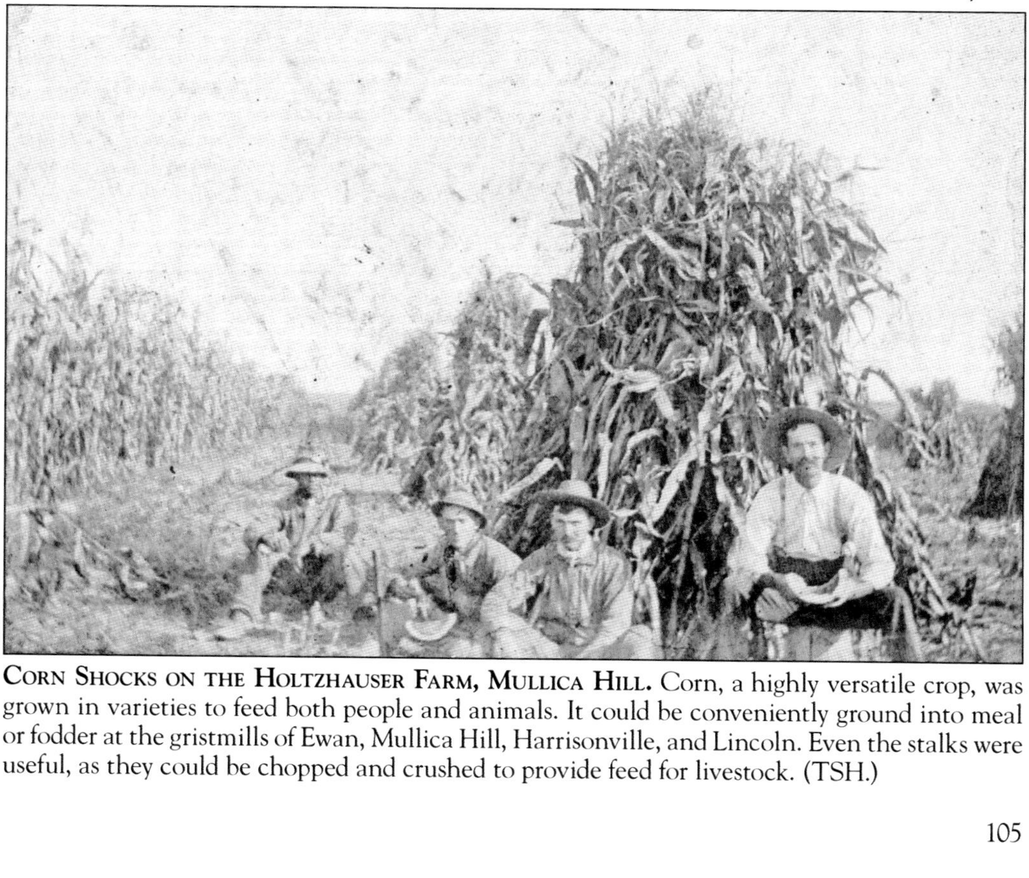

Corn Shocks on the Holtzhauser Farm, Mullica Hill. Corn, a highly versatile crop, was grown in varieties to feed both people and animals. It could be conveniently ground into meal or fodder at the gristmills of Ewan, Mullica Hill, Harrisonville, and Lincoln. Even the stalks were useful, as they could be chopped and crushed to provide feed for livestock. (TSH.)

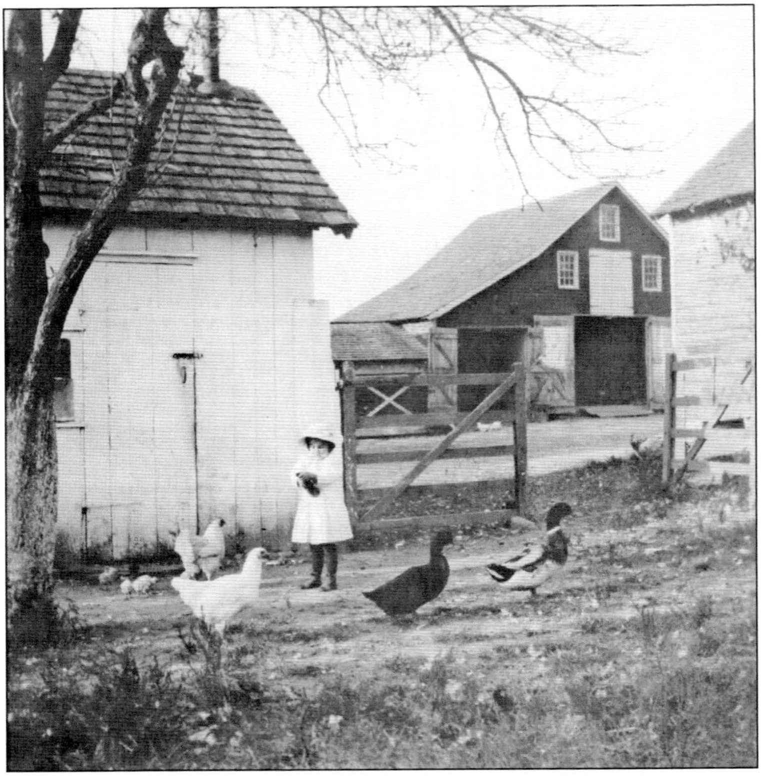

FEEDING THE POULTRY, C. 1905. Chickens and ducks were kept on most local farms in the 19th and early 20th centuries and children, like Ella Evans at Cherry Grove, were often responsible for their care. Poultry supplied the family's needs, and their surplus eggs could be bartered or sold at the local general store.

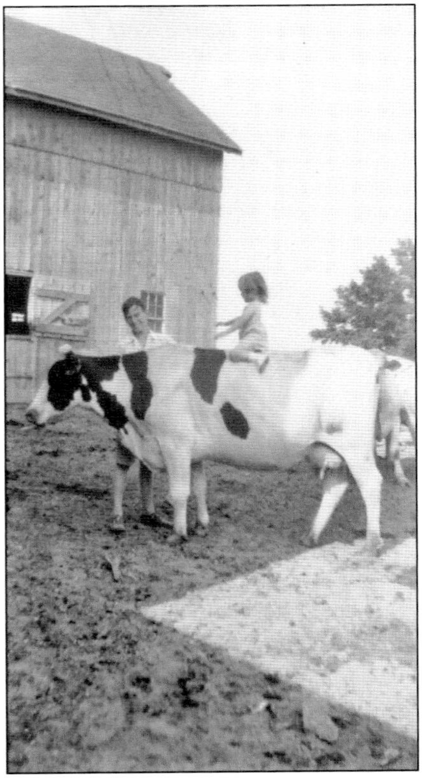

FERGUSON FARM, C. 1944. Dairy was an important industry through much of the 20th century, and several farms were located in the Harrisonville area. Here, Judy Ferguson and Bob ? tend to a cow on the Ferguson farm. Bob was a "taken boy," a term used at the time to refer to a child being fostered by a family. (JF.)

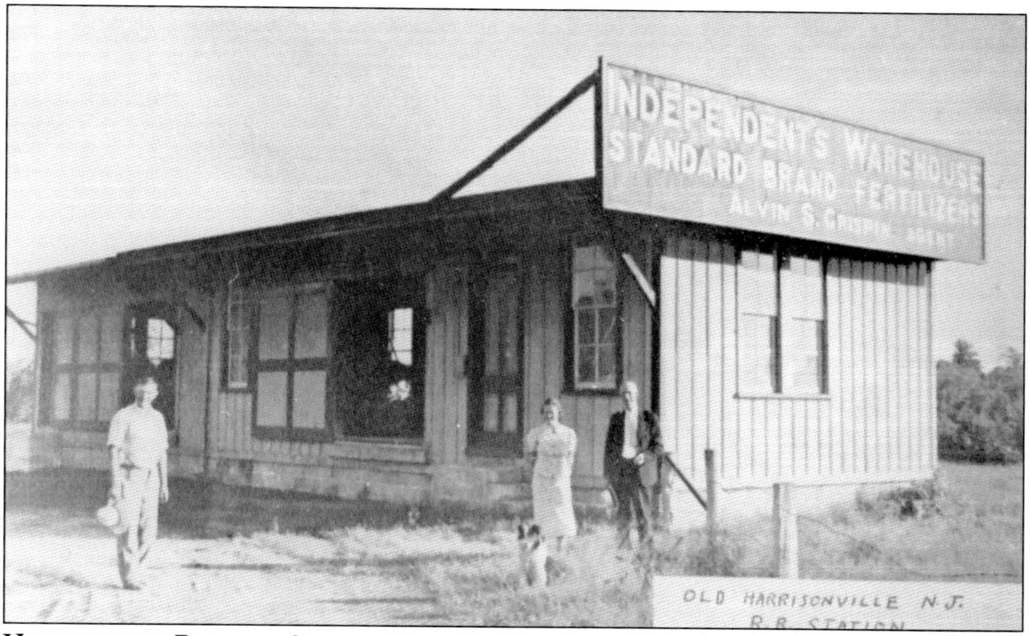

HARRISONVILLE RAILROAD STATION. Part of the West Jersey & Seashore Railroad, it was originally called Bassett Station and served as a milk stop for dairy farms in the area. The Independent Fertilizer Company later purchased the building and moved it to the Alvin Crispin farm on Porch's Mill Road, where it was used as a warehouse. It is now a private home. (FSC.)

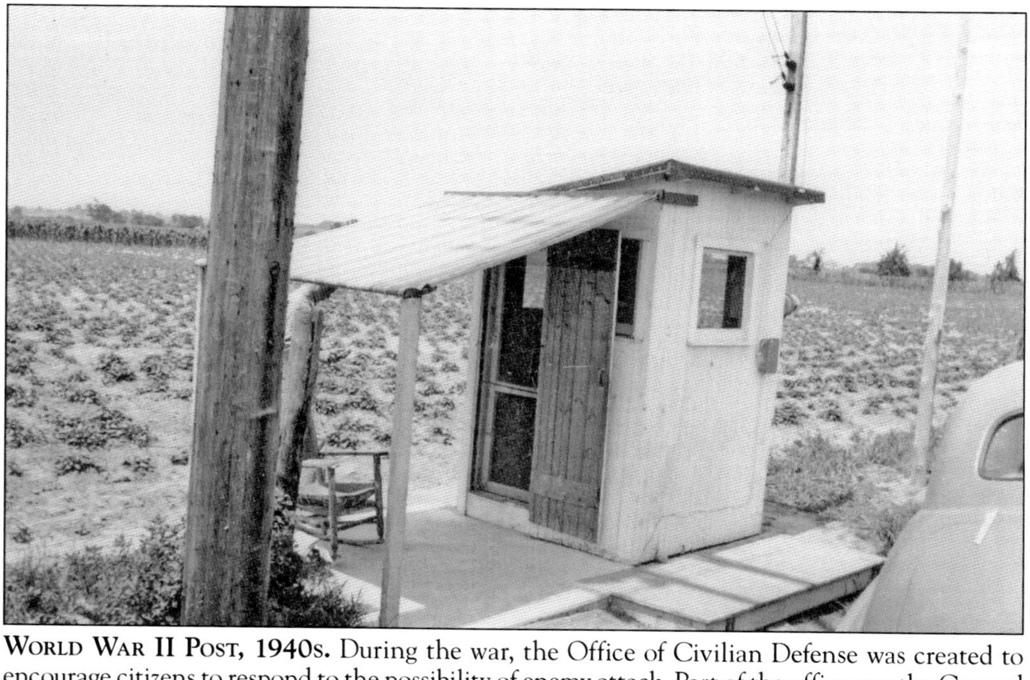

WORLD WAR II POST, 1940s. During the war, the Office of Civilian Defense was created to encourage citizens to respond to the possibility of enemy attack. Part of the office was the Ground Observer Corps, which set up posts to watch for enemy aircraft. This one, by a farm field, was not far from the Harrisonville School. (GCHS.)

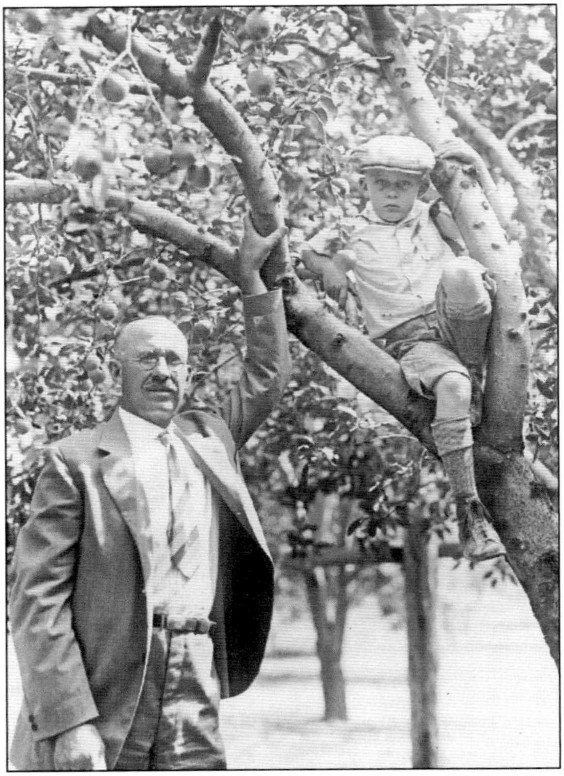

Lewis Mood Farm, 1925. In the early 1920s, Ferrell farmer Lewis Mood Sr. noticed that the fruit on one limb of a Delicious apple tree had turned completely red while all the others were still green. Stark Brothers Nursery in Missouri bought the tree for $6,000 and named the new variety Starking Delicious. It revolutionized the industry and helped popularize the Red Delicious apple.

Starking Delicious Apple Celebration at Old Town Hall, 1925. Stark Brothers made arrangements for a celebration of the new apple that included noted horticulturalists, representatives from apple-growing states, and dignitaries from Great Britain. According to a contemporary newspaper account, 1,500 people gathered in front of the town hall in Mullica Hill on August 31 before proceeding to the Mood farm for the presentation of the new apple.

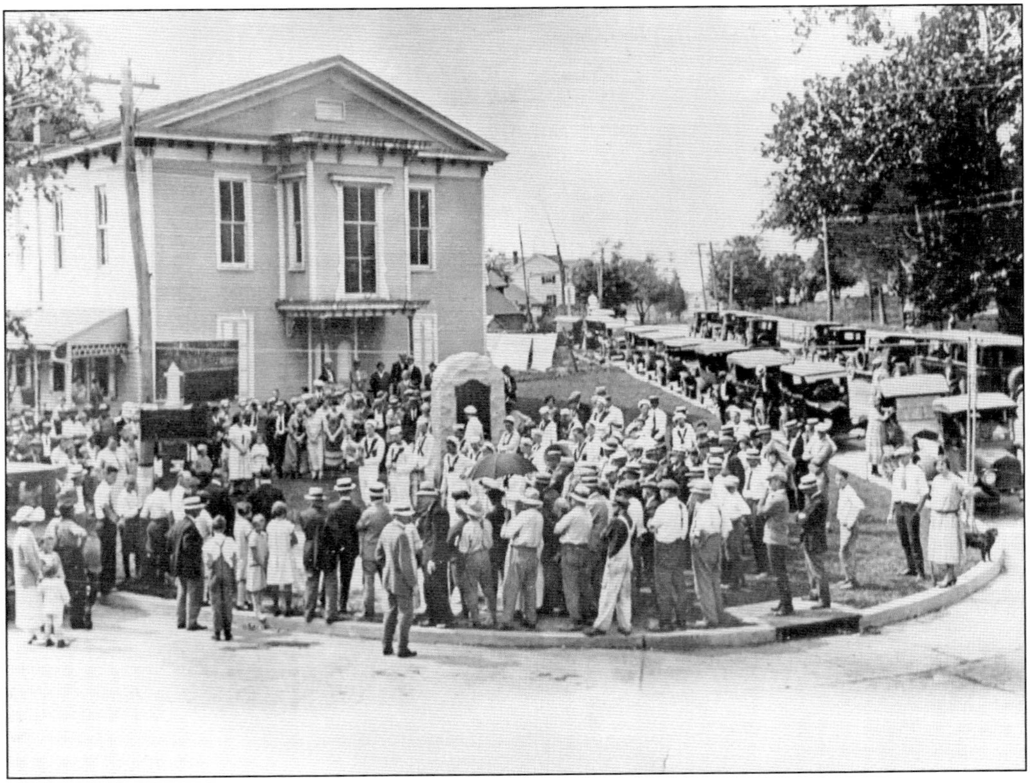

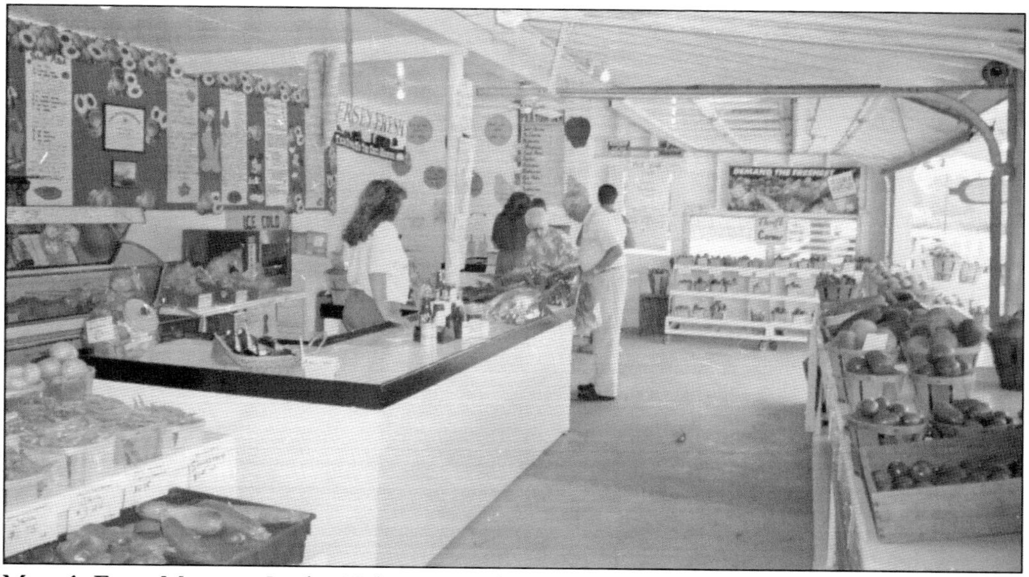

MOOD'S FARM MARKET. In the 20th century, farmers developed roadside markets to sell freshly harvested produce to local customers. Mood's opened in 1925 and was the first market in the area. A cider press was added in 1967 that still produces the apple cider sold there and distributed to other markets.

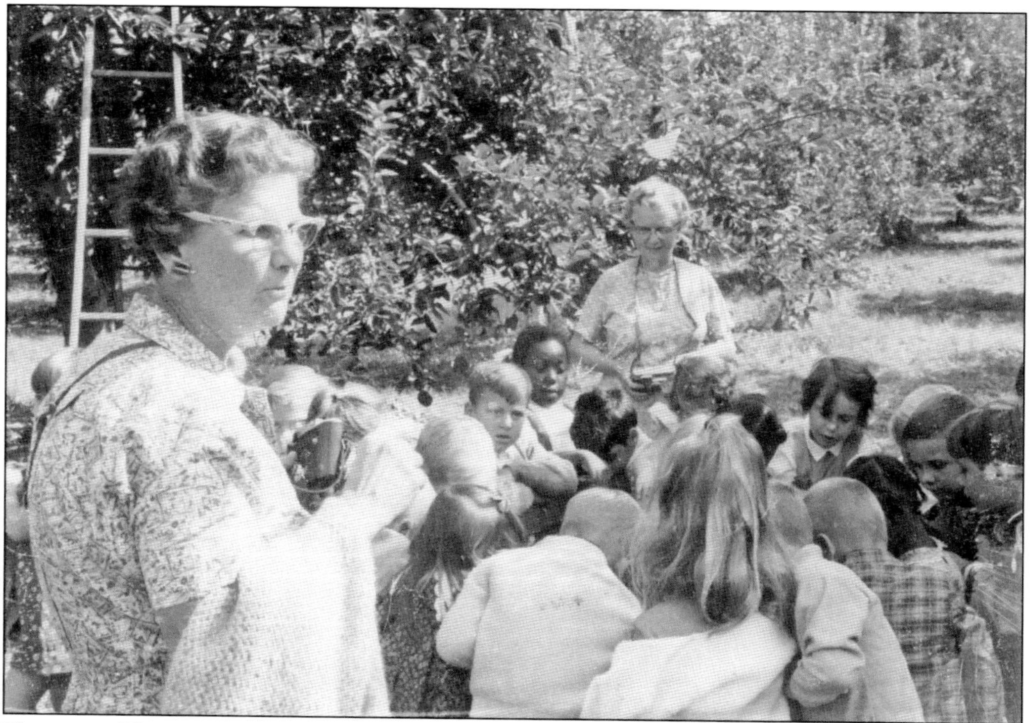

HARRISON TOWNSHIP KINDERGARTEN CLASS TRIP, 1967. Although the township was still mostly rural in the late 1960s, development was beginning to take place and not all children were intimately familiar with the workings of a farm. As a form of community outreach, schools sponsored field trips like this one that Margaret Smith's class took to the Schleicher farm in Richwood. Smith is in the background, and Doris Schleicher is on the left.

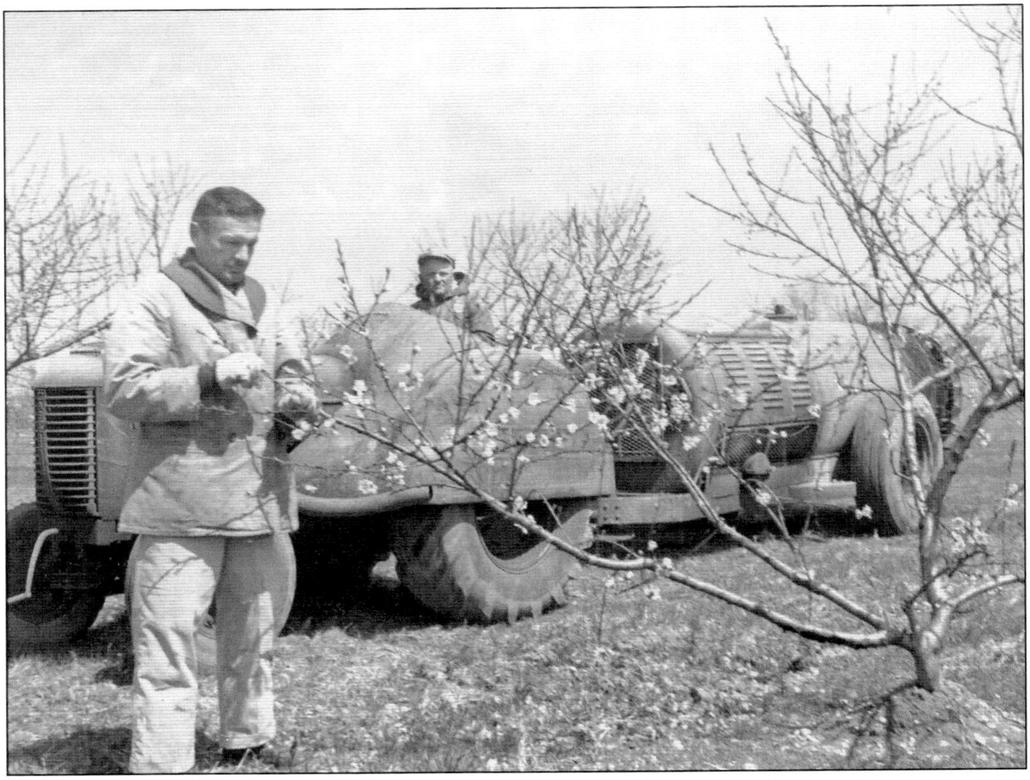

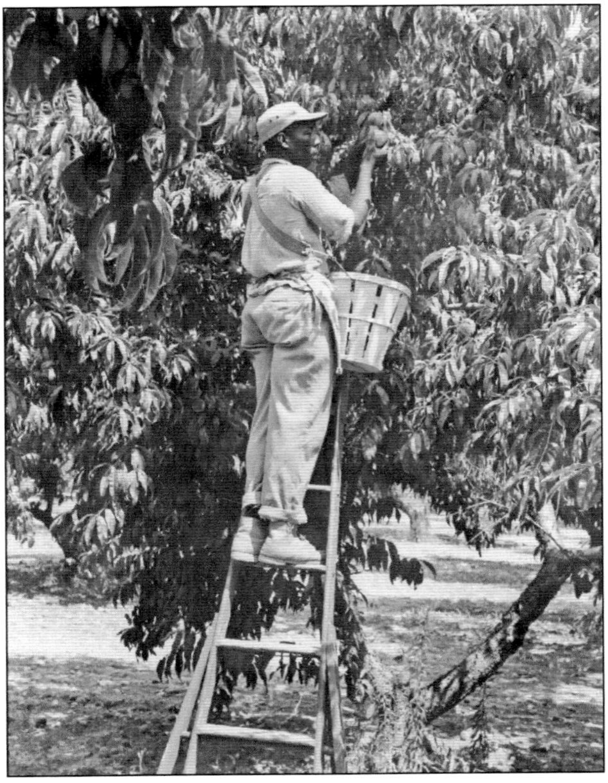

Peaches in Bloom, Mount Pleasant Orchards. Peaches have been grown in the township since Colonial times, but it was only in the first two decades of the 20th century that production began on a large scale. Farmers in Richwood were the first to plant extensive orchards and to specialize in fruit on farms such as Mount Pleasant, where Lou and Jake Reuter examined blooming trees.

Picking Peaches, c. 1957. Charles J. Roth Sr. planted the first peach orchard on his Richwood farm in 1915. He, like most other farmers in the area, had grown a variety of crops and had also kept chickens and hogs. By the 1940s, after he had passed away and his son Charles J. Roth Jr. had taken over operations, the farm was producing only tree fruit. (NJSA.)

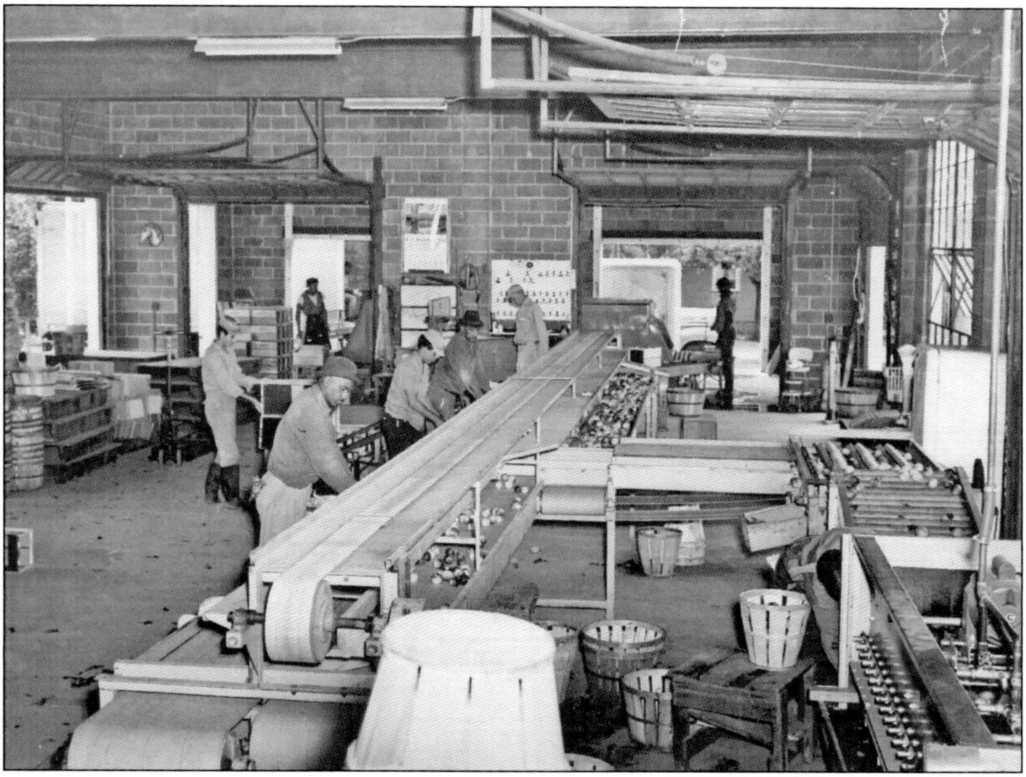

Packing Peaches, c. 1957. From the 1950s through the 1960s, the township was the center of one of the largest peach-producing areas in the United States. To facilitate shipment of their fruit throughout the Northeast, local growers began to build their own packinghouses with modern mechanized equipment, like the one on the Roth farm on Harrisonville Road. (NJSA.)

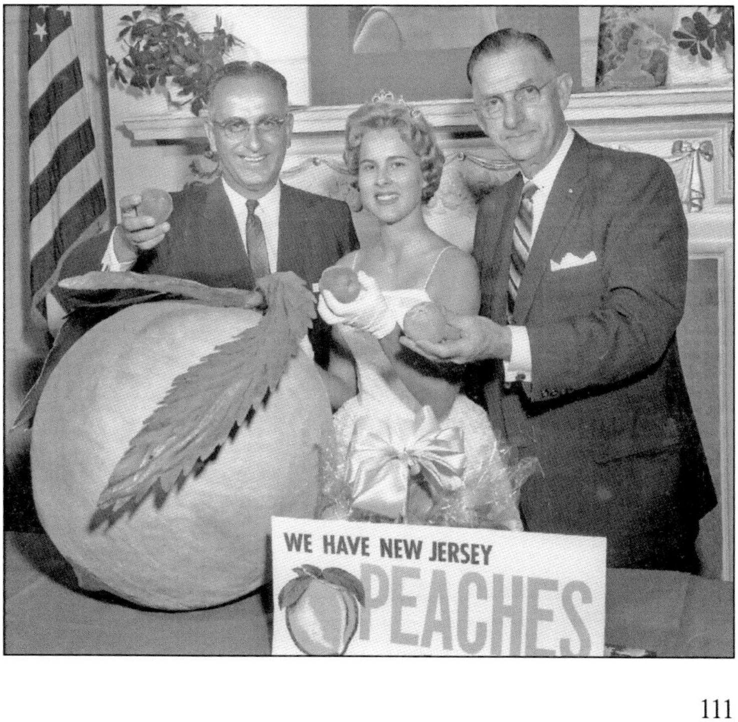

Northeastern Peach Marketing Conference, 1962. The marketing and promotion of peaches became an important business by the middle of the 20th century. Rosemary Mood, daughter of J. Richard Mood Sr., was named National Peach Queen and poses with Phillip Alampi (left) and Dr. William Henning at the conference in Philadelphia on July 19. (NJSA.)

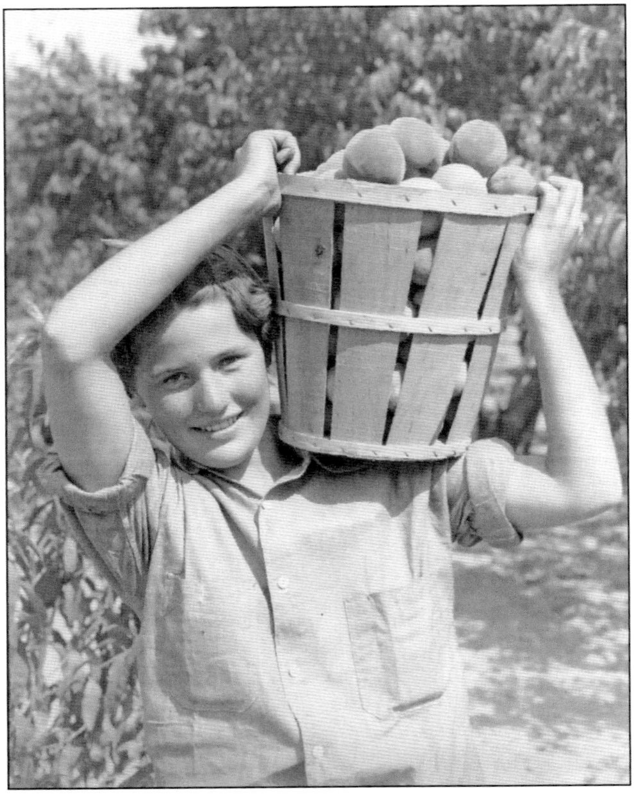

Mary Esther Edge, 1944. The Women's Land Army formed in 1943 to address the war-related shortage of male farmworkers. Mary Esther Edge, 18-year-old daughter of Gov. Walter E. Edge, was a member and spent a week in August picking and packing peaches on the Henry Reuter farm in Richwood. (PU.)

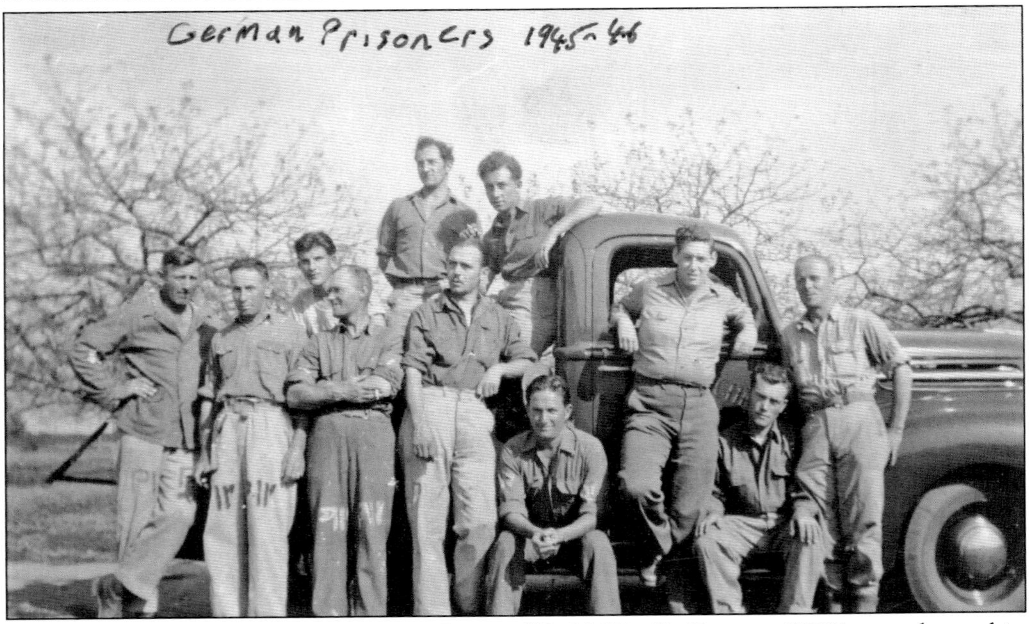

German Prisoners of War, c. 1945. During World War II, German POWs were housed in America when camps became overcrowded in England. The Civilian Conservation Corps camp in nearby Glassboro was put in service to house prisoners, who worked on several farms in the township, including John Schleicher's in Richwood. Their guard stands in front of the truck door window.

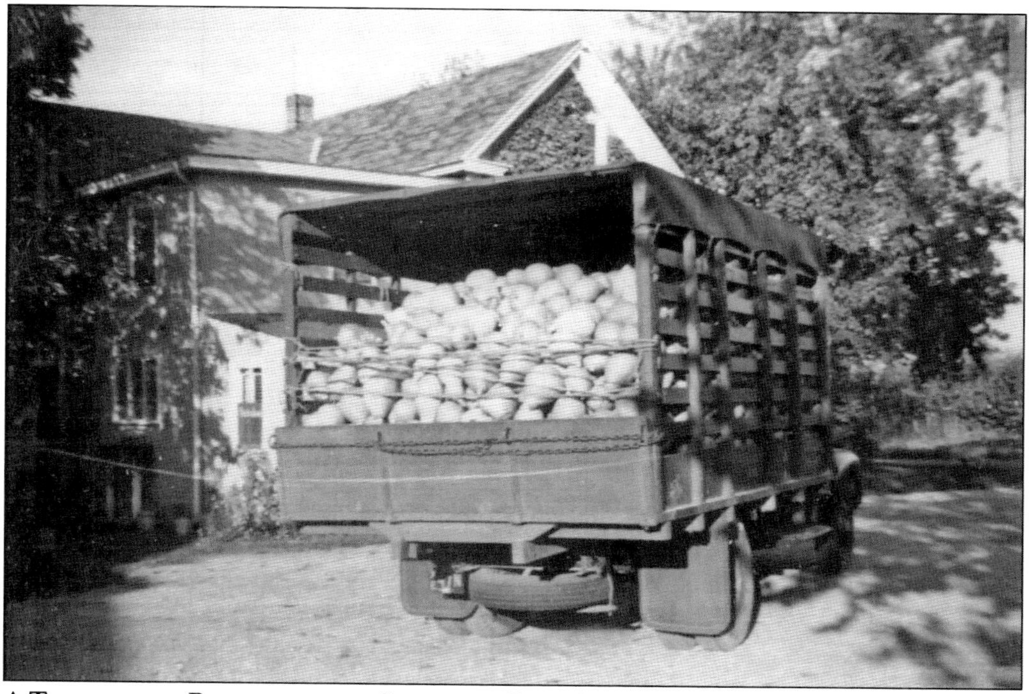

A Truckload of Pumpkins at the Schleicher Farm, Richwood. Trucks and improved roadways transformed fruit and produce distribution. This marked the beginning of the end for the railroad lines that previously had helped make farming a profitable business in the township. (NS.)

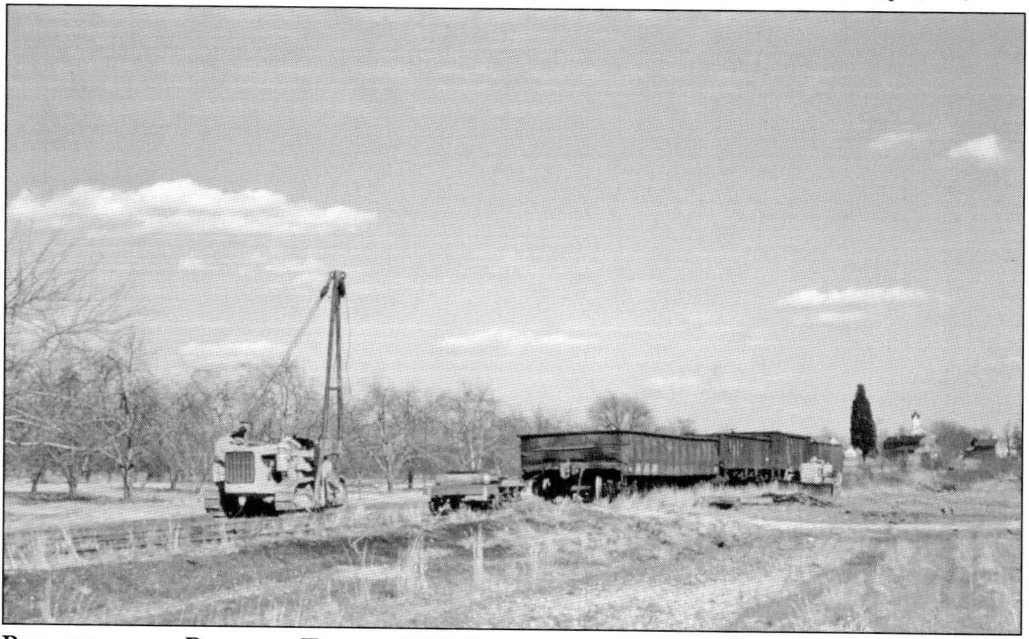

Removal of the Railroad Tracks, 1950. Four passenger trains a day traveled between Mullica Hill and Philadelphia at the height of rail service in the township. Passenger service on the Glassboro to Mullica Hill line was discontinued in 1933 but freight service continued until 1950. With the rise of trucking, the railroad was no longer a profitable business and the tracks were removed in 1950.

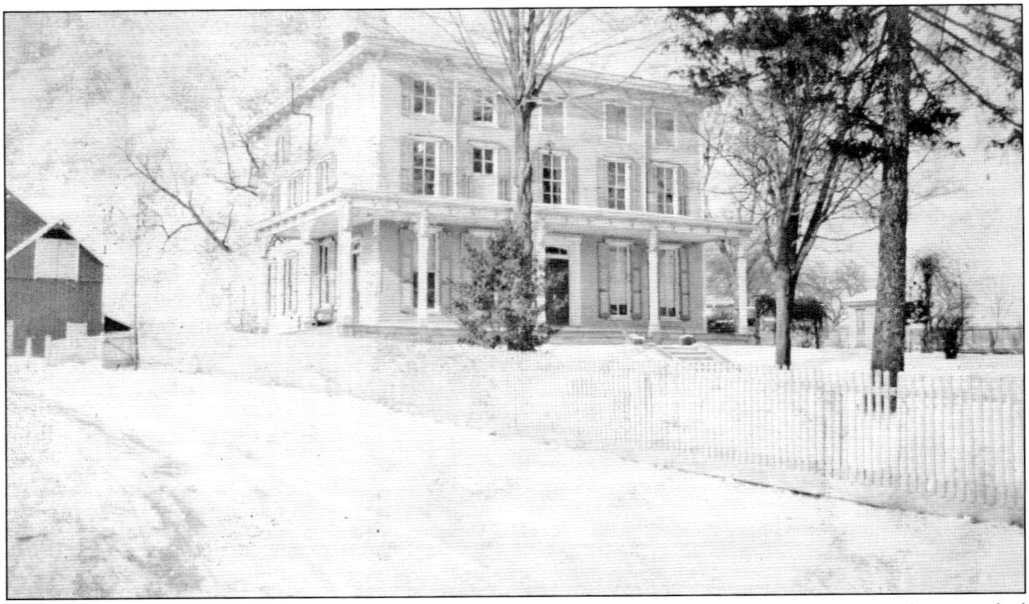

Horner Farm. George Horner Sr. established his farm in Harrisonville in 1857 and expanded it in 1865. Into the first decade of the 21st century, it was a dairy farm but now is an equestrian center called Fertile Green Farms. The fine Italianate farmhouse anchors a traditional courtyard-style farmstead. The farm remains in the Horner family and was designated a Century Farm by the New Jersey Agricultural Society in 1987. (KH.)

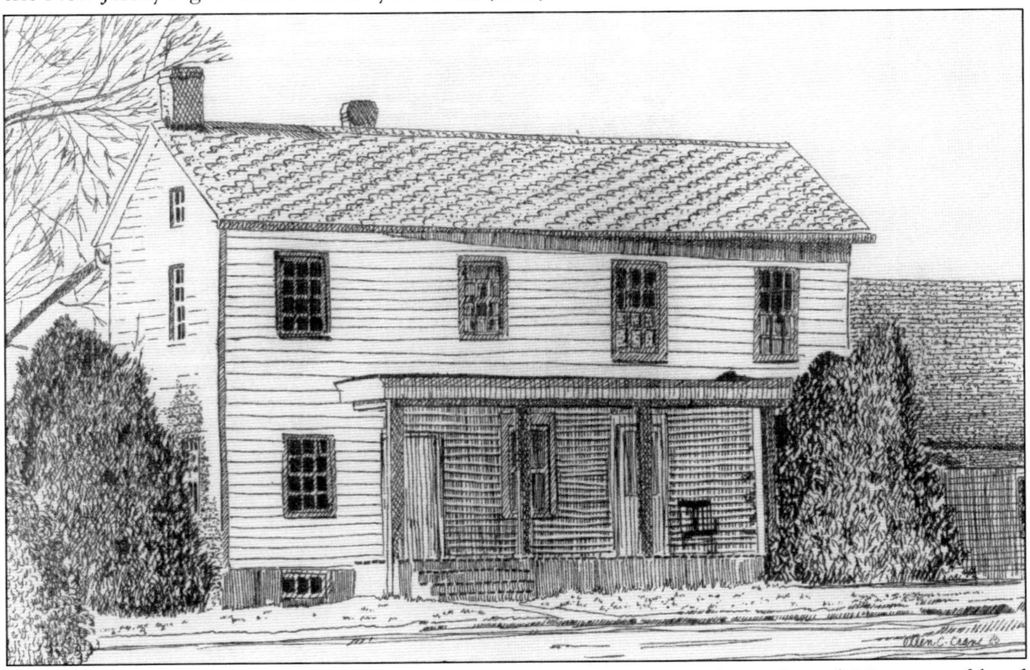

Mood Homestead. George Mood emigrated from Germany and purchased 30 acres of land near Ferrell in 1865. The farmhouse, depicted here by Ellen C. Crane, was built in 1870 and still stands. His grandson expanded the farm in 1945 when he bought 112 acres of land that included the old Pine Tavern. The farm, with its thriving market, remains in the Mood family and was designated a Century Farm in 1986. (JRM.)

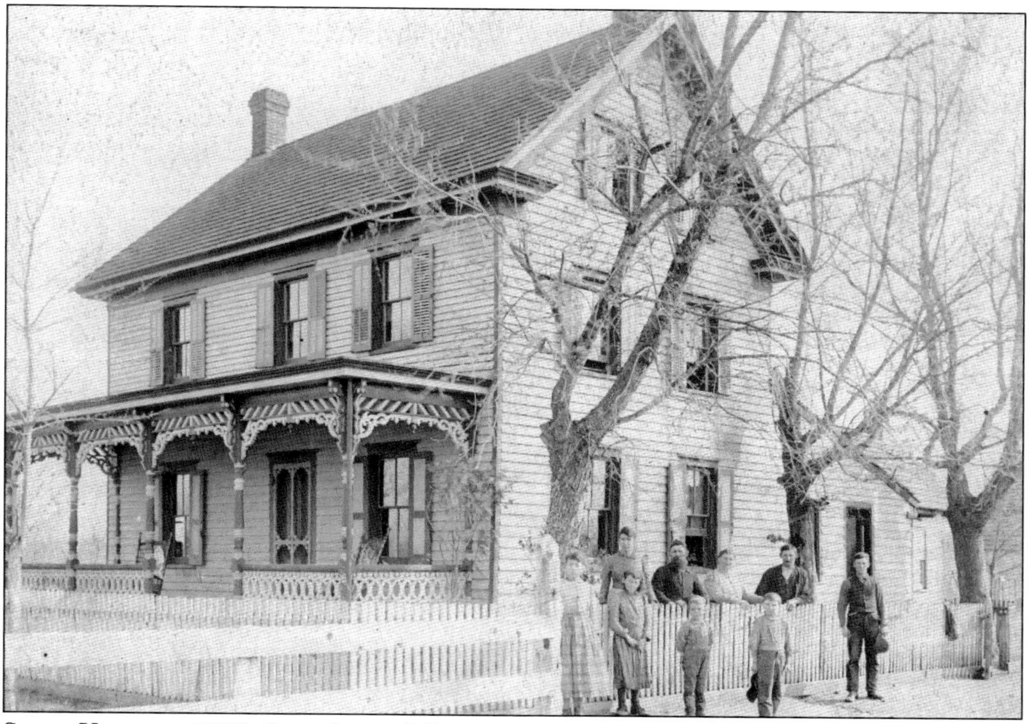

Stony Knoll, c. 1890. One of several German immigrants to settle in Richwood, Philipp Jacob Reuter arrived in 1865. He lived at first with a family in Ewan and then, in 1879, purchased a farm from Richard Skinner. The farm remains in the Reuter family and was designated a Century Farm in 1991.

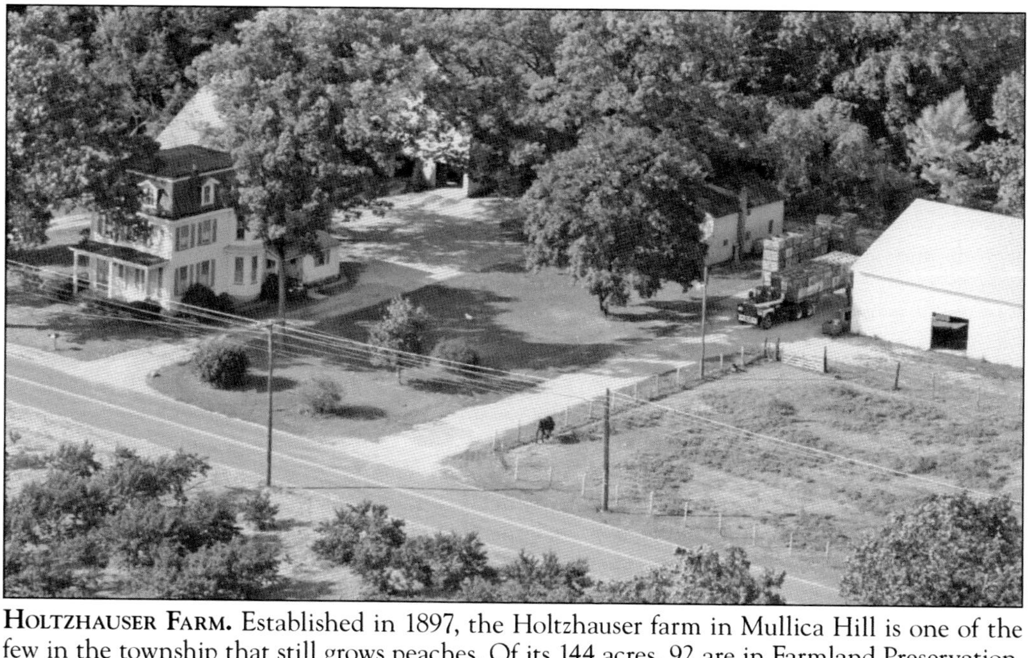

Holtzhauser Farm. Established in 1897, the Holtzhauser farm in Mullica Hill is one of the few in the township that still grows peaches. Of its 144 acres, 92 are in Farmland Preservation, assuring that they will remain in production for years to come. It was designated a Century Farm in 2014. (TSH.)

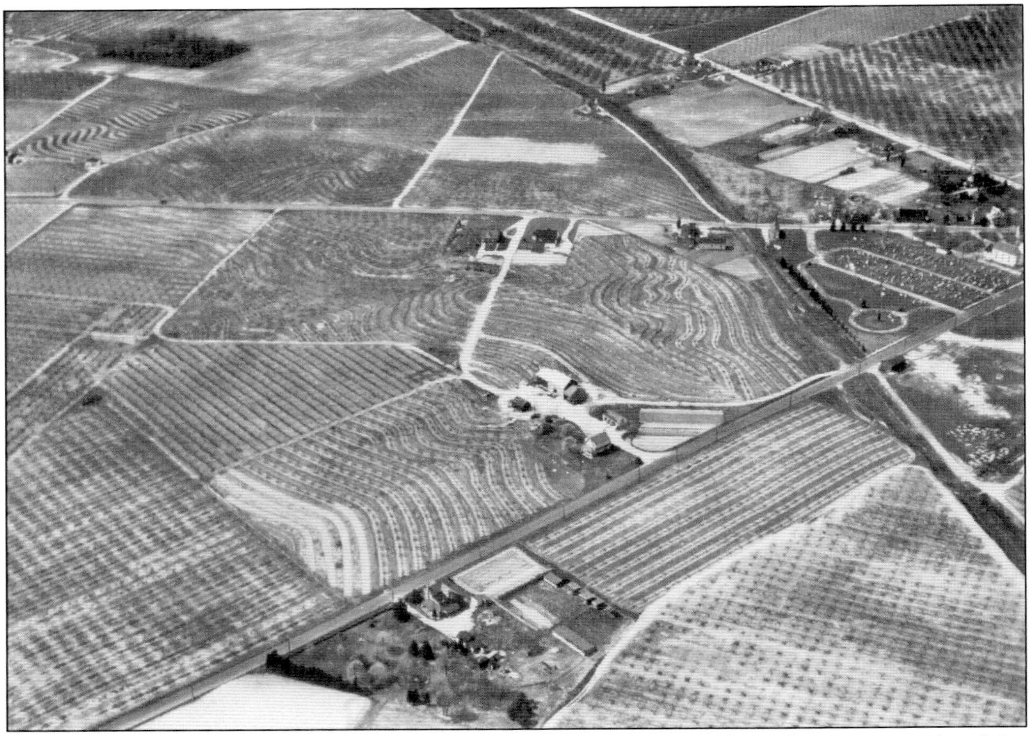

W. W. Heritage & Sons Farm, 1952. The Heritage farm in Richwood is an example of the evolution of farming in the township over the last century and a half. The family began farming vegetables in the 1850s and then planted peaches and apples in the 1930s. The market for peaches declined in the 1990s, and the family discovered that the soil and climate were conducive to growing grapes. A winery was established in 2001, and the farm was designated a Century Farm in 2015.

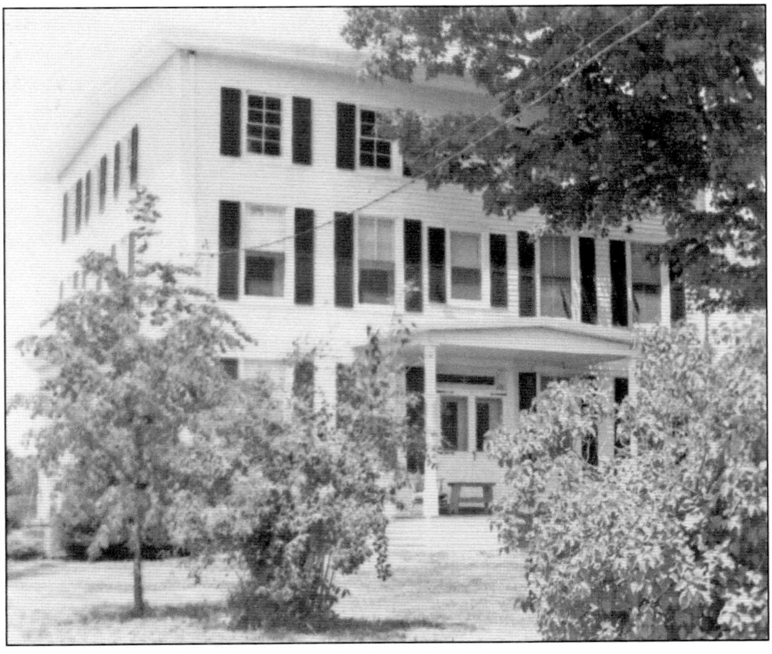

Sunnybrook. Although not a Century Farm, Sunnybrook on Woodstown Road in South Harrison also provides an example of how farming has changed in the township. Through the first half of the 20th century, it was a dairy farm and in 1959 became a nursery. As vineyards proliferated in the first two decades of this century, it has followed the trend and houses a winery.

Six

Old Harrison in Transition

The latter part of the 20th century witnessed the greatest changes in the community's history since the arrival of the first European settlers. While farming continued as an important part of the local economy, housing developments began to replace orchards and farm fields. Along with the increasing population came the need for additional schools and infrastructure. New recreation and sports fields opened in both Harrison and South Harrison that hosted annual family and community events—outgrowths of the US bicentennial and subsequent township sesquicentennial and centennial celebrations.

In the midst of this growth, interest in protecting and preserving the community's history also emerged. The Harrison Township Historical Society was founded in 1971 at the behest of the mayor and township committee as a means of assuring preservation of Mullica Hill's historic Old Town Hall. In 1993, the society in partnership with the township secured a New Jersey Historic Trust grant to finance a major restoration of the hall. Today, Old Town Hall Museum presents exhibitions and programs on Old Harrison Township's cultural heritage and houses an extensive local history collection.

In addition to the Mullica Hill Historic District, Richwood United Methodist Church and four additional sites were placed in the New Jersey and National Registers of Historic Places. Two of these sites have since been demolished.

Today, Old Harrison continues to evolve. New roadways and major developments in Richwood, including Rowan University's West Campus, signal a new chapter in the township's long history. In the midst of all this change, however, Old Harrison's rich heritage is still valued and continues to contribute to its unique character and quality of life.

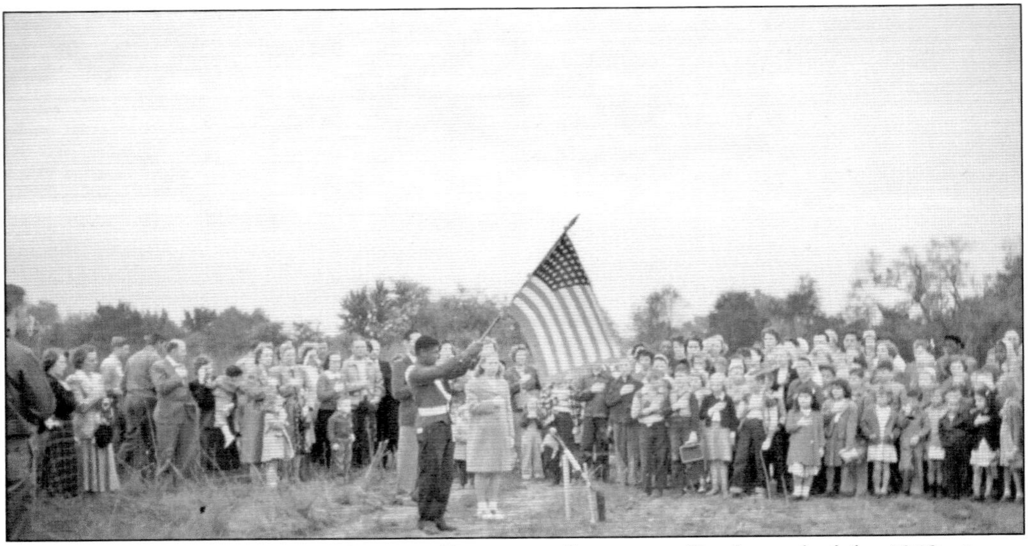

Harrison Township School Ground-Breaking Ceremony. By the end of the 1940s, it was decided to replace all the antiquated schoolhouses with a single, modern elementary school to serve the entire township. A site was selected north of Mullica Hill, and a festive ceremony was held in October 1949. This was a community-wide event; local officials and dignitaries, parents, and children all had a hand in breaking ground for the new building.

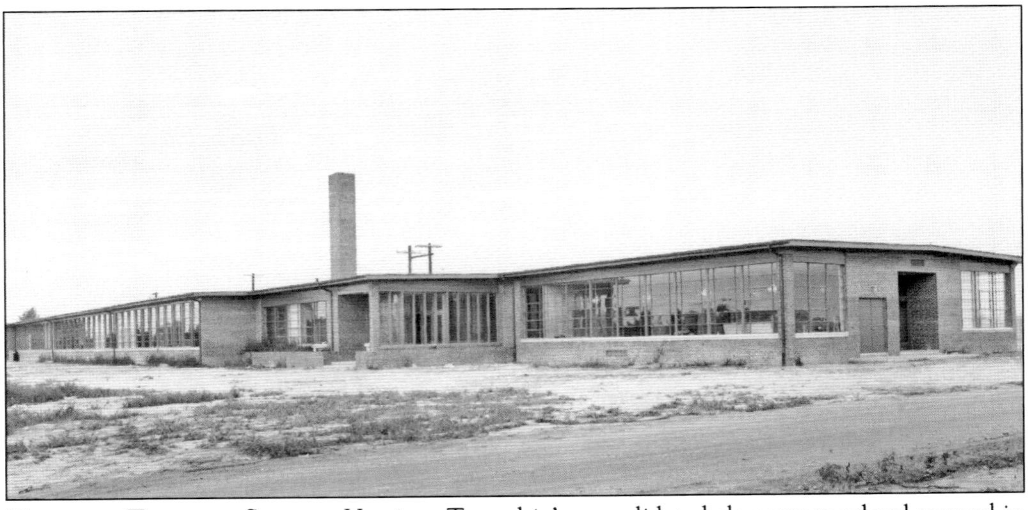

Harrison Township School. Harrison Township's consolidated elementary school opened in 1950. The new school featured wide corridors, abundant windows, and classrooms for manual training and home economics. Within a few years, the building was enlarged with an additional wing of classrooms and an all-purpose room, the first of several subsequent renovations over the next 60 years.

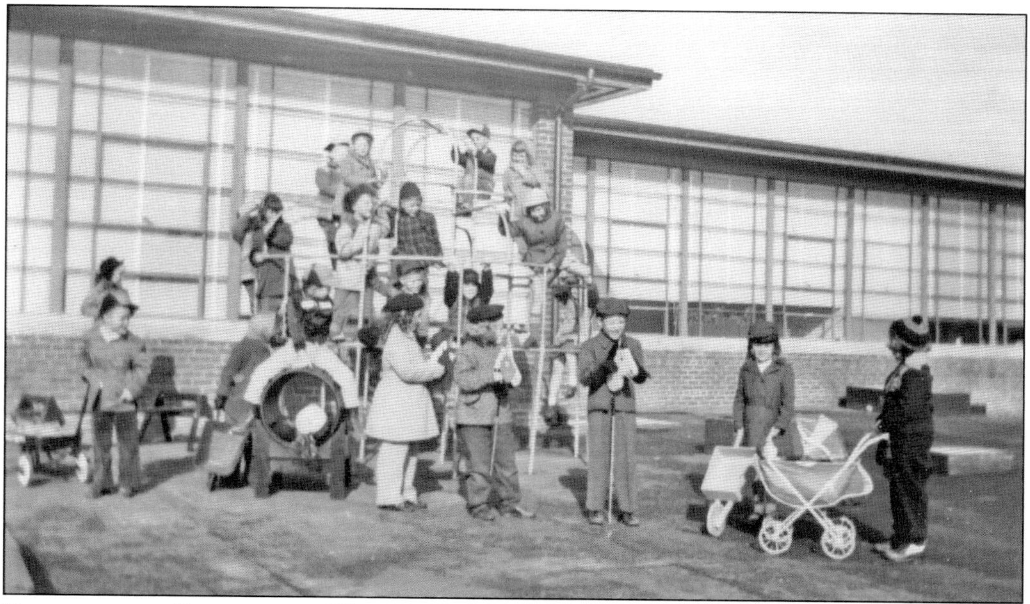

Kindergarten Playground, Harrison Township School. The large kindergarten classroom was self-contained with its own outdoor playground separated from the other students. There was also an indoor play area with a slide, which, at the time, was considered state of the art.

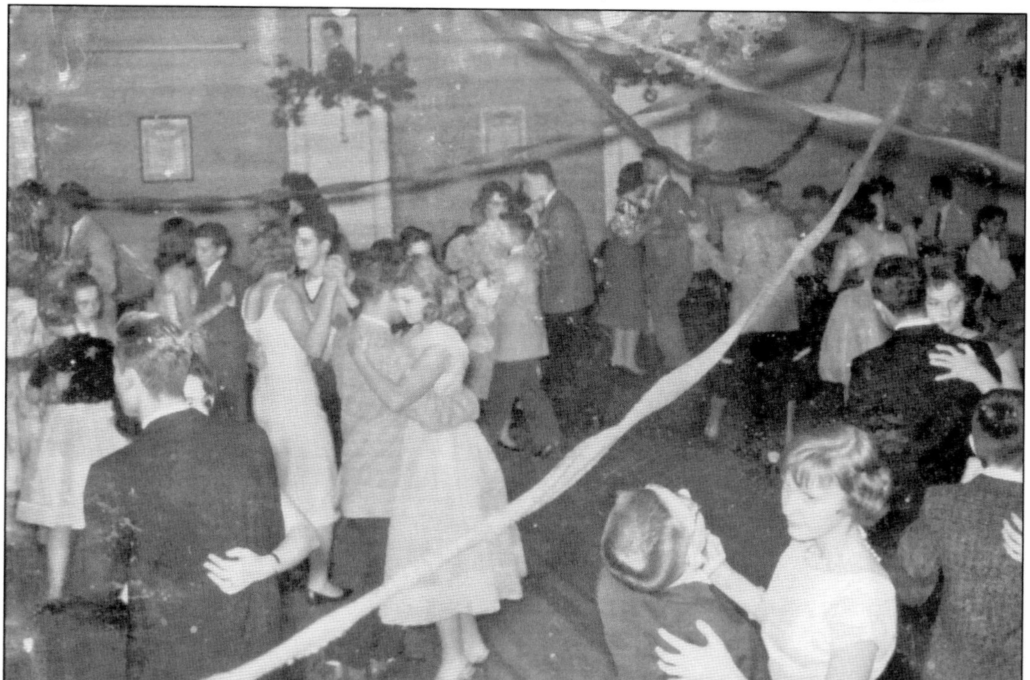

The American Legion Teen Club. Recognizing the lack of chaperoned social activities for teenagers, members of the Robert W. Mills Post No. 452 organized the teen club and, in October 1957, sponsored the first teen dance. Club members organized the dances, which featured both live bands and records. Initially, the dances were very popular, but attendance declined after Clearview Regional High School opened. The club disbanded in 1962.

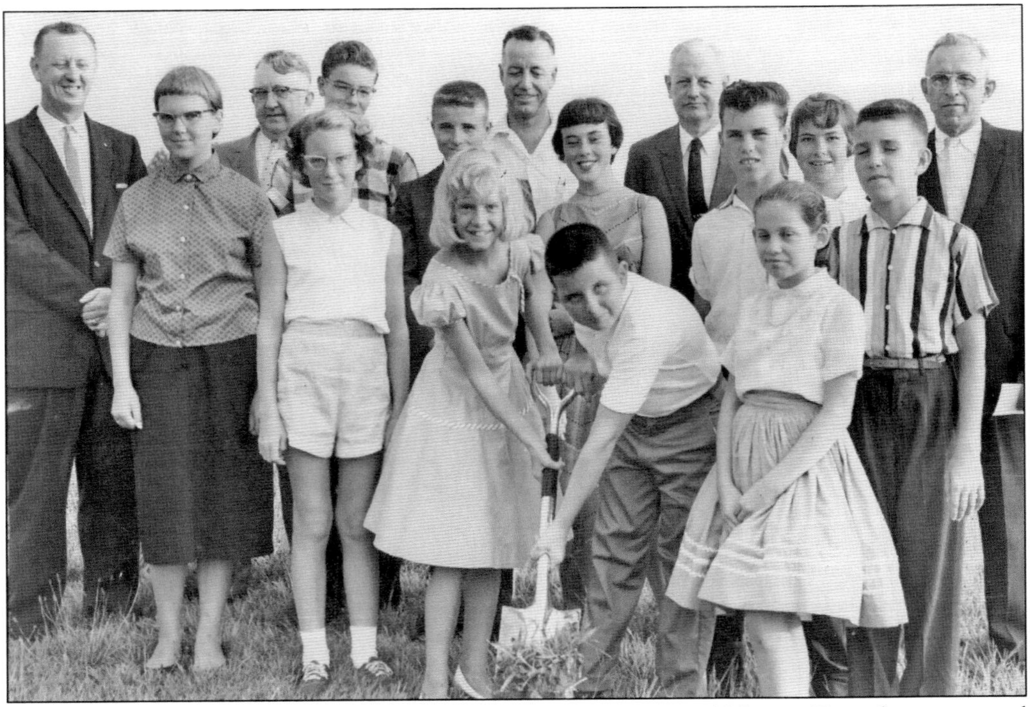

Building Clearview. Faced with growing populations, Harrison and Mantua Townships requested approval in 1958 to form a regional district for seventh through twelfth grades. A group of young people who would attend the new school broke ground in 1959; pictured from left to right are Susan Barrett, John Lippincott, and Mary Beth Muhlbaier; (second row) Toby Gegenheimer, Barbara Boone, Paul Reitz, Joanne Moore, Kenneth Vogt, and Brian Nealy; (third row) Supt. Ward Broomall, architect Edwin Brumbaugh, Marvin Harris, board members Melvin Boone and Norman Thompson, Joan White, and county superintendent Harvey Shue. (MM.)

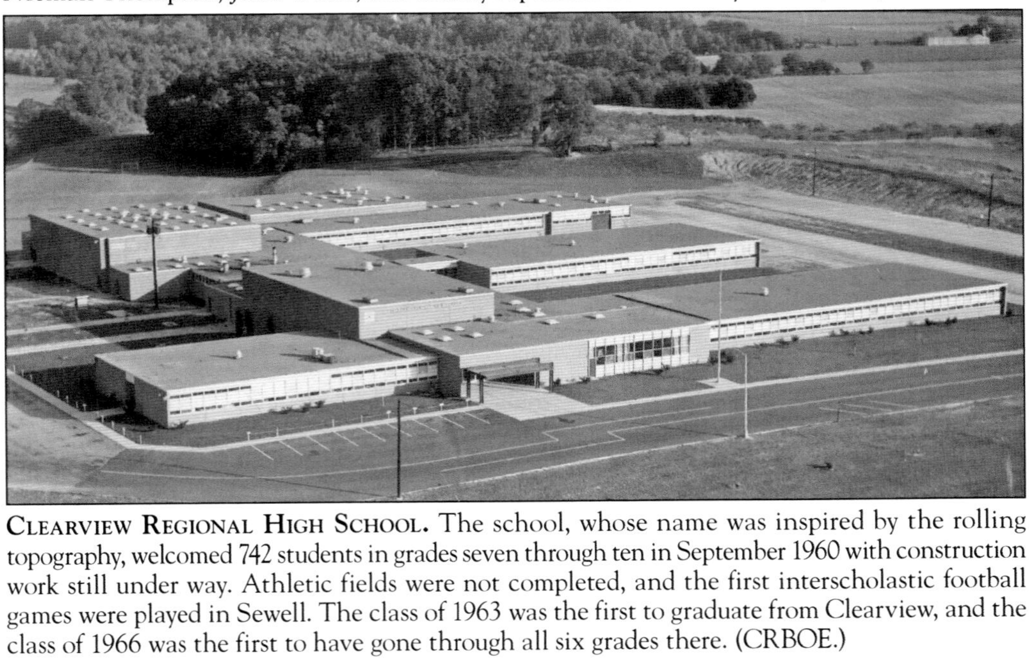

Clearview Regional High School. The school, whose name was inspired by the rolling topography, welcomed 742 students in grades seven through ten in September 1960 with construction work still under way. Athletic fields were not completed, and the first interscholastic football games were played in Sewell. The class of 1963 was the first to graduate from Clearview, and the class of 1966 was the first to have gone through all six grades there. (CRBOE.)

William "Peanut" Gaines. A Mullica Hill native, Gaines was Clearview's first state, national, and international champion athlete. Between 1966 and 1968, he set local, national, and world track records. He was inducted into the Gloucester County Hall of Fame in 1981, and the South Jersey Track and Field Hall of Fame in 2010. (CRBOE.)

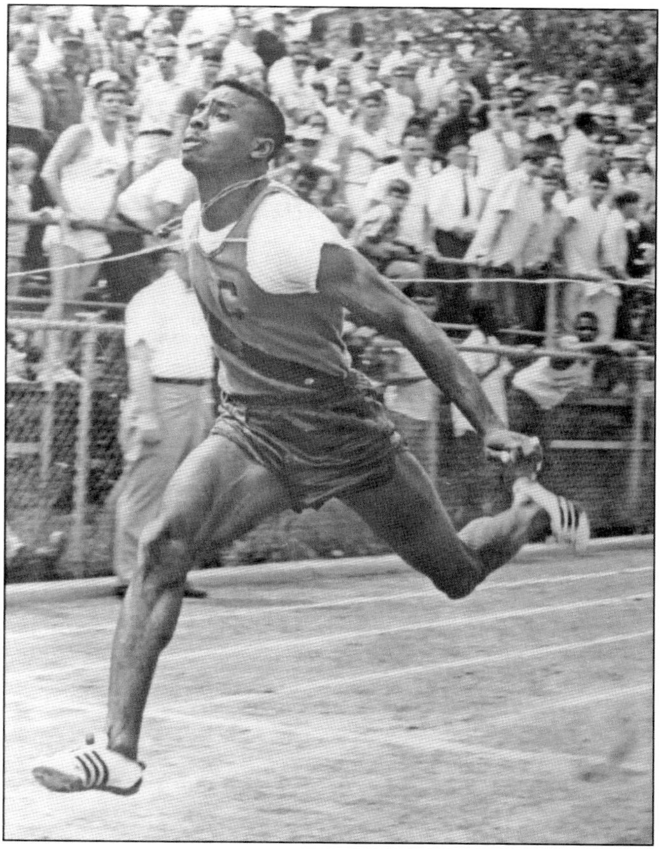

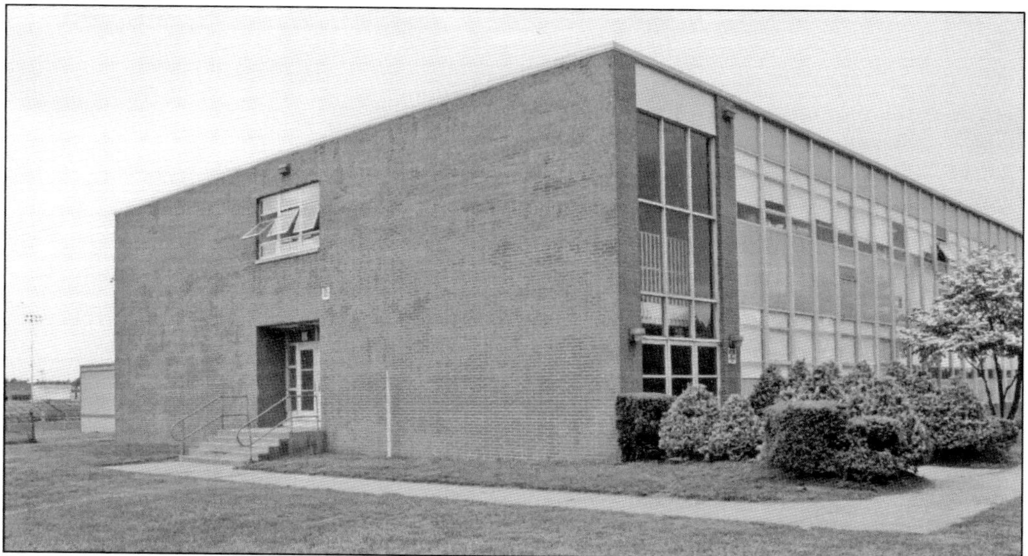

Clearview Regional Junior High School. Within five years of opening, the new high school's increased enrollments necessitated implementing half sessions in 1965. The following year, approval was granted to construct and equip a junior high school in the amount of $2 million. The new school was built on the eastern edge of the campus on Jefferson Road. Both Clearview's school buildings have subsequently been enlarged as student populations continue to grow. (CRBOE.)

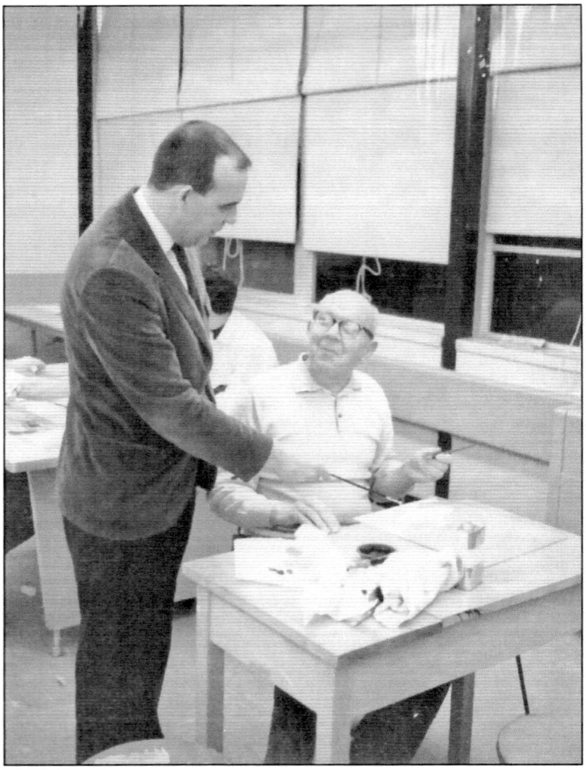

Clearview Adult School. Shortly after it opened, the high school began offering enrichment classes for adults. William Aitken, chair of the art department, taught a class in drawing, with Mullica Hill's Thomas Lippincott in attendance. (CRBOE.)

Friends School, Eighth-Grade Class, 1977. Quaker education in Mullica Hill can be traced back to the 18th century, but the present Friends School was established in 1969 in the former Union Academy. Seen here from left to right are members of the eighth-grade class and their teacher in 1977: Mark Guidotti, teacher Tom Kent, Karen Heritage, Ross Vecchio, Frank Giraffe (seated); Sarah Porter and Stephanie Willson (standing).

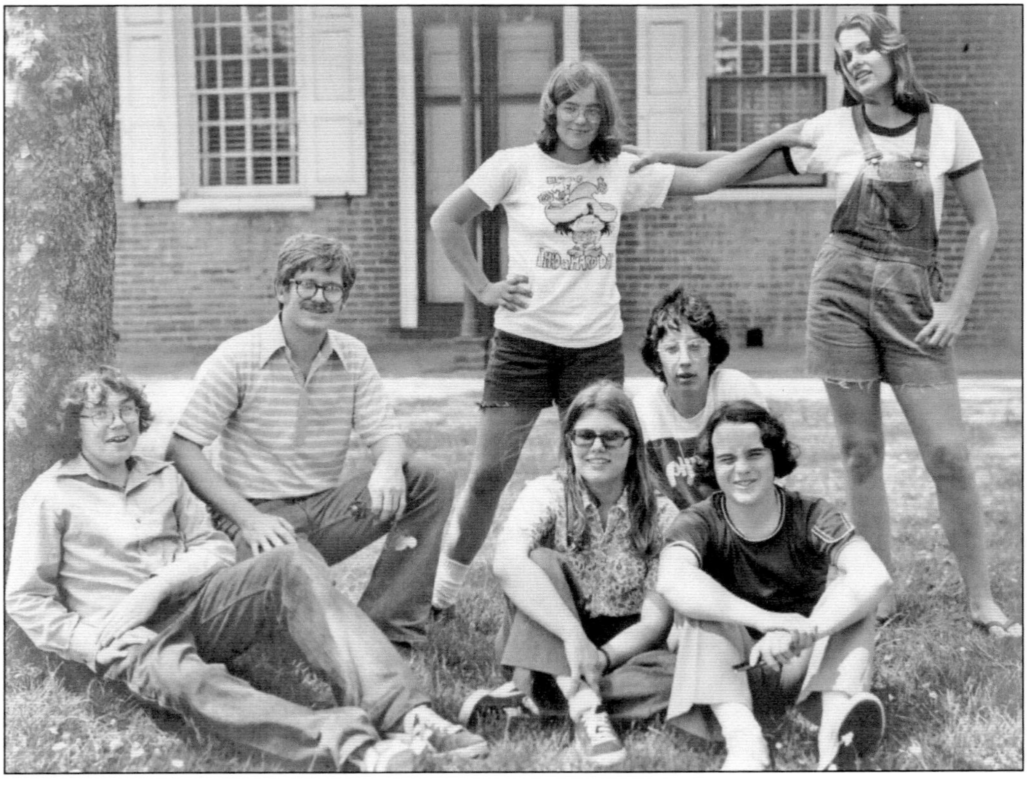

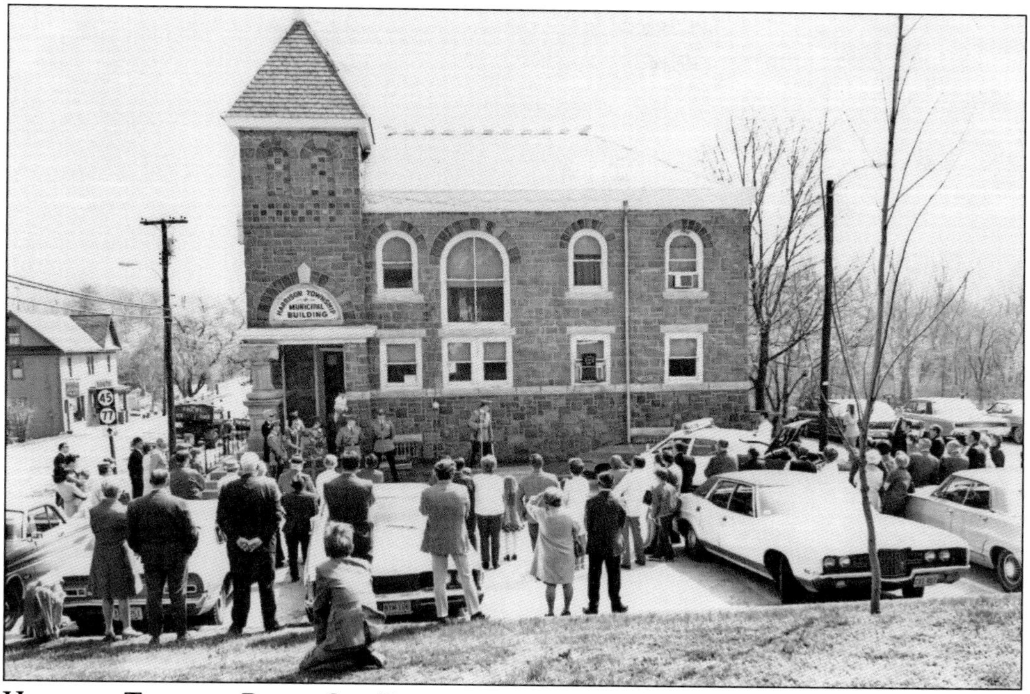

HARRISON TOWNSHIP POLICE CAR DEDICATION, 1972. By the second half of the 20th century, Old Town Hall was no longer adequate to meet the needs of local government. After Farmers National Bank relocated its headquarters north of town in 1963, the township moved into the bank's imposing old building. The acquisition of the new police car was cause for celebration, which was attended by local, county, and state officials.

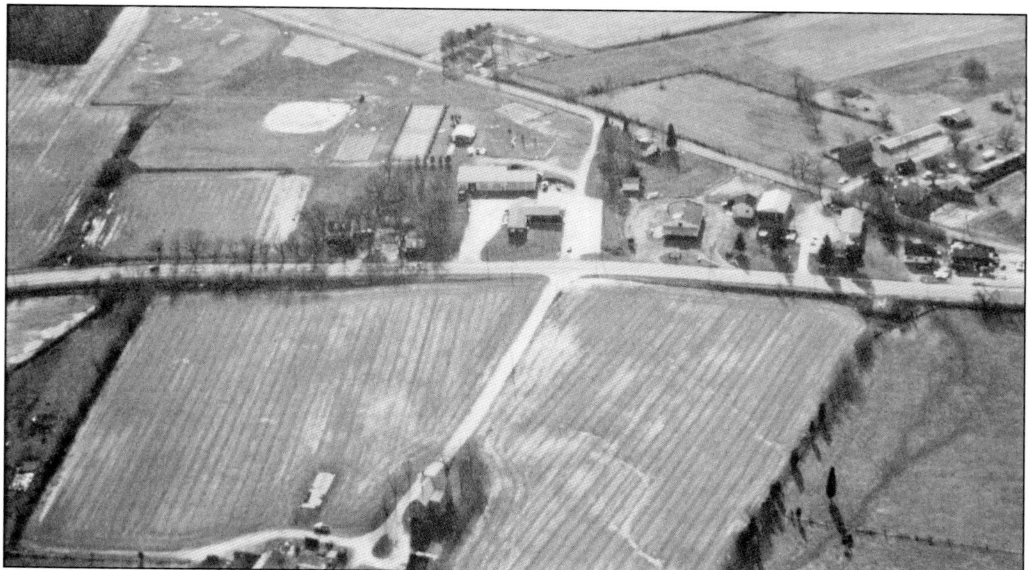

HARRISON TOWNSHIP MUNICIPAL BUILDING AND ELLA HARRIS PARK. By the mid-1970s, government services had outgrown the old bank building, and so the township acquired an old agricultural supply business on Bridgeton Pike and converted it into offices and the police station. The adjacent open field became the township's first public park, a project of the township's US bicentennial committee that honored civic leader Ella Harris.

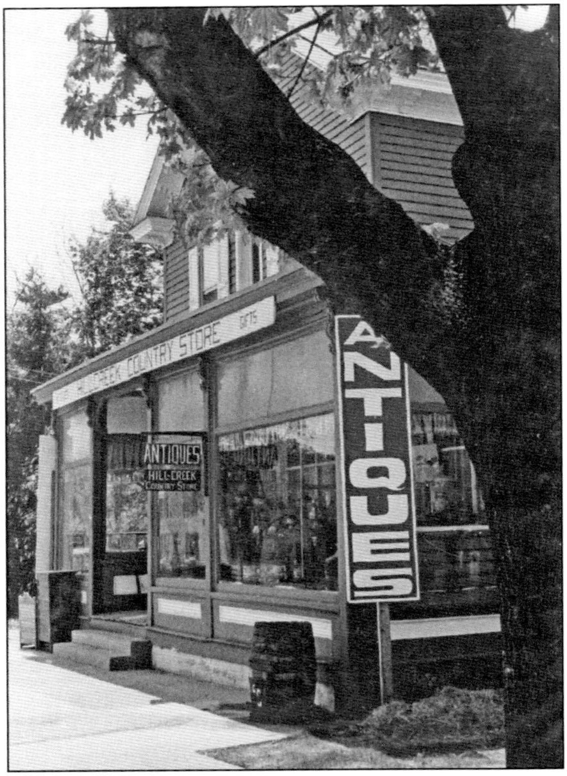

Antique Country. Mullica Hill's reputation as an antiques center began in the late 1960s when Hillcreek House opened at 32 North Main Street. By the 1970s, shops proliferated throughout the village, which became widely known throughout the Northeast. These businesses also awakened recognition of the town's heritage, resulting in the Mullica Hill Historic District. (GCHS.)

The Bicentennial Parade. Harrison Township's US bicentennial celebration took place June 26–27, 1976, with a grand parade, country fair at the 4-H Fairgrounds, chicken barbecue, square dance, horse show, and ecumenical religious heritage service. The Robert W. Mills American Legion Post's grand marshal float led off the parade.

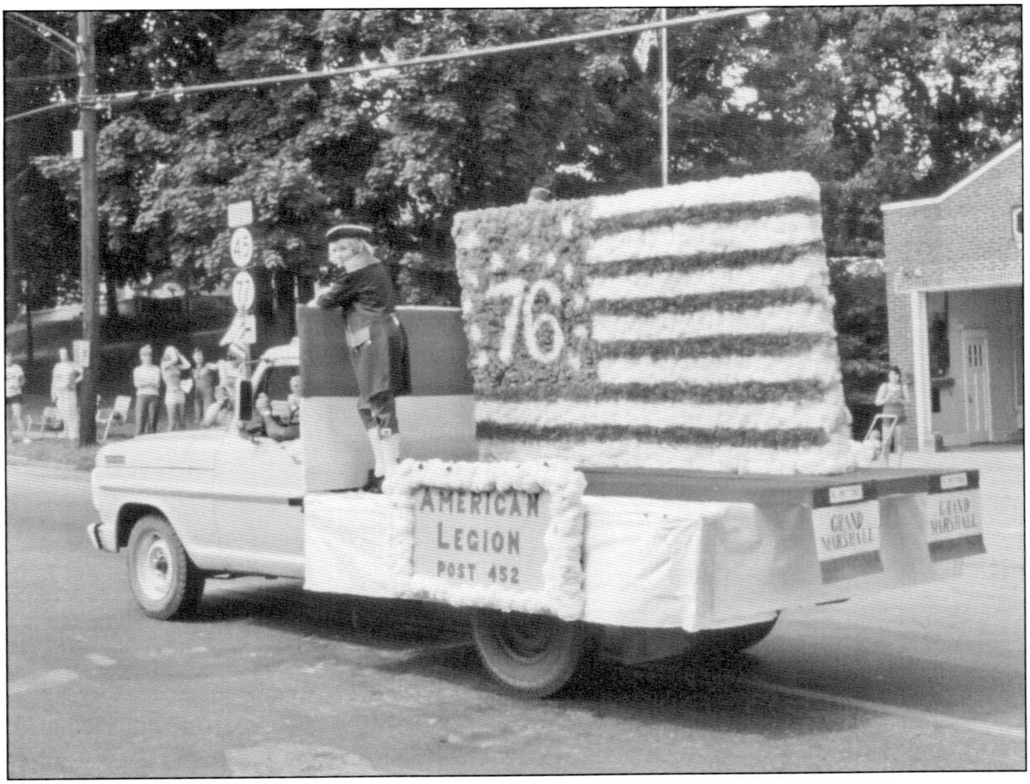

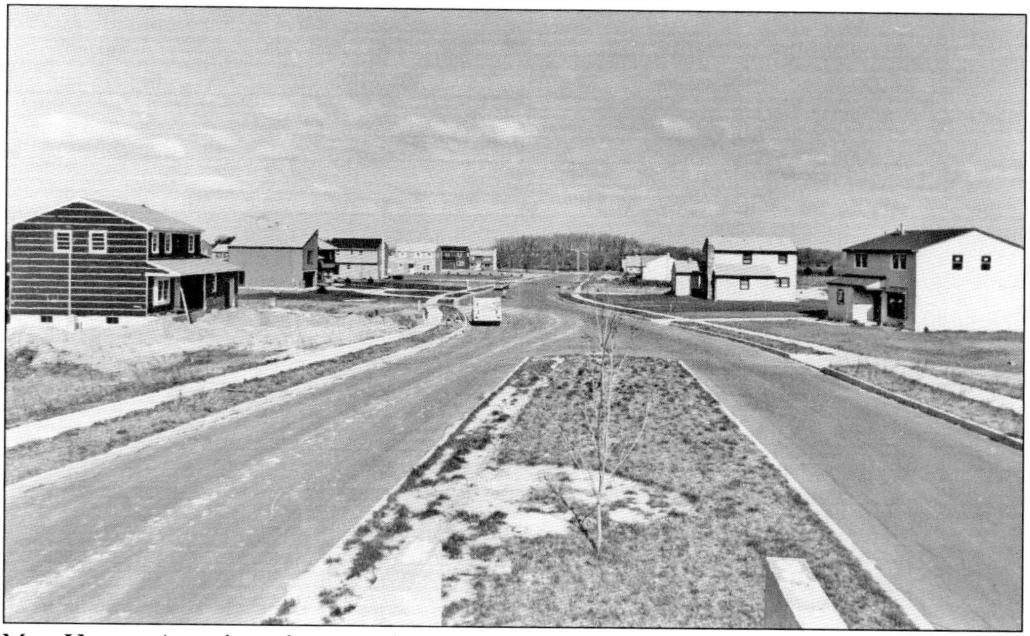

MILL VALLEY. As early as the 1920s, housing developments had been occasionally proposed, but none came to fruition until the 1970s. Mill Valley south of Jefferson was the township's first major housing development. Initially, projects proliferated around the perimeter of Mullica Hill, but they have since spread outward to all the larger villages, except Harrisonville. This growth has spurred interest in open space and farmland preservation programs. (GCHS.)

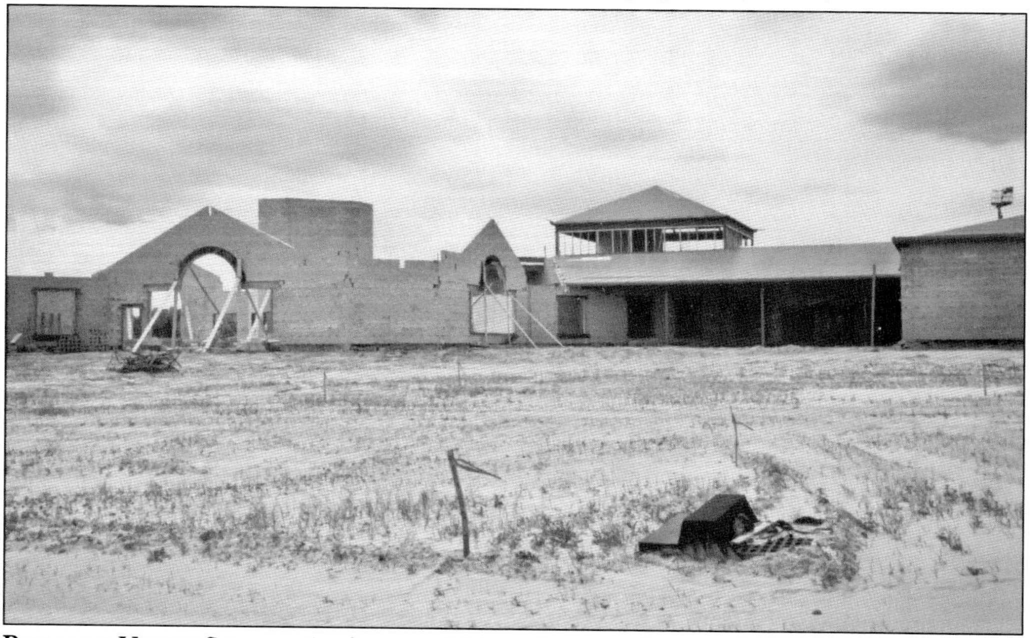

PLEASANT VALLEY SCHOOL. As the township's student population continued to grow, so did the need for additional elementary classrooms, despite a major addition to Harrison Township School. The answer was a new school on Walters Road in Jefferson. Pleasant Valley opened for grades five and six in 2004. It was built on land that was once part of the historic Colson Farm, which was called Pleasant Valley. (HTBOE.)

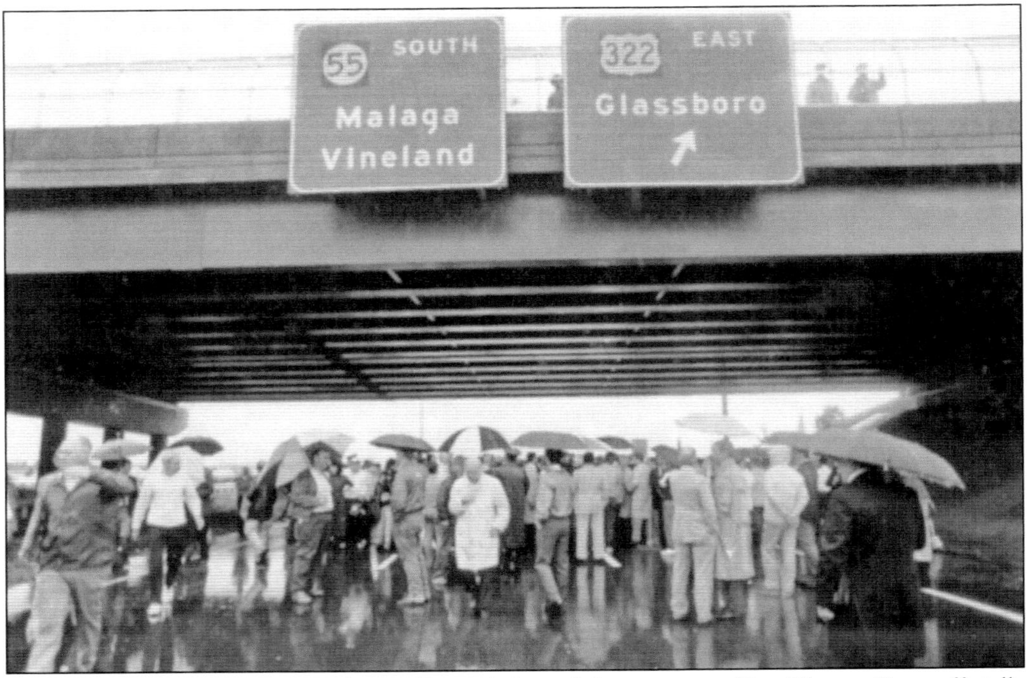

ROUTE 55. On October 2, 1989, about 250 people braved the rain to see Gov. Thomas Kean officially open Route 55 through Gloucester County at the Richwood interchange. The village of Richwood was immediately impacted. Route 322 became a four-lane highway and century-old buildings gave way to new commercial ventures. Rowan University's West Campus and a new regional hospital have recently located here as longtime farmlands give way to development. (GCHS.)

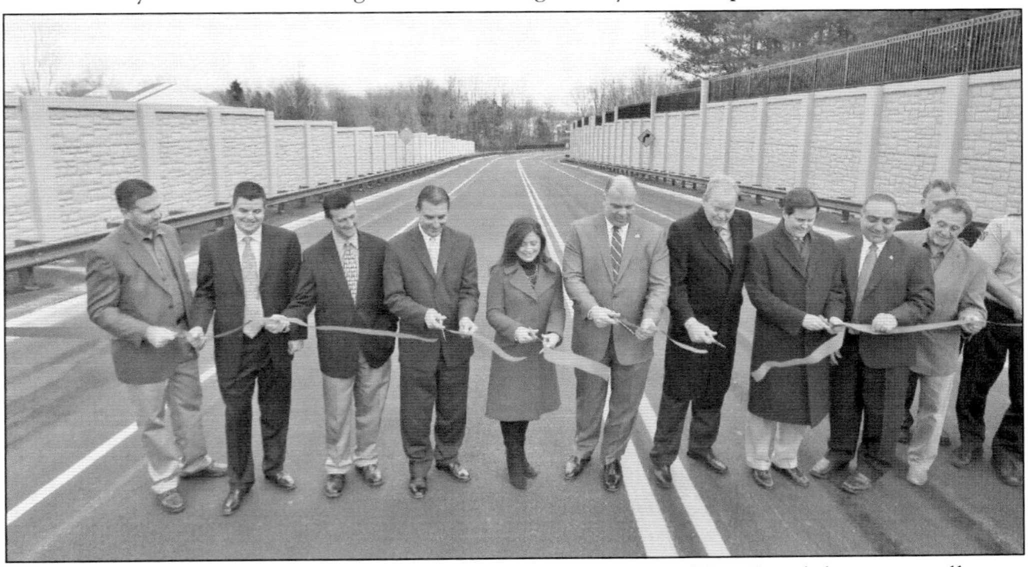

OPENING THE BYPASS. January 12, 2012, marked the culmination of decades of planning to alleviate traffic congestion through Mullica Hill's historic district. From left to right, Committeemen Matthew Diggons, Robert Shearer, and Don Heim; Mayor Lou Manzo; Freeholder Heather Simmons; New Jersey state senate president Steve Sweeney; Freeholder Robert Damminger; New Jersey state senator Donald Norcross; Freeholder Joe Chila, former mayor Mike Koestler; and Sheriff Carmel Morina cut the ribbon to open the long-awaited Route 322 bypass. (SJT.)

About the Harrison Township Historical Society

In 1971, the Harrison Township Committee under the leadership of Mayor Philip J. Reuter appointed a committee to organize a historical society to preserve and provide a new purpose for Mullica Hill's historic Old Town Hall. Since that time, the Harrison Township Historical Society has not only restored the building (a key contributing structure in the Mullica Hill National Register Historic District) but has also established an award-wining community museum.

The society's mission focuses on collecting, preserving and interpreting the history and cultural heritage of Old Harrison Township as defined by the municipality's original 1844 borders, which encompassed present-day Harrison, South Harrison, and the western edge of Elk Township. Since its founding, it has developed an extensive local history collection comprised of museum, library, and archival holdings. The majority of the photographs featured in this book were drawn from the society's rich photograph archive. The excellence of the work of the society and its volunteers has been recognized with awards from the American Association for State and Local History, the New Jersey Historic Trust, the New Jersey Historical Commission, and the League of Historical Societies of New Jersey.

The museum features long-term and changing exhibitions exploring the area's rich history from prehistoric times to the present day. The galleries are open seasonally on weekends in the spring and fall. Annual events include the Groundhog Day dinner, a revival of an old farming tradition from Richwood featuring sausage (the "ground" hog), and the Mullica Hill Ghost Walk, a storytelling event drawing on regional folklore. The society also provides free educational programming for local elementary school students and Scout troops.

Through its work at the museum and in the community, the Harrison Township Historical Society is an important cultural institution in the region, having successfully brought new life to Old Town Hall, just as it was charged to do almost 50 years ago.

For program and membership information contact:
Harrison Township Historical Society
Old Town Hall Museum
62–64 South Main Street
Mullica Hill, NJ 08062
856-478-4949
www.harrisonhistorical.com

Discover Thousands of Local History Books Featuring Millions of Vintage Images

Arcadia Publishing, the leading local history publisher in the United States, is committed to making history accessible and meaningful through publishing books that celebrate and preserve the heritage of America's people and places.

Find more books like this at
www.arcadiapublishing.com

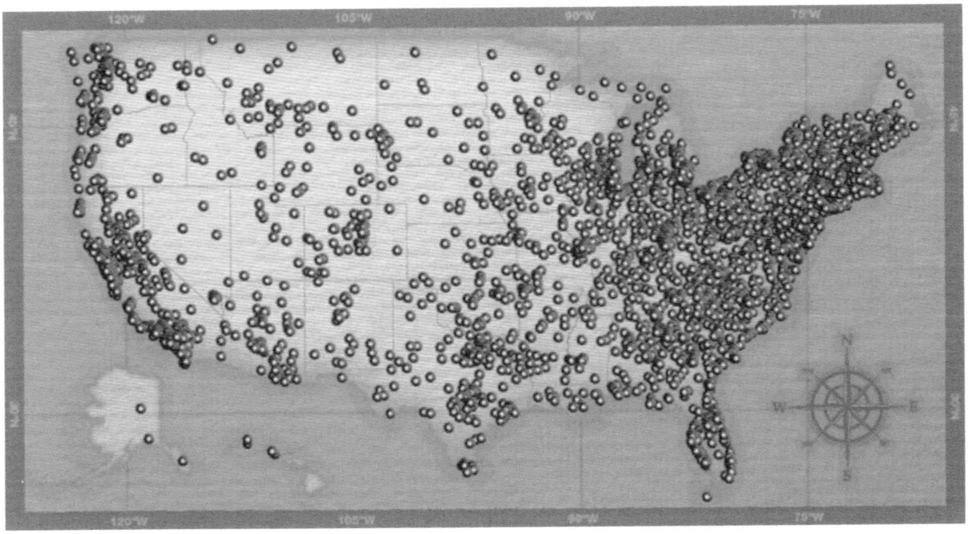

Search for your hometown history, your old stomping grounds, and even your favorite sports team.

Consistent with our mission to preserve history on a local level, this book was printed in South Carolina on American-made paper and manufactured entirely in the United States. Products carrying the accredited Forest Stewardship Council (FSC) label are printed on 100 percent FSC-certified paper.

MADE IN THE USA